IDEOLOGY

This **volume** explores and explains the complex concept of ideology. David Hawkes traces the history of the concept, arguing that 'ideology' **ultimately** refers to a distortion of the relationship between ideas, matter and representation.

In **his** clear, concise volume, the author examines the debates **around** ideology, using examples throughout to illuminate his **argument**. He discusses key thinkers in the field, from Luther to **Baudrillard**, and sets ideology within the critical frameworks of **empiricism**, idealism, Marxism, post-Marxism and postmodernism. **Crucially**, the volume asks why ideology matters, and looks at the **implications** of the terrorist attacks of 11 September 2001 for the **theory** of ideology.

A **knowledge** of the tradition through which people have attempted to **describe** the phenomenon of ideology is essential for an understanding of contemporary philosophy, art and literature. With a **newly** updated bibliography and fresh suggestions for further reading, *Ideology* offers the ideal foundation for such an understanding.

David Hawkes teaches at Lehigh University, Pennsylvania. His **recent** publications include *Idols of the Marketplace: Idolatry and Commodity Fetishism in English Literature, 1580–1680*.

THE NEW CRITICAL IDIOM

SERIES EDITOR: JOHN DRAKAKIS, UNIVERSITY OF STIRLING

The New Critical Idiom is an invaluable series of introductory guides to today's critical terminology. Each book:

- provides a handy, explanatory guide to the use (and abuse) of the term
- offers an original and distinctive overview by a leading literary and cultural critic
- relates the term to the larger field of cultural representation.

With a strong emphasis on clarity, lively debate and the widest possible breadth of examples, *The New Critical Idiom* is an indispensable approach to key topics in literary studies.

Also available in this series:

Autobiography by Linda Anderson
Class by Gary Day
Colonialism/Postcolonialism by Ania Loomba
Crime Fiction by John Scaggs
Culture/Metaculture by Francis Mulhern
Discourse by Sara Mills
Genders by David Glover and Cora Kaplan
Gothic by Fred Botting
Historicism by Paul Hamilton
Humanism by Tony Davies
Interdisciplinarity by Joe Moran
Intertextuality by Graham Allen
Literature by Peter Widdowson
Metre, Rhythm and Verse Form by Philip Hobsbaum
Modernism by Peter Childs
Myth by Laurence Coupe
Narrative by Paul Cobley
Parody by Simon Dentith
Pastoral by Terry Gifford
Romanticism by Aidan Day
Science Fiction by Adam Roberts
Sexuality by Joseph Bristow
Stylistics by Richard Bradford
The Unconscious by Antony Easthope

IDEOLOGY

Second Edition

David Hawkes

Routledge
Taylor & Francis Group

LONDON AND NEW YORK

First published 1996 by Routledge
11 New Fetter Lane, London EC4P 4EE

This edition first published 2003 by Routledge
11 New Fetter Lane, London EC4P 4EE

Simultaneously published in the USA and Canada
by Routledge
29 West 35th Street, New York, NY 10001

Routledge is an imprint of the Taylor & Francis Group

© 1996, 2003 David Hawkes

Typeset in Adobe Garamond and Scala Sans by
Keystroke, Jacaranda Lodge, Wolverhampton
Printed and bound in Great Britain by
Biddles Ltd, Guildford and King's Lynn

British Library Cataloguing in Publication Data
A catalogue record for this book is available from the British Library

Library of Congress Cataloging in Publication Data
has been applied for

ISBN 0–415–29011–2 (hbk)
ISBN 0–415–29012–0 (pbk)

In memory of my grandmother, Betty Roberts

Contents

SERIES EDITOR'S PREFACE

The New Critical Idiom is a series of introductory books which seeks to extend the lexicon of literary terms, in order to address the radical changes which have taken place in the study of literature during the last decades of the twentieth century. The aim is to provide clear, well-illustrated accounts of the full range of terminology currently in use, and to evolve histories of its changing usage.

The current state of the discipline of literary studies is one where there is considerable debate concerning basic questions of terminology. This involves, among other things, the boundaries which distinguish the literary from the non-literary; the position of literature within the larger sphere of culture; the relationship between literatures of different cultures; and questions concerning the relation of literary to other cultural forms within the context of interdisciplinary structures.

It is clear that the field of literary criticism and theory is a dynamic and heterogeneous one. The present need is for individual volumes on terms which combine clarity of exposition with an adventurousness of perspective and a breadth of application. Each volume will contain as part of its apparatus some indication of the direction in which the definition of particular terms is likely to move, as well as expanding the disciplinary boundaries within which some of these terms have been traditionally contained. This will involve some re-situation of terms within the larger field of cultural representation, and will introduce examples from the area of film and the modern media in addition to examples from a variety of literary texts.

PREFACE

This second edition of *Ideology* contains much new material, written to reflect intellectual and political developments since the appearance of the first edition in 1996. The friends and colleagues at Lehigh University who have assisted me are multitudinous, but I am especially indebted to Gordon Bearn, Betsy Fifer, Scott Gordon, Barry Kroll, Carol Laub, Seth Moglen, Donna Warmkessel, Viv Steele and Barbara Traister. The patient assistance of Liz Thompson has been indispensable. My gratitude to Terry Eagleton, who first taught me about ideology, and to John Drakakis, who first asked me to write about it, has only increased over the years.

INTRODUCTION
Ideology and Globalization

It is only in the world market that money first functions to its full
extent as the commodity whose natural form is also the directly
social form of realization of human labor in the abstract. Its mode
of existence becomes adequate to its concept.

(Karl Marx, *Capital* [1867] 1976, 240–1)*

When this book was first published in 1996 its argument seemed, even to
the author, a trifle Quixotic. My claim was, and is, that the market
economy produces a systematically false consciousness: an ideology.
Global exchange for profit, and more especially the exchange of money –
which is itself the medium of exchange – for profit, is the root cause and
prime example of today's ideological errors. While market exchange
is obviously present in and necessary to any civilized society, our
postmodern society is historically unique in elevating the mercantile
principle to a position of complete dominance over the economy and, I
argue, over every area of public and private experience. When it attains

* Dates in square brackets are those of first publication. Those in round parentheses are
those of the modern editions listed in the Bibliography and page numbers refer to these.

this degree of power, the market ceases to fulfil its necessary but subordinate function as a means towards the end of civilized life. It becomes, rather, an end in itself, and in consequence it takes on the aspect of a tyrannous, destructive force, whose impact is felt within each of our minds as well as in our material lives. The market becomes an ideology.

In the 1990s it seemed to many that to oppose the market was to oppose life itself. The recent collapse of socialism, which had been the only significant anti-capitalist movement for over a century, appeared to inaugurate a permanent reign of trade and usury. Francis Fukuyama's influential *The End of History* (1992) made a convincing case that market ideology had finally exterminated any viable alternative, and that it therefore constituted the 'end point of mankind's ideological evolution' (xi). The most extreme claims of libertarian capitalists verged on idolatry; Blair Hoxby (1998) declared that 'the market is a means by which imperfect men may, in the long term, approximate the wisdom of God' (188). In the 1990s, only slightly less bizarre beliefs achieved something approaching orthodoxy among professional economists. As Thomas Frank remarks in *One Market Under God* (2000):

> Only when people act within the marketplace, such thinkers told us, do they act rationally, choose rightly, and make their wishes known transparently. Only then could business give us what we wanted, cater to our freely expressed choices. Markets are where we are most fully human; markets are where we show that we have a soul. To protest *against* markets is to surrender one's very personhood, to put oneself outside the family of mankind.
>
> (xiii)

Under such conditions, it seemed that the best that could be done was to remember how perverse and unnatural such beliefs would have looked to every previous epoch of human history. The first edition of *Ideology* tried to show that global capital and its ideology violated the fundamental tenets of Western thought from Aristotle and the Bible on, but it could offer little prospect that capitalism's philosophical falsehood might cause it any practical concern. That situation has now changed, although it would be a hardhearted observer who could take much satisfaction from the fact. In the 1996 edition of this book I observed that '[i]nstitutions dedicated to the interests of capital, such as the IMF and the World Bank, have become far more important than any national government' (7). Many others had said the same thing before, but in the mid-1990s this was still considered a fairly controversial, or at least a contestable, claim. In 2003 it is regarded as a truism so obvious as to be unworthy of repetition. These organizations, of which many people had barely heard ten years ago, are now unable to convene meetings near major population centres for fear of being torn apart by an angry mob.

Perhaps that is progress of a sort, but in the absence of practical alternatives, popular awareness of the machinations of capital can easily spawn nihilism and social psychoses. Fyodor Dostoevsky's *Devils* [1872] tells the story of a group of youthful terrorists who, unable to engage in legitimate politics under Czarist tyranny, resort to increasingly absurd and violent tactics of destruction. They are not idealists who believe in an ideology; they are nihilists who believe in nothing. One of their number, Kirillov, advocates a politics of revolutionary suicide: 'He who doesn't care whether he lives or dies – he'll be the new man' (2000, 121). Their leader, Peter Verkhovensky, proudly proclaims the abolition of traditional culture in his future utopia: 'Cicero's tongue will be cut out, Copernicus's eyes will be gouged out, Shakespeare will be stoned' (442). This kind of dysfunctional but formidable nihilism has infected many opponents of capitalism from Seattle to Kabul, and nobody expects 11 September's assault on the centre of world trade to be the final such atrocity.

It seems that we have reached a stage of history when neither capitalism nor anti-capitalism can any longer be understood as a narrowly 'economic' matter. The rule of money is part of a more general phenomenon, which we might term the dictatorship of representation. It is obvious enough that everybody's economic life is determined by the intricate and subtle coils of purely symbolic money, but it is less immediately apparent that our cultural and psychological lives are also so determined. Spheres of life that were once thought to lie beyond the realm of the 'economy' now clearly exhibit the influence of market ideology. The political culture of the West, for example, is taken up exclusively by discussion of spin, image and presentation. Corporations sponsor everything from art galleries to rock concerts. Psychology must take account of the fact that the consumption of particular brand identities is central to the formation of the personality. The discourse of marketing creeps into diverse areas of intellectual life. The various academic tendencies collectively known as 'postmodernism' are united by their belief that the media of representation determine our experience of the world. A glance at any popular entertainment confirms that the line between reality and fiction is increasingly blurred, and not just in the minds of overt lunatics.

The most perspicacious contemporary novelists remark pointedly on this tyranny of representation. American works like Brett Easton Ellis's *Less than Zero* (1985) or Douglas Coupland's *Generation X* (1991) provide nihilistic descriptions of a subjectivity reduced to a repository of niche marketing and brand identities. British novels like Martin Amis's *Money* (1984) or Irvine Welsh's *Filth* (1998) offer post-Joycean interior monologues to illustrate the degeneration of the psyche when exposed to the full impact of commerce and media. In Will Self's *My Idea of Fun* (1993), the protagonist comes under the influence of a sinister Svengali known as the Fat Controller. This mentor scorns traditional culture, remarking after a visit to the theatre: 'How risible it is that art cannot provide a better imitation of life, when we know that life itself is so illusory' (86). Instead, he encourages his protégé to take up a career in marketing, which is described as 'the dialectical materialism of the [Thatcher] regime' (143). Self understands that the autonomous, non-referential and self-generating character of postmodern capital chimes perfectly with the constitutive role that postmodern philosophy assigns to representation in general. Finance, in Self's view, has become just another branch of aesthetics:

> At this fag end of the millennium money had begun to detach itself from the very medium of exchange. Money was lagging behind. Ian knew – because he had read about it in the press – that there was approximately $800 trillion that had simply winked into existence. It had never been earned by anyone, or even printed by any government. Everywhere you looked you saw advertisements screaming: 'Value for Money'. That such an obvious *non sequitur* should have become a benchmark of credibility was beyond Ian's, and indeed anyone's, understanding. This 'value' was as insubstantial as the $800 trillion. It was linked to no commonly perceived variable; instead it was chronically relativised. The merchant banks and brokerage firms that made up the City had long since given up on employing even the

most flamboyant and intuitive of economic forecasters. Instead they
had fallen back on the self-styled 'money critics', refugees from the
overflowing newsprint sector, who offered their services to provide
'purely aesthetic' judgements on different mediums of exchange.

(223–4)

Money is a language, a system of signs. The material forms taken by
these signs can vary; previous ages have incarnated them in the form of
conch shells, precious metals or banknotes. In our time, though, it has
become clear that money exists only in our minds. It is a medium of
representation and, as recent works of economic theory such as Dierdre
McClosky's *Knowledge and Persuasion in Economics* (1994) have shown,
this implies that money can be subjected to the modes of analysis
and critique that have been developed by philosophers of language and
semioticians. Equally, the theories and methods of economists can
profitably be applied to the study of linguistic and visual modes of
signification. The school of literary theory known as the 'New Economic
Criticism' testifies to this recognition of 'parallels and analogies between
linguistic and economic systems' and 'the existence of homologies
between language and money' (Woodmansee and Osteen, 1999, 14, 15).
The proliferating pupils of this school take inspiration from two philosophers whose seminal work appeared in the 1970s, but whose profound
importance has only recently been appreciated: Marc Shell and Jean-
Joseph Goux.

In *Symbolic Economies* (1990), Goux recalls the origin of his project in
the revelation that 'Marx's analysis [of financial value] held the lineaments
of a general and elementary logic of exchange which far exceeded the
sphere of economic value for which it was initially produced' (3). The
fertile intellectual ambience of Paris in the 1960s and 1970s, in which
structuralism and deconstruction called attention to the constitutive role
of signification, produced in Goux the epiphany that Marx's theory of
money applied to semiotic as well as to financial value. His work focuses
on Marx's view of money as a 'general equivalent' that facilitates the
exchange of all other objects. As he traces the historical development
of the general equivalent, Goux finds that a similar logic operates in
psychology and linguistics: 'what had previously been analysed separately
as phallocentrism (Freud, Lacan), as logocentrism (Derrida), and as the

rule of exchange by the monetary medium (Marx), it was now possible to conceive as part of a unified process' (4).

Goux argues that postmodern representation is characterized by 'the inconvertibility of the sign' (7). Until the early twentieth century, it was officially declared and popularly believed that all the money in the world could theoretically be converted into gold. Money was a sign, but it had an ultimate, material referent. In postmodernity, however, money has become an autonomous, self-generating, inconvertible sign – a signifier with no signified. Postmodern linguistics and semiology likewise portray the sign as arbitrary and non-referential, and its meaning as relational rather than essential. The history of money and the history of language are elements within a more general history of signification, and this general history has a logic of development that determines each of its parts. In *Money, Language and Thought* (1982), Marc Shell describes a similar narrative of money's historical development:

> Between the electrum money of ancient Lydia and the electric money of contemporary America there occurred a historically momentous change. The exchange value of the earliest coins derived wholly from the material substance (electrum) of the ingots of which the coins were made and not from the inscriptions stamped into those ingots. The eventual development of coins whose politically authorized inscriptions were inadequate to the weights and purities of the ingots into which the inscriptions were stamped precipitated awareness of quandaries about the relationship between face value (intellectual currency) and substantial value (material currency). This difference between inscription and thing grew greater with the introduction of paper moneys. Paper, the material substance on which the inscriptions were printed, was supposed to make no difference in exchange, and metal or electrum, the material substance to which the inscriptions referred, was connected with those inscriptions in increasingly abstract ways. With the advent of electronic fund-transfers the link between inscription and substance was broken. The matter of electronic money does not matter.
>
> (1)

It appears, from the accounts of Shell and Goux, that history involves the progressive detachment of signs from referents and a growing autonomy and determining power of signification. The postmodern era, in which images of various kinds have attained the power to constitute reality itself, is often said to represent the culmination or *telos* of this process. This is why many postmodern thinkers declare that the concept of 'ideology' has outlived its usefulness. The term 'ideology' usually refers to a systematically false consciousness. But if representation is the only reality, if truth is merely, as such precursors of postmodernism as Nietzsche claimed, a rhetorical device by which the powerful maintain their dominance, then how are we to distinguish between true and false modes of thought? This case is summarized in Nietzsche's famous argument:

> What then is truth? A mobile army of metaphors, metonyms, and anthropomorphisms – in short, a sum of human relations, which have been enhanced, transposed and embellished poetically and rhetorically, and which after long use seem firm, canonical, and obligatory to a people: truths are illusions about which one has forgotten that is what they are; metaphors which are worn out and without sensuous power; coins which have lost their pictures and now matter only as metal, no longer as coins.
>
> (1954, 46–7)

This is, in essence, the postmodernist position on truth and ideology. It is impossible to distinguish between these categories because both are constructed out of the manipulation of empty signifiers; truth and falsehood are merely effects produced by non-referential signs. Shell takes up the question of how to identify ideology in *The Economy of Literature* (1978). He describes ideology as undialectical thought: that is to say, thought that seeks to reduce a mutually definitive binary opposition to one of its poles. The first such ideology Shell discusses is materialism:

> Those discourses are ideological that argue or assume that matter is ontologically prior to thought. Astrology, for example, looks to the stars, phrenology to the skull, physiognomy to the face, and palmistry to the hand. In the modern world, ideological discourses look to the biochemistry of the brain, sexual need, genes, and social class; they seek to express how matter 'gives rise to' thought by employing metaphors such as 'influence', 'structure', 'imitation', 'sublimation', 'expression', and 'symptom'.
>
> (1)

Ideas and matter form a mutually definitive binary opposition and so it is false, or 'ideological', to claim that one of these elements determines the other. If it is false to reduce ideas to matter, however, it is equally false to reduce objective reality to subjective ideas. Shell therefore goes on to attack the sceptical relativism that characterizes postmodernity:

> Finding no salve for the wound of the desire to know, they retreat to comfortably relativistic or uncomfortably nihilistic lookouts, from which, grandly surveying the combatants, they argue that all ideologies are equally valid and therefore equally invalid. Who has not heard the liberal injunction to 'do your own thing', the rule that 'you have your opinion and I have mine'?
>
> (1)

Shell's dual definition of ideology echoes Hans Barth's statement of some thirty years earlier: 'The principle of ideological interpretations of cultural and intellectual life is to deny the autonomy of mind and the existence of universal truths' [1951] (1976, 162). This kind of materialist relativism, which reduces thought to matter in order to deny the possibility of identifying any mode of thought as systematically false or 'ideological', is indeed prevalent in postmodernity. Alan Bloom's *The Closing of the American Mind* (1987) is a devastating critique of contemporary ideology that has gone largely unrecognized as such because it is perceived as having come from the political 'right'. But people of all political shades should hear a chord striking when Bloom identifies relativism as the postmodern form of false consciousness:

> There is one thing a professor can be absolutely certain of: almost every student entering the university believes, or says he believes, that truth is relative. If this belief is put to the test, one can count on the students' reaction: they will be uncomprehending. That anyone should regard the proposition as not self-evident astonishes them, as though he were calling into question $2 + 2 = 4$. These are things you don't think about. . . . The relativity of truth is not a theoretical insight but a moral postulate, the condition of a free society, or so they see it.
>
> (25)

To say that a certain kind of consciousness is 'false', to speak of 'ideology', is thus to violate the most fundamental tenet of postmodern society. As Bloom puts it: 'The true believer is the real danger' (26). Bloom's attitude recalls that of the literary critic F.R. Leavis, who dedicated his career to exposing the degeneration of moral and aesthetic taste which, as he saw it, a commercial society must produce. In *Mass Civilization and Minority Culture* (1930), Leavis notes the kinship of authentic, essential aesthetic value to the financial gold standard: 'The accepted valuations are a kind of paper currency based upon a very small proportion of gold. To the state of such a currency the possibilities of fine living at any time bear a close relation' (4). There is, however, a 'psychological Gresham's law' (8) whereby, under market conditions, bad taste inexorably drives out good. This is more than a metaphor. The deterioration of essential value into relativism is *the same thing* as the unmooring of money from its physical referent.

For Shell, like Leavis and Bloom, relativism is just as reductive as materialist determinism, since it reduces objective truth to subjective preference. In contrast to both forms of reductionism, Shell proposes 'to understand dialectically the relationship between thought and matter by focussing . . . on economic thought and literary and linguistic matters' (1982, 2). The shifting relationship between thought and matter is made manifest in the development of signification, whether financial or linguistic. The various stages through which the history of representation passes can thus be evaluated according to the criteria of ideological criticism. There can, in other words, be a false and a true mode of representation, and a good and an evil deployment of signs. The absence of such an ethics of representation has hampered attempts to critique the free-floating money of global capitalism. As Werner Bonefeld and John Holloway observe, 'money has too often been treated as an aspect of "economics", as an element of the framework within which class struggle takes place rather than as being a form of class struggle itself' (1995, 3). Money is not merely a convenient vehicle for exchange; money has significance, it *means* something. In short, money talks, and it speaks the language of ideology.

If money has grown progressively more abstract and less material over the course of its historical development, the same might be said of the things people buy with it. For millennia, most things that people exchanged were simple means of subsistence. With the beginnings of a global market in the sixteenth century, it soon became possible to conceive of almost any thing as a commodity. And with the complete triumph of the market in our own time, the most valuable commodities traded are not things at all, but ideas, images and brands. This dematerialization of the economy gives it unprecedented power over the minds of individuals. As Naomi Klein observes in *No Logo* (2000):

> The astronomical growth in the wealth and cultural influence of multinational corporations over the last fifteen years can arguably be traced back to a single, seemingly innocuous idea developed by management theorists in the mid-1980's: that successful corporations must primarily produce brands, as opposed to products . . . this corporate obsession with brand identity is waging a war on public and individual space: on public institutions such as schools, on youthful identities, on the concept of nationality and on the possibilities for unmarketed space.
>
> (16)

My main argument in this book is that the postmodern sign, whether financial or linguistic, is epistemologically false and ethically degenerate. Postmodernism is thus the veritable apotheosis of ideology. I ended the Introduction to *Ideology*'s first edition with the contention that 'postmodernism is nothing more than the ideology of consumer capitalism' (12). Many postmodernists consider themselves to be political radicals, and my statement provoked howls of protest. Today, however, a burgeoning awareness of the repressive political power of financial representation, and of its kinship with the modes of autonomous linguistic and semiotic representation that postmodernism promotes, has provoked many investigations of the complicity between global capitalism and postmodernist philosophy. Peter Burnham points out that academic trends towards multiculturalism and philosophical relativism suggest that 'the phenomenon of "globalization" was absolutely compatible with post-modernist ideology' (2000, 9), but the word 'compatible' seems unnecessarily weak. It would be more accurate to say that postmodernism *is* the ideology of globalization. In *Empire* (2000), Michael Hardt and Antonio Negri observe that:

> Many of the concepts dear to postmodernists and postcolonialists

find a perfect correspondence in the current ideology of corporate capital and the world market. The ideology of the world market has always been the anti-foundational and anti-essentialist discourse par excellence. Circulation, mobility, diversity, and mixture are its very conditions of possibility. Trade brings differences together and the more the merrier! Differences (of commodities, populations, cultures, and so forth) seem to multiply infinitely in the world market, which attacks nothing more violently than fixed boundaries: it overwhelms any binary division with its infinite multiplicities.

(150)

One of postmodernism's most subtle manoeuvres has been to present such tendencies as liberating and progressive. The humanities departments of Western universities ring with denunciations of the dominant, or 'hegemonic', culture, and postmodernism allies itself firmly with the 'oppositional' and the 'counterculture'. We are asked, in richly suggestive terms, to applaud the 'free play' of 'difference' and eschew the rigidity of philosophies that 'totalize' – a term which has acquired a connotative association with totalitarianism. The rhetoric of 1960s libidinal revolt merges imperceptibly into theoretical celebrations of the body, and the works of canonical culture are routinely interrogated for the degree of 'subversion' or 'containment' they putatively express. Although the details are left suspiciously vague, there is a sense across the intellectual spectrum that postmodernism is a radical, subversive and oppositional mode of thought.

Thomas Frank discusses a comparable sleight of hand in *The Conquest of Cool* (1997). He argues that the explosion of a 'counterculture' and the proliferation of 'alternative lifestyles' that the West has witnessed since the 1960s are merely the ultimate subordination of identity to the market, in which people purchase personality traits as they would any other commodity. Frank's title does not suggest that the countercultural concept of 'cool' has been co-opted by capital so much as that the notion of 'cool' itself originates as a marketing slogan that has invaded and conquered the popular mind. He claims that the 'counterculture served corporate revolutionaries as a projection of the new ideology of business, a living embodiment of attitudes that reflected their own' (1997, 33). A similar point is made by Hardt and Negri, who remark of multinational corporations that: 'The "culture" within these organizations has also adopted the precepts of postmodernist thinking' (2000, 153). This affinity between capitalism and counterculture was barely visible to most observers in the 1960s and 1970s, but today it is becoming overt. At the end of the twentieth century, Frank remarks:

> rebel youth culture remains the cultural mode of the corporate moment, used to promote not only specific products but the general idea of life in the cyber-revolution. Commercial fantasies of rebellion, liberation, and outright 'revolution' against the stultifying demands of mass society are commonplace almost to the point of invisibility in advertising, movies, and television programming.
>
> (1997, 33)

Naomi Klein's *No Logo* provides a detailed history of corporate America's cultivation of 'cool'. As she presents it, the construction of cool involves the assimilation of racial difference through symbolic multiculturalism:

> Just as the history of cool in America is really (as many have argued) a history of African-American culture – from jazz and blues to rock and roll to rap – for many of the superbrands, cool hunting simply means blackculture hunting. Which is why the cool hunters' first stop was the basketball courts of America's poorest neighborhoods.
>
> (2000, 23)

Nor is capitalism's association with libidinal liberation and aestheticized rebellion confined within the purview of popular culture. The union of the commercial and the aesthetic achieved respectable, canonical status with Andy Warhol's paintings of baked bean tins. In *Privatising Culture* (2001), Chin-tao Wu documents the current, unprecedented influence of business over the institutions of traditional art: 'Never before has the corporate world in America and Britain exercised such sway over high culture, in which business involvement had previously been thought of as inappropriate, if not completely alien' (2). This influence is particularly glaring in the visual arts, where patrons like Charles Saatchi astutely perceive the ideological usefulness of aesthetic radicals like Damien Hirst.

Infatuation with the avant-garde is hardly a new tendency in capitalism, which has always lived by constant innovation and the ruthless rejection of the accumulated wisdom of the past. In the *Communist Manifesto* [1848] (1975), Karl Marx and Friedrich Engels view the permanent revolution which capitalism sets in motion as a necessary clearing of the ground prior to the establishment of socialism:

> Constant revolutionizing of production, uninterrupted disturbance of all social conditions, everlasting uncertainty and agitation distinguish the bourgeois epoch from all earlier ones. All fixed, fast frozen relations, with their train of ancient and venerable prejudices and opinions, are swept away, all new-formed ones become antiquated before they can ossify. All that is solid melts into air, all that is holy is profaned, and man is at last compelled to face with sober senses his real condition of life and his relations with his kind.
>
> (VI, 135)

The postmodern condition resoundingly corroborates all of these statements except the last. Marx and Engels imagined that the destruction of traditional beliefs, identities and relationships would bring about an accurate knowledge of the 'real conditions of life'. They thought they were witnessing the coalescence of all previous contradictions into the single opposition between capital and labour power, as these abstract forces became embodied in the respective social classes of bourgeoisie and proletariat. They believed that the overthrow of capital by labour would resolve the ancient, artificial alienation between human beings and their subjective activity, and thus inaugurate a utopian era of human history in which life would at last be 'real'. As it turned out, however, the proletarian revolution, which Marx and Engels predicted would break out in the advanced industrial economies of the West, never took place. Instead, the opposition between capital and labour power hardened and spread, colonizing every corner of the earth as well as the innermost recesses of the mind. The most important fact that anti-capitalists must grasp today is that the contradiction between capital and labour can no longer be identified with the class struggle between the bourgeoisie and the proletariat. That contradiction is certainly real and irreconcilable, but in postmodernity it has become internalized. The conflict between capital and labour is, today, an ideological struggle.

The above understanding of history is anathema to postmodernist philosophy. Postmodernists disdain the dialectic: they deplore the idea that history and logic proceed by means of the continual posing and resolution of 'binary divisions', such as that between capital and labour. In place of dialectic, philosophers such as Jacques Derrida proffer *différance*, a never-ending chain of deferred and displaced significance, as the element through which thought and history move. It is easy to identify the ideological purport of this manoeuvre. Postmodernism is designed to deny the binary opposition that frames and structures our contemporary experience: the contradiction between capital and labour. Elision of the contradiction between capital and labour is postmodernism's *raison d'être*. To understand that capital is objectified labour, that it stands in logical contradiction to human subjective activity, to life itself, is accurately to comprehend the dilemma of our epoch. There are, naturally, many powerful and determined modes of thought that seek to obscure this comprehension. The name we give to such modes of thought is 'ideology', and the aim of this book is to delineate some of ideology's sinuous historical mutations.

1

ORIGINS

Among them he a spirit of phrenzie sent,
Who hurt their minds,
And urg'd them on with mad desire
To call in haste for their destroyer
                    (John Milton, *Samson Agonistes*, 1673, ll. 1675–8)

IDOLATRY

Twin colossi once stood at the centre of world trade. To the merchants and brokers who gazed on them as they went about their business, the two enormous structures must have seemed emblems of an entire civilization. Perhaps this was why the Taliban government of Afghanistan made the destruction of the twin statues, the Buddhas of Bamiyan, one of their highest priorities. Ruling a war-torn nation with no infrastructure and paltry food supplies, they nevertheless devoted an incredible amount of time and effort to the removal of these icons. It was far from easy: the statues were hewn from solid rock, 53 and 38 metres tall, and they had presided over that part of the ancient Silk Road for 1,500 years. The Taliban treated them as physical enemies, blasting them with rockets, mortars and tank shells, drilling holes in their heads and filling them with dynamite, burning tyres on their lips in order to blacken their faces. Finally, in May 2001, they succeeded in destroying their stone foes, thus ironically proving the truth of the Buddha's central teaching that nothing on earth can aspire to permanence.

The Taliban Minister of Culture responded to the consequent international protests by remarking, somewhat dejectedly, that: 'The statues are no big issue. They are only objects made of mud and stone.' This, it appears, is a defect that agents of his government remedied six months later with the more terrible abnegation of the dual symbol of another civilization. The destruction of the Buddhas, it emerged, had been merely an admonitory rehearsal for the most ferocious act of iconoclasm since the seventeenth century. The people who sent this message were fanatics straight out of Dostoevsky's *Devils*, but the message itself was clear enough. The citadels of capital, we were being told, were idols of the same nature as the Bamiyan Buddhas, and the Western world's adoration of money repeated the sin, and invited the fate, that monotheistic religions have assigned to idolaters since the demolition of the golden calf at Sinai.

History shows that all philosophical or ideological developments call forth their own refutation. In Europe between 1700 and 1800, for example, religious faith was challenged by enlightened reason, which in turn provoked the reaction of Romanticism. This process involves a series of clashes between binary oppositions, but it would be naive (and ideological) to see these oppositions as mutually exclusive. On the contrary, the struggle between opposites reveals their mutual dependence, and the result of the struggle is never the victory of one side and the extirpation of the other, but rather the emergence of an entirely new element, forged from their collision. If today there is an aggressive spirit of iconoclasm abroad in the world, it has been summoned by the apparently complete triumph of its antithesis: idolatry.

In the past, civilizations have generally evolved sophisticated criteria to demonstrate the errors of their victims or rivals. The Greeks declared foreigners to be uncivilized, primitive barbarians who lacked the capacity for rational thought; the early Christians portrayed pagans as worldly, sinful idolaters, addicted to the things of this world and the pleasures of the flesh. It is beyond the scope of this book to analyse such ancient discourses in detail. For our purposes the relevant task is to describe the theories of false consciousness which typify the modern and postmodern worlds. In order to do this, however, we will first need to mention the essential Greek and biblical conceptions of the relation between spirit and matter.

The sacred books of all three monotheistic religions take the oscillation between idolatry and iconoclasm as their primary theme, and they all condemn idolatry on the grounds that it involves the adoration of the products of human labour. The fetishization of the products of labour is the great, all-encompassing sin of humanity. Such idolatry involves a fetishistic attitude towards the self, it implies the objectification of the human subject. Psalm 135 is typical:

> The idols of the heathen are silver and gold, the works of men's hands.
> They have mouths, but they speak not; eyes have they, but they see not;
> They have ears, but they hear not; neither is there any breath in their mouths.
> They that make them are like unto them: so is every one that trusteth in them.
>
> (ll. 15–18)

In Judaism, Christianity and Islam, to take an image for true reality is the most heinous of all sins. In Greek philosophy, it is the most damaging of all epistemological errors. It is the error of the prisoners in Plato's cave and of those who substitute material causes for Aristotle's *telos*. It is also the predominant, even the definitive, characteristic of postmodern society. It is often remarked that our society is dominated by the 'economy', and that this 'economy' is dominated by money. The most salient characteristic of money is that it does not exist. Or rather, it exists only as a symbol, an idea in people's minds, as opposed to a physical object that one could see or touch. Money, in short, is an image that has attained the status of reality: it is an idol.

The Hebraic tradition, which along with Hellenic thought is the primal influence on Western philosophy, ascribes false consciousness to a misconstrual of the relation between matter and spirit. In the Hebrew Bible, the Israelites are distinguished from the Gentiles by the prohibition on material representations of their deity. Due to the attraction which sensual things hold for fallen humanity, such representations will inevitably become fetishes; that is, people will forget that they are merely representations, and idolize them, venerating them as though they were incarnations of the divine. Yahweh makes this clear when, in the first two commandments, He makes the abandonment of images a precondition of monotheism:

> **Exodus 20:3**. Thou shalt have no other gods before me. **4**. Thou shalt not make unto thee any graven image, or any likeness of any thing that is in heaven above, or that is in the earth beneath, or that is in the water under the earth. **5**. Thou shalt not bow down thyself to them, nor serve them: for I the Lord thy God am a jealous God, visiting the iniquity of the fathers upon the children unto the third and fourth generation of them that hate me.

The ferocity of the aniconic commandment is necessary because, due to our faulty understanding of the relation between signs and things, we will inevitably mistake an image of God for God Himself. Representations of the deity are thus incompatible with Judaic monotheism, which asserts that the source of all meaning is an absolute *logos* which is necessarily incorporeal. It is therefore fundamentally erroneous to worship an image. But it is also immoral to do so, for two reasons. First of all, an image is a material object, and thus ethically inferior to the ideal dimension of the divine. Second, an image is the product of human labour – it has been 'graven', or manufactured. In worshipping an icon, then, we are really worshipping the objectified manifestation of our own labour.

This aspect of idolatry was particularly stressed under the Babylonian captivity. The book of Isaiah contains lengthy descriptions of the various kinds of labour which go into manufacturing the Babylonian icons, and the fact that they have been produced by human labour is cited as the clearest possible proof of the absurdity of worshipping images:

> **Isaiah 41:18**. To whom then will ye liken God? Or what likeness will ye compare unto him? **19**. The workman melteth a graven image, and the goldsmith spreadeth it over with gold, and casteth silver chains. **20**. He that is so impoverished that he hath no oblation chooseth a tree that will not rot; he seeketh unto him a cunning workman to prepare a graven image, that shall not be moved.

> **Isaiah 46:5**. To whom will ye liken me, and make me equal, and compare me, that we may be like? **6**. They lavish gold out of the bag, and weigh silver in the balance, and hire a goldsmith; and he maketh it a god: they fall down, yea, they worship.

What is being criticized here is the attempt to establish an equivalence between the ideal and the material through the use of representation. Such an enterprise succeeds only in fetishizing the products of human labour, bestowing upon them a superstitious power and an illegitimate influence over human life. In the New Testament, the Hebraic proscription of idols blends with Hellenic idealism, issuing in a generalized mistrust of all earthly perception, which will only be corrected by posthumous heavenly revelation. Thus Paul, writing to the Corinthians: 'For now we see through a glass, darkly; but then face to face: now I know in part; but then shall I know even as I am known' (I Cor. 13:12).

The centuries immediately before and after the birth of Christ witnessed a syncretic union between Greek rationalism and Jewish monotheism, and Christianity is its most momentous progeny. Philo Judaeus was one thinker who consciously tried to unite the Greek and Hebrew traditions. In his view, God could be equated with Plato's Absolute Idea, and as such He could have no effect on the world that He made possible. The world, rather, was created and governed by God's 'reason', 'word', or *logos*. *Logos* is the term used in the Gospel of John to designate what Christianity metaphorically calls the 'son' of God. The notion that this *logos* could be incarnated in human form indicates a yearning to escape the false consciousness of the flesh, but the earthly fate of Jesus of Nazareth implied that no such liberation was possible in this world.

IRRATIONALISM

Greek philosophy eventually arrived at the same pessimism as Christianity regarding the possibility of achieving a true consciousness on earth, although its route to this destination was long and circuitous. The concept of a systematically false consciousness predates philosophy. At first, it is identified with a particular kind of person rather than with a specific mode of thought. For example, Homer's *Iliad* (*circa* 720 BC) begins with two challenges to the authority of King Agamemnon. In book I, Achilles attacks his tyrannical rule and inequitable lust for plunder, and Thersites criticizes him on identical grounds in book II. There is a marked difference, however, in the ways in which the two rebels are treated. The dispute between Agamemnon and Achilles is presented as a conflict between equals, and the rebellious soldier is accorded as much deference and respect as the proud monarch. Thersites' harangue is indistinguishable in content from Achilles', but his outburst is met with scornful laughter and a blow from Agamemnon's sceptre, wielded by Ulysses. The difference is not in their arguments but in the propriety of their speaking. While Achilles is of semi-divine descent, Thersites' physical ugliness associates him with the lower social ranks, and hence his intervention is unequivocally located outside the realm of acceptable discourse.

In Socrates, by contrast, physical ugliness is said to reflect a laudable commitment to matters of the mind rather than the body. With the development of abstract speculation about concepts – that is to say, of philosophy – the veridical status of consciousness ceased to be connected to personal qualities and was instead equated with the ability to think rationally. In philosophy, very broadly, thinkers tend to claim that others are mistaken by trying to show that they have misunderstood the relation between matter and ideas. The opposition between idealism and materialism structures Western philosophy from its very inception.

The earliest philosophers, known as the Ionics, were materialists who denied the reality of ideas, and also monists who reduced all life and thought to one element. Thales (*circa* 620–550 BC) argued that all things were forms of water, while Anaximenes (*circa* 590–520 BC) claimed that the fundamental principle of the universe was air. Later, by contrast, the Orphics and Pythagoreans concentrated their attention on the soul, which they claimed was spiritual rather than material, and whose purpose was to escape from the material world. These schools therefore preached asceticism and the illusory nature of transient matter. The tendency, which we discussed in the Introduction, to reduce the opposition between ideas and matter to one of its elements is thus as old as Western philosophy itself.

The first thinker to refract the opposition between matter and ideas into an internal contradiction within the human mind was Parmenides (born *circa* 510 BC). He argued that our minds are divided between the senses and reason, with the former responding to the world of matter and the latter inhabiting the realm of ideas. Parmenides gave ethical precedence to the rational function. He regarded reason as the 'way of truth', and sense experience as leading to error, via the 'way of opinion'. The philosophical distinction between truth and falsehood thus originally derives from the dichotomy between matter and spirit. The world of sense experience is illusory, and reality must be sought in the extrasensory operations of reason.

Philosophers after Parmenides can be divided into three groups: those who hold that matter is the true reality, those who claim that the true reality lies in ideas and those who deny the distinction between matter and ideas altogether. Democritus (*circa* 460–370 BC) is an example of the first approach. In his opinion, which is shared by modern science, everything in the universe is made up of atoms which, although invisible, are material. In contrast, Anaxagoras (*circa* 500–430 BC) argued that the universe was created and is moved by an all-powerful mind, or *nous*. Democritus, that is to say, was a mechanist, who sought material, mechanical causes of effects, while Anaxagoras had a teleological approach to the world, viewing it as the product of intelligent design. Where mechanism explains things by studying their origins at a microscopic level, teleology explains things by examining their end or final purpose: their *telos*.

We can find a more recent instance of this debate in the nineteenth-century controversy over natural selection. Pre-Darwinian evolutionists such as William Paley, whose *Natural Theology* [1802] was for fifty years the most highly respected work of evolutionary theory, observed that living organisms had, through evolution, become perfectly adapted to their environments. A process of natural selection was thus indisputably at work. Paley's reflections on the fact were teleological in nature. He asked *why* such exquisite adaptation occurred, and he was inexorably led to the conclusion that the universe has an intelligent designer, whom he labelled the 'great watch-maker'. In the *Origin of Species* [1859], Charles Darwin examined the same data as Paley from a materialist perspective. For Darwin, the competitive adaptation of individual organisms to their environment was the only cause of evolution. He therefore posited a mechanistic universe with no place for any directing intelligence or *nous*.

The difference between Paley and Darwin is thus essentially method-ological. The same data led them to such divergent conclusions because they sought after different causes. Paley sought the *final* cause of evolution and found it in the design of *nous*, while Darwin looked for evolution's *material* cause, which he found in the principle of 'the survival of the fittest'. As he freely admitted, Darwin reached this conclusion by applying the economic theories of Thomas Malthus and Adam Smith to the natural world. The conclusions even of scientists are determined by the methodology they employ.

Today, most natural science and philosophy are committed to the mechanistic, materialist approach to truth. The world as it is perceived by the senses is, to most philosophers as well as to the general public, the real world. But this does not seem to result in any agreement about the nature of that world, or about the role of human beings within it. On the contrary, the twenty-first century is characterized by an extreme relativism with regard to questions of truth and falsehood, and this sceptical attitude is reinforced by an emphasis on the determining power of representation. People often have the impression that scientific empiricism is somehow opposed to linguistic determinism. This notion is encouraged by such cases as the 'Sokal affair' of 1996, in which a physicist tricked the editors of the postmodernist journal *Social Text* into printing his parodic argument for the arbitrary nature of scientific truth. In fact, however, empiricist natural scientists and postmodernist philosophers share the assumption that surface appearances constitute the only knowable reality. Scientists examine the world as it is immediately given to the senses, while postmodernist philosophers claim that immediately perceptible signs construct our experience of the world.

For a historical example of how these approaches can happily cohabit, we can turn to the group of ancient philosophers known as the Sophists. They were not a unified school of thinkers, and our knowledge of them is largely filtered through the fierce criticisms of Plato and Aristotle. Broadly speaking, however, the Sophists agreed that sense perception was more reliable than rational ideas and also, in an argument that would be picked up by Nietzsche, that truth was merely the effect of the subtle manipulation of linguistic or rhetorical techniques. They did not believe in absolute truth, but claimed that truth was radically contingent. They thought of themselves as practising the art of persuasion rather than as following the path to objective truth, and one of the reasons for their castigation by the followers of Socrates was the fact that they happily commodified this art, selling their rhetorical skills to the highest bidder.

The Sophists have frequently, and plausibly, been identified as precursors of postmodernism. Jacques Derrida's essays on such Platonic dialogues as the *Gorgias* argue that Plato himself has recourse to rhetorical shifts in order to refute his Sophist opponents in the name of a spuriously absolute truth. For Derrida the history of Western philosophy is, as A.N. Whitehead famously put it, a series of footnotes to Plato. But Derrida believes that those footnotes comment on a basically fallacious text. The Platonic dream of an absolute distinction between truth and falsehood has, many would argue, finally been exposed as illusory by the brutal facts of the postmodern condition, and the subjectivist relativism of Shakespeare's Hamlet rings out across the centuries: 'There's nothing good or bad but thinking makes it so' (II, ii, 259).

Works of 'New Historicist' literary criticism such as Stephen Greenblatt's *Renaissance Self-fashioning* (1983) have convincingly argued that the literature of the early modern period prefigures postmodernity's concern with the indeterminacy and relativism of truth. Shakespeare's plays are particularly rich in this regard. Hamlet, for example, is regarded by his friends and family as insane. The play's audience is asked to consider whether he is really crazy or just pretending, and Shakespeare leads us to the conclusion that it does not much matter. Hamlet *seems* to be insane, and in the moral universe he heralds, appearance and reality have become indistinguishable. In fact, his insanity is defined by his inability to distinguish between reality and appearance, as in his rebuke to his mother: 'Seems, Madam! Nay, it is; I know not "seems"' (I, ii, 77). In *Macbeth*, the witches prophesy the collapse of binary oppositions, telling of a world where 'Fair is foul and foul is fair' (I, i, 11). *The Tempest* gives an insight into the mutual dependence of moral relativism and mechanistic empiricism. The villain Antonio describes his usurpation of power in the duchy of Milan. 'But for your conscience?' asks his confidant. 'Ay sir,' replies Antonio, 'where lies that? If 'twere a kibe, / 'Twould put me to my slipper; but I feel not / This deity in my bosom' (II, i, 275–8). The conscience is not an empirically perceptible thing, like a 'kibe' or chilblain, and for this reason Antonio concludes that it does not exist, and that he therefore has licence to act on his subjective desires.

In *King Lear* the evil Edmund declares a similar subjective secession from objective morality when he announces 'all with me's meet that I can fashion fit' (I, iv, 183–4).

In Shakespeare's time, such relativist materialism was often called 'sophistical'. Whereas the Sophists founded knowledge on sense perception, Socrates and his pupil Plato founded it upon reason – that is to say, on an objective rather than a subjective approach to truth. All theories of false consciousness claim that it is produced by an imbalance in the relationship between the subject (which is the realm of ideas) and the object (the world of substantial, material things). When one set of ideas intends to label another as false, it generally declares that its opponent has misunderstood the relations between these elements. In Plato's *Republic*, for example, ideas are held to be more authentic than the material world. If we take the objective world for reality, we therefore commit an error which is simultaneously an ethical transgression. Plato likens the way human beings perceive the material world to the vision of prisoners chained by the neck in a cave. A fire burns behind them, and a wall runs between the prisoners and the fire. Plato then describes

> men carrying along that wall, so that they overtop it, all kinds of artefacts, statues of men, reproductions of other animals in stone or wood fashioned in all sorts of ways, and . . . some of the carriers are talking while others are silent.
>
> (514b–515a)

The prisoners would only be able to see the shadows thrown on the wall by these artefacts, and would thus naturally take these shadows to be real things and assume that the voices of the men emanated from the shadows. Any prisoner who escaped into the sunlight and returned to tell his fellows about the real world would be treated as a malicious lunatic by the denizens of the cave. Plato means to indicate that the visible world is made up of mere shadows of ideal forms, which are inaccessible to normal human perception. Not only is this perception flawed, he suggests, but it is in the nature of this flaw to disguise itself, so that it appears self-evident to human beings that the visible world is the only real one. We should also note that the shadows are cast by man-made objects: carved figures, which are carried by human beings. Deliberate deception is thus involved in constructing this pattern of illusion, and this theme will recur frequently in the history of ideology.

After Plato, Hellenic thought generally takes for granted the superiority of the ideal over the material. This means that the mutually definitive binary opposition between ideas and matter has become a hierarchy, in which the former pole is privileged over the latter. We can see some of the consequences of this in Aristotle's *Politics*. In that work, all forms of power are justified by analogy with the mind / body hierarchy:

> It is then in an animal . . . that one can first discern both the sort of rule characteristic of a master and political rule. For the soul rules the body with the rule characteristic of a master, while intellect rules appetite with political and kingly rule; and this makes it evident that it is according to nature and advantageous for the body to be ruled by the soul, and the passionate part [of the soul] by intellect and the part having reason, while it is harmful to both if the relation is equal or reversed.
>
> (1254b, 2–10)

From the presupposition that the mind's subjective ideas are naturally superior to the objective material body, Aristotle proceeds to deduce the necessary dominance of masters over slaves, of Greeks over barbarians, and of men over women. A bias in the relation of the ideal to the material gives credence to the claim that certain human beings are fit only to be ruled by others, as well as to the assertion that certain forms of conscious-ness are systematically false. Aristotle goes on to identify further errors in thought, which he also traces to distortions of the relations between subjective ideas and objective things. He claims, for instance, that every piece of property can be regarded in two ways:

> Every possession has a double use. Both of these uses belong to it as such, but not in the same way, the one being proper and the other not proper to the thing. In the case of footwear, for example, one can wear it or one can exchange it.
>
> (1257a, 7–10)

If the use of the shoe is simply to be worn, it can be regarded as a material object. If on the other hand the shoe is to be exchanged for another object, or sold, an ideal form must be grafted on to the material thing. The shoe is then not simply a shoe, it must be conceived as equivalent to the object for which it is to be exchanged. We must impose an idea on the object which does not naturally belong to its material properties. For this to be possible on any large scale, a common denominator is necessary. We need a sphere of representation which can mediate between the shoe in itself and our idea of the shoe. According to Aristotle, this medium is money. As long as it retains its proper place as a go-between for the ideal and the material, Aristotle looks benignly upon money. When it becomes an end in itself, however, when money is used merely to generate more money, he considers that a fundamental logical and ethical error has been made:

> expertise in exchange is justly blamed since it is not according to nature but involves taking from others, usury is most reasonably hated because one's possessions derive from money itself and not from that for which it was supplied. For it came into being for the sake of exchange, but interest actually creates more of it. . . . So of all sorts of business this is the most contrary to nature.
>
> (3258b, 1–8)

Once again, this error results from an imbalance in the proper relations between ideas, matter and the sphere of representation that mediates between them. When the medium of representation becomes autonomous, when it is exalted above the elements between which it supposedly mediates, an unnatural and perverse view of the world is the result. In the ethics of Plato and Aristotle, this misperception that signs are ends in themselves is equated with sensuality: an irrational attachment to the transient and therefore illusory pleasures of the flesh.

The Platonic–Christian tradition thus assumes that it is impossible for human beings to see things in their true nature. It establishes an 'idealist' hierarchy, in which earthly, material knowledge is necessarily imperfect. But Greek thought also offers a more sanguine view of the possibility of overcoming false consciousness. In the *Magna Moralia*, Aristotle considers the relationship between 'nature' and 'custom'. The distinction rests on the difference between innate and acquired characteristics, and Aristotle suggests that the former are the more durable:

> For nothing that is by nature becomes other by custom. For instance, a
> stone, and heavy things in general, naturally go downwards. If anyone,
> then, throws them up repeatedly, and tries to accustom them to go up,
> all the same they would never go up, but always down.
>
> (I, 1186a, 4–7)

Clearly, to attempt to alter the nature of natural objects is a task of
Sisyphean futility. In the sphere of human nature, however, the nature /
custom dichotomy becomes less absolute. Human beings habitually
conduct themselves in ways which, while they may remain constant, are
evidently not 'natural' in the same sense as the law of gravity. In book II of
the *Magna Moralia*, Aristotle restates the primacy of nature over custom,
but this time with a rather different emphasis: 'For what comes by nature
is harder to cure than what comes by custom (for the reason why custom
is held to be so strong is that it turns things into nature)' (1203b, 30–1).

It seems that we are to distinguish between two kinds of nature. On
the one hand the term refers to intrinsic, immutable qualities, such as
weight in the stone. On the other, there are customary modes of
behaviour which can become so habitual that they come to appear
natural. This 'second nature' is different from the first in that it can be
changed, and manipulated. It therefore has a powerful potential as an
agent of social control. In fact, in the *Nicomachean Ethics*, Aristotle
presents the cultivation of this 'second nature' as a fundamental element
of statecraft:

> This is confirmed by what happens in states; for legislators make the
> citizens good by forming habits in them, and this is the wish of every
> legislator; and those who do not effect it miss their mark, and it is in
> this that a good constitution differs from a bad one.
>
> (1103b, 2–6)

This operation on the part of political leaders may strike modern readers
as underhand, even sinister. If it does, this testifies to our assumptions
that social change and adaptation are, broadly speaking, good things; that
people ought to evaluate situations and determine courses of action by
means of rational analysis; and that it is foolish to continue doing things
in a certain way merely because that is how they have been done in the

past. To Aristotle, on the contrary, habit and custom are the foundations of morality and civilization, and any legislator who neglects to cultivate these qualities in his subjects is failing in his duty. Despite this, we can find in the Aristotelian concept of a 'second nature' the basis of a theory of false consciousness which allows for the possibility that such faulty thinking, being the product of human invention, might be overcome.

THE DAWN OF MODERNITY: LUTHER AND MACHIAVELLI

As the term implies, the postmodern ideas we discussed in the Introduction emerged as a reaction against the characteristic assumptions of the 'modern' age. The modern period begins with the sixteenth century and stretches until the middle of the twentieth. It is the era of production-based capitalism, as opposed to the exchange-oriented, postmodern economy. Unlike postmodernity, the philosophy of the modern period is deeply interested in the identification and refutation of false consciousness. During the 'early modern' period of the sixteenth and seventeenth centuries, Western Europe began its long process of mutation from an agricultural, largely feudal society into one organized around a capitalist, money-based economy. People began to think about themselves and the world around them in new ways, ways that are characteristic of the modern world. The rediscovery of ancient Greek philosophy, combined with the translation of the Bible into the vernacular, provided the thinkers of the early modern period with ammunition against the entrenched ideas of Church and state.

But the people of the sixteenth century were attempting to come to terms with dramatic changes in the organization of social life. A simple transposition of Greek and biblical notions seemed inadequate to explain the unprecedented experiences of modernity. One way of differentiating modern ways of thinking about false consciousness from earlier ones is to chart people's changing attitudes towards precedent, or 'custom'. Around the beginning of the sixteenth century, the idea began to be formulated that, far from guaranteeing ethical action as Aristotle had argued, a blind adherence to custom represented a superstitious and unwarranted reverence for past forms of social behaviour. This notion at first emerged only haltingly, out of the need to explain and legitimate local civil and ecclesiastical innovations. The chaos inflicted on Italy in 1494 by the invasion of Charles VIII of France, for instance, produced extremely sudden and dramatic political changes, which called forth new theories of secular power. Following the flight of Florence's hereditary ruler, Piero de' Medici, the affairs of the city-state were briefly directed by a fanatically puritanical monk named Girolamo Savonarola. In accordance with scholastic tradition, Savonarola justified his seizure of power in Aristotelian terms:

> Habit, indeed, is second nature, and as the rock's nature is to fall and it cannot alter this and cannot be raised except by force, so habit too becomes nature, and it is very difficult if not impossible to change men, especially whole peoples, even if their habits are bad, for their habits spring out of their character. . . . Now the Florentine people, having established a civil form of government long ago, has made such a habit of this form that, besides suiting the nature and requirements of the people better than any other, it has become habitual and fixed in their minds. It would be difficult, if not impossible, to separate them from this form of government.

(1978: 237)

In fact, as Savonarola and his audience were well aware, Florence had not had 'a civil form of government' – that is to say, it had not been a republic – for sixty years. But because the only available vocabulary for legitimating power involved an appeal to custom, Savonarola was forced into the paradoxical position of invoking tradition to justify revolutionary innovation. In practice, Savonarola's four-year rule was characterized by rather bizarre and obsessive attempts to destroy and obliterate all manifestations of the nefarious 'second nature'. A particular target of the monk's ire was the practice of wearing make-up, or 'face painting', and cosmetics were frequently incinerated, along with other sinful, worldly artefacts, in public 'bonfires of the vanities'.

The principal objection to wigs, powder and face-paint was that they made it possible to fabricate a new identity, and thus appeared to be an arrogation of the divine prerogative of creation. This 'second nature' was understood to be idolatrous, because it replaced the works of God with the work of human beings. In his anti-cosmetic diatribes, Savonarola was able to formulate an account of 'second nature' as a distortion and perversion of the God-given 'first' nature. Perhaps this explains the priority he gave to what today may seem a peripheral issue: it provided an opportunity for theoretical advances which was unavailable in overtly political discourse. By thus attempting to reform long-established, customary behaviour while lacking a theoretical justification for political innovation, Savonarola soon made himself unpopular, and he was overthrown and executed in 1498. A younger Florentine, Niccolò Machiavelli, drew from this the conclusion that an innovative ruler must disseminate a systematic illusion among his subjects if he is to retain power. Savonarola, declares Machiavelli in *The Prince*, was an 'unarmed prophet' 'who was ruined in his new orders when the multitude began not to believe in him, and he had not the means of keeping firm those who had believed, or to make unbelievers believe' (1969, 28).

The Prince considers the question of how a reforming ruler can legitimate his reign. Machiavelli claims that the issue does not arise in the case of hereditary princes, or with regard to a ruler who does not seek to introduce social or cultural change. In such circumstances, an appeal to custom is sufficient to forestall rebellion. To keep people obedient:

> it is enough, not to transgress the arrangements of their ancestors . . . it is reasonable that . . . [the prince] will be well liked by his subjects, and the memories and causes of innovations are lost in the ancientness of the continuation of his Dominion . . . in maintaining their old condition, and there not being differences in customs, men will live quietly.
>
> (238–9)

The question raised by the recent history of Florence, however, was how a government which desires to abolish old customs and introduce new ones might justify itself in the eyes of its subjects. Obviously, such a government cannot honestly invoke established custom. And yet Machiavelli did not have access to any other vocabulary in which power could be legitimated. The only possible solution for an innovative government, he concludes, is to deceive the people. As he puts it in the *Discourses*:

> He who desires or wants to reform the State of a City, and wishes that it may be accepted and capable of maintaining itself to everyone's

satisfaction, it is necessary for him at least to retain the shadow of ancient forms, so that it does not appear to the people that the institutions have been changed, even though in fact the new institutions should be entirely different from the past ones: for the general mass of men are satisfied with appearances, as if it exists, and many times are moved by the things which appear to be rather than by the things that are.

(330)

When skilfully deployed, it seems, mere representations can pass themselves off as reality. Machiavelli has thus described two distinct forms of false consciousness. There is, first of all, the tendency of the people to make a fetish out of their past modes of behaviour, or custom. Machiavelli perceives a natural human urge to continue doing things as they have, apparently, always been done. This essentially involves mistaking the second nature for the first nature. It is as if the actions people have performed in the past acquire an animate power in the present and work to frustrate progress and disguise society's real interests, so that, as Machiavelli puts it later, 'the People desire their own ruin' (363). But this self-deception on the part of the people necessitates a second deception which is deliberately instigated by their ruler, who must falsely represent any innovations as if they were continuations of established practice. It thus appears that ideology (to use the anachronism) can arise spontaneously out of quotidian social life, and that it can also be inculcated through a conscious manipulation of 'appearances' by the powers that be. This attribution of a deceptive element to the civil power was so shocking to Renaissance sensibilities that Machiavelli's name soon became a byword for cunning and intrigue in general. Thus, in Marlowe's *The Jew of Malta* [1590], the prologue uses the Florentine's name as a noun, which tells the audience all they need to know about the villainous protagonist, Barabas: 'you shall find him still / In all his projects a sound Machevill / And that's his character' (ll. 7–9).

Despite his unsavoury reputation over the century following his death, Machiavelli's work both described and facilitated a radical change in political thought. The ideas that the people's attachment to custom can constitute a brake on good government, and that it can be desirable for the government to deceive the people, amounted to a transformation in the conventional conception of civil power. One good reason for locating the decisive historical break between the 'medieval' and the 'modern' worlds in the early sixteenth century is the fact that an analogous development in religious thought took place simultaneously with Machiavelli's breakthrough in the secular realm. *The Prince* was written in 1512, and in 1517 Martin Luther nailed his ninety-five theses to the church door at Wittenberg.

The intellectual revelation which initiated the Reformation came when Luther recognized the causal link between the two great problems which beset him: his inability to free himself from guilt through any amount of monastic discipline, and the presence in Wittenberg of the indulgence-seller Johann Tetzel. As an Augustinian monk, Luther had distinguished himself by his insatiable zeal for penance. His exasperated confessor would frequently dismiss him with the injunction not to return until he had some real sins to expiate. And yet Luther found that he was unable to convince himself of God's forgiveness, or to assure himself of his salvation, through the performance of penitential labour, or 'works'.

The idea that absolution from sin can be achieved by carrying out certain ecclesiastically mandated tasks was central to Catholic belief, and penance was a holy sacrament. It was thus in the Pope's power to impose penitential fasts, pilgrimages, banishments and so on, to enable sinners to expiate their transgressions. As well as imposing them, the Pope could also excuse offenders from these penalties. This was often done by calculating a cash equivalent of the penance imposed, and substituting this fine for the performance of the penitential works. This remission became known as an 'indulgence'. This practice was widely deemed acceptable, as long as it was made clear that the money bought remission only from the temporal punishment, and that to buy an indulgence was to participate in a purely legal transaction with the worldly aspect of papal power. Over the two centuries preceding Luther, however, the talismanic potency attached to indulgences increased to the degree that they were believed to be capable of purchasing for the owner a reduction of the time he or she would have to spend in purgatory. Although the papacy disclaimed such views, unscrupulous indulgence-peddlers found it paid to encourage them. The rhyme against which Luther complains in the ninety-five theses – 'when you hear the money's ring, the soul from purgatory springs' – accurately summarizes the popular misconception fostered by indulgence-hawkers.

An indulgence, then, was a certificate denoting a specific amount of human activity. The indulgence system represented these penitential works in the form of a currency. Salesmen like Tetzel attributed to these certificates the power to ameliorate the condition of the soul in the afterlife. Indulgences, in short, represented fetishized labour. They were representations of human actions, which were ascribed supernatural, magical power in the popular imagination. Their role was essentially financial. Just as money establishes a medium of representation which enables us to conceive of an equivalence between human labour and various objects, so indulgences provided a common denominator which made it possible to imagine an equivalence between penitential tasks and divine grace. The Church was supposed to control a kind of capital treasury of the surplus good works of the saints, from which it could dole out specific amounts in exchange for the cash of the indulgence-purchasers. Luther's initial protest was against a local 'abuse' of this system perpetrated by Tetzel on the people of Wittenberg. Following the punitive response of the papacy, however, he was impelled to consider the wider ramifications of the exchange of 'works' for grace. His personal experience of the inadequacy of penance to liberate him from guilt convinced him that no such equation could legitimately be drawn. As a result, Luther concluded that the entire penitential system of the Catholic Church was nothing more than a systematic and blasphemous confidence trick.

In *The Babylonian Captivity of the Church* [1521] Luther elaborates a detailed critique of the idea that grace can be earned by human actions, an idea which he calls 'works righteousness'. In his opinion, this 'carnal' or 'fleshly' mode of thought has polluted virtually every aspect of Catholic doctrine. In the mass, for example, the ceremonial actions of the priest are believed to bring about a 'transubstantiation', exchanging the bread and wine for the body and blood of Christ. In Luther's view, this doctrine perniciously misconstrues the relationship between the material and the spiritual. It suggests that the priest can transform a representation of God into physical reality. According to Luther, the Catholic mass thus fits the Old Testament definition of idolatry; it establishes an illusory equivalence between ideas and matter through the medium of representation, and it does so by fetishizing human activity. This belief in the magical efficacy of the priestly acts is necessary, according to Luther, to enable the priest to sell his labour and perform masses for money. As he puts it in the *Commentary on Galatians*:

> The pope has taken away the true use of the Mass and has simply turned it into merchandise that one must buy for the benefit of another person. There stood the Mass priest at the altar, an apostate who denied Christ and blasphemed the Holy Spirit; and he was doing a work not only for himself but for others, both living and dead, even for the entire church, and that simply by the mere performance of the act.
>
> (1959, XXVI, 135)

It is necessary to conceive of the mass as a miraculous 'work' performed by the priest in order that it may be exchanged for money. Such a belief blasphemously removes salvationary power from Christ's sacrifice and bestows it on a fetishized human act. Throughout his polemical career, Luther dwells on the contention that this fetishization serves the purposes of an ecclesiastical market economy:

> there is no opinion more generally held or more firmly believed in the church today than this, that the mass is a good work and a sacrifice. And this abuse has brought an endless host of other abuses in its train, so that the faith of this sacrament has become wholly extinct and the holy sacrament has been turned into mere merchandise, a market, and a profit-making business. Hence participations, brotherhoods, intercessions, merits, anniversaries, memorial days and the like wares are bought and sold, traded and bartered, in the church. On these the priests and monks depend for their entire livelihood.
>
> (1959, XXXVI, 35–6)

This ecclesiastical market was more intimately involved with secular capital than even Luther was aware. Unbeknownst to him, the great banking house of Fugger had organized Tetzel's trip to Wittenberg as a means of ensuring the collection of debts owed by the Church. The transfer of profits from the indulgence trade was the foundation upon which the Fuggers built their fortune. Luther may have been ignorant of the details, but he was certainly cognizant of a close relationship between secular and ecclesiastical capital. In his writing the distinction between them often evaporates. The Church's idolatry and the capitalist fetish of money are, for Luther, one and the same:

the business is now to be transferred, and sold to Fugger of Augsburg. Henceforward bishoprics and livings for sale or exchange or in demand, and dealings in the spiritualities, have arrived at their true destination, now that the bargaining for spiritual or secular properties has become united into a single business. But I would like to hear of a man who is clever enough to discover what Avarice of Rome might do which has not already been done. Then perhaps Fugger would transfer and sell to someone else these two lines of business which are now to be combined into one.

(1959, 430)

The effect of this 'business' on the minds of the congregation was, according to Luther, to produce an earth-bound, objectified or 'fleshly' consciousness, in which faith is occluded and replaced by a belief in the efficacy of 'works'. Fallen humanity is under a constant temptation to lapse into this false consciousness, but Luther believes that a consistent, thoroughgoing awareness of this pernicious tendency will force the believer to place his or her faith in divine agency.

This resistance to the idolatrous fetishization of human works informed the consciousness of Protestant Europe for centuries. For example, in John Bunyan's allegory *The Pilgrim's Progress* [1678] (1984), the wayfaring Christian is misdirected by 'Mr Worldly-Wiseman' to seek the counsel of one 'Legality', who dwells in the village of 'Morality'. He discovers his error when 'Evangelist' informs him that Worldly-Wiseman is of a 'carnal temper':

This Legality therefore is not able to set thee free from thy burden [i.e. of sin]. . . . No man was as yet ever rid of his burden by him, no, nor ever is like to be: ye cannot be justified by the Works of the Law; for by the deeds of the Law no man living can be rid of his burden: therefore Mr. Worldly-Wiseman is an alien, and Mr. Legality a cheat; and for his Son Civility, notwithstanding his simpering looks, he is but a hypocrite, and cannot help thee.

(19–20)

For Luther as for Machiavelli, then, false consciousness arises when human beings make fetishes of their own deeds. In the arena of secular politics, Machiavelli describes a transformation of established patterns of behaviour, or 'custom', into an immutable 'second nature', and he identifies this manoeuvre as the principal obstacle to innovative government. In the field of theology, Luther finds the root of error in the belief that human actions can save our souls. As we shall see, these criticisms of mortal hubris provide solid foundations for later thinkers, when they set about the tasks of criticizing and dismantling the ecclesiastical and secular institutions of medieval Europe.

In Francis Bacon's *Novum Organon* [1620] (1959), the originally religious concept of 'idolatry' is adapted into a fully secular theory of false consciousness. Bacon divides the various kinds of mistaken ideas into four classes of 'idols'. The 'idols of the tribe' refer to the presuppositions and prejudices which enter the mind as a result of living in society. Mere social conventions are taken for eternal verities, and so the products of the mind are mistaken for absolute truths: 'the human understanding is like a false mirror, which, receiving rays irregularly, distorts and discolours the nature of things by mingling its own nature with it' (70). Since this kind of error results from the intrinsic qualities of human nature, it cannot be altogether avoided. We can, however, guard against it by scrupulously resisting the temptation to idolize our own ideas or arrogantly regard them as eternal or absolute. The second class of idol, the 'idols of the cave', are the mistakes which arise from the purely personal predilections of individuals and the third, the 'idols of the Market-place', indicate the mental distortions which result from ignorance of the creative power of linguistic representation: 'For men believe that their reason governs words; but it is also true that words react on the understanding' (80). Any coherent theory of knowledge must therefore take into account the signs which mediate between ideas and things.

These three kinds of 'idol' Bacon labels 'native', or inherent in the human mind, and he therefore sees them as unavoidable. In contrast, the fourth class, which Bacon terms the 'idols of the theatre', and which includes all closed philosophical systems which try to force empirical reality to accord with their own formal patterns, is termed 'adventitious'. That is to say, these idols are originally extraneous to the mind and they can therefore be expelled. Bacon's division of the idols into two classes anticipates a distinction often found in later discussions of ideology, between those false ideas which arise spontaneously out of everyday social life, and those which are introduced with a degree of calculation, usually with the purpose of perpetuating a particular form of power or control. This distinction became an extremely pressing issue when, in the middle of the seventeenth century, a section of the English nation found itself attempting to replace its ancient system of government by force of arms.

2

EMPIRICISM

Divinity, adieu!

(Christopher Marlowe, *Dr Faustus*, I, i, 48)

MILTON AND THE ENGLISH REVOLUTION

The English Revolution of the mid-seventeenth century was the first modern attempt to reorder the political affairs of an entire nation, while simultaneously reforming the consciousness of its citizens. John Milton, the official propagandist for Cromwell's revolutionary government, was compelled to enlist ancient and medieval ideas in the service of political innovation, just as Machiavelli had done in Renaissance Florence. Milton's work combines the Platonic dichotomy between ideal and material spheres with the Aristotelian concept of custom to offer an explanation of why people collude in their own oppression. For a time, Milton believed that by purging monarchy and prelacy out of the Commonwealth it might be possible to build a reformed society, and to people it with virtuous citizens. Milton was convinced, to use the twenty-first-century vernacular, that the personal was political. In 'The First Defence of the English People', he saw an indissoluble connection between the spiritual condition of the individual and the political condition of the state:

> My fellow countrymen, your own character is a mighty factor in the acquisition and retention of liberty. Unless your liberty is such as can neither be won or lost by arms, but is of that kind alone which, sprung from piety, justice, temperance, in short true virtue . . . there will not be lacking one who will surely wrench [it] from you.
>
> (1962, IV, ii, 680)

Like most revolutions from above, however, the Cromwellian state soon foundered on the rocks of popular conservatism, and the monarchy was restored in 1660. The revolutionary regime's intellectual apologists were thus faced with the weary task of comprehending 'an inconstant, irrational and Image-doting rabble'. How was it possible to account for people who, as it seemed, voluntarily chose slavery over freedom? The most readily available explanation was the Christian myth of the Fall, and in *Paradise Lost* Milton undertakes a long meditation on the nature of the post-lapsarian mind. Milton's epic endorses the common assumption that Adam and Eve's alienation from God had obscured humanity's *oculus intellectualis*, or 'eye of understanding'. Their posterity is therefore doomed to reverse the Platonic hierarchy, and allow their fleshly appetites to dominate their intellect. As they are being expelled from Eden, Adam and Eve are informed that this mental error will result in political oppression:

> Therefore since hee permits
> Within himself unworthy Powers to reign
> Over free Reason, God in Judgment just
> Subjects him from without to violent Lords;
> Who oft as undeservedly enthral
> His outward freedom.
>
> (XII, ll. 90–5)

Paradise Lost represents this false consciousness as a universal human trait, and this doubtless reflects Milton's pessimism after the Restoration. But such a universal false consciousness could not account for the political and religious divisions within the English nation. How could it be that some people were quite able to perceive what Milton took to be the moral and godly way to organize Church and state, while others were so utterly deluded? In the speech quoted above, Milton has the archangel Michael inform Adam that mankind is condemned to live under tyranny because 'inordinate desires' and 'upstart Passions' will usurp the place of reason in the human mind. In *Paradise Lost* these disruptive forces are identified primarily with sensual appetite and undisciplined emotion. However, the work Milton produced during the more hopeful days of the Commonwealth indicates that his understanding of sensuality has a political dimension which extends far beyond any censorious exhortations to an austere personal morality.

In the prose works which Milton composed in his capacity as polemical pamphleteer during the 1640s and 1650s, the Aristotelian notion of custom subtly modifies the Platonic denigration of sensuality. According to Milton's *The Judgement of Martin Bucer Concerning Divorce*, 'the prostrate worshippers of Custom' (II, 439) commit idolatry. That is to say, they genuflect before merely human practices and institutions, treating them as if they were divinely ordained and hence immutable. A blind adherence to 'custom' is, in fact, a form of sensuality. Like the pleasures of the flesh, the traditions of man are material, earthly things, and to fetishize them by allowing them to inhibit the free exercise of reason is therefore idolatrous.

Milton's explicitly political conception of the link between custom and idolatry is an important moment in the history of ideology. The Scriptural injunction against adoring 'the work of men's hands' could be interpreted as a command that no human traditions, institutions or assumptions should be regarded as sacrosanct. During the crisis of the mid-seventeenth century the 'idol' or 'tyrant' custom became a topical concern. Meric Casaubon's *A Treatise of Use and Custome* [1638] alludes to the ancient idea that

> custome having once got the strength of long continuance, insinuates errors and impostures (bee they never so grosse) into the minds of most men under the shape and representation of genuine truth: so Justin Martyr; who fetcheth hence especially the origine of Idolatrie.
>
> (cit. Milton, 1962, II, 222n1)

Milton began his polemical career by applying this idea to the organization of the Church. In *The Reason of Church Government* [1642] he notes that the Gospel warns against heeding 'the pride and wisdom of the flesh', which 'consists in a bold presumption of ordering the worship and service of God after man's own will in traditions and ceremonies' (1962, I, 826). The episcopal hierarchy and the conducting of services according to conventional 'set forms' are declared to be barriers to the true knowledge of God, on the grounds that they subject His worshippers to merely human traditions.

In the tumultuous 1640s, criticism of the Church could rapidly be extended into other spheres. By 1642 Milton was generalizing from his criticism of the Anglican hierarchy into wider epistemological issues: 'the service of Prelaty', he remarks, 'is perfect slavery, and by consequence perfect falsehood' (I, 853). By the following year, in *The Doctrine and Discipline of Divorce*, he had extended his iconoclasm to the most intimate areas of private conduct. 'The greatest burden in the world', he writes, 'is superstition; not only of Ceremonies in the Church, but of imaginary and scarecrow sins at home' (II, 228). Arguing for the legalization of divorce on the grounds of mental incompatibility, Milton declares that marriage must no longer be 'worshipt like some Indian deity' (II, 277).

Under the pressure of simultaneous upheavals in his personal life and in the political life of the nation, Milton was driven to broaden his originally liturgical attack on idolatry, so that the concept could be applied to any human practice with pretensions to immutability. In *Areopagitica* [1644], Milton arrives at the radical conclusion that truth is necessarily historical: 'Truth is compar'd in Scripture to a streaming fountain; if her waters be not in a perpetual progression, they sick'n into a muddy pool of conformity and tradition' (II, 543). Innovation is thus to be welcomed, and even when it appears shockingly radical, this can be attributed to our faulty perception: 'our eyes blear'd and dimm'd with prejudice and custom' (II, 565) will be unable to discern new truths.

Milton not only saw that idolatry and custom can deform the mind as well as the institutions of Church and state; he also suggested that there is a causal relationship between external oppression and internal error. In *Areopagitica* he worries lest 'while we still affect by all means a rigid external formality, we may as soon fall again into a gross conforming stupidity' (II, 564), and *The Tenure of Kings and Magistrates* [1650], in which Milton achieves a fully fledged theory of revolution, opens with a lengthy consideration of how mistaken ideas are linked to political repression:

> If men within themselves would be govern'd by reason, and not generally give up their understanding to a double tyrannie, of Custom from without, and blind affections within, they would discerne better, what it is to favour and uphold the Tyrant of a Nation. But being slaves within doors, no wonder that they strive so much to have the public State conformably govern'd to the inward vitious rule, by which they govern themselves.
>
> (III, 190)

The regicidal *Eikonoklastes* [1649] makes explicit the connection between Milton's attacks on established ecclesiastical and secular government: 'the People, exorbitant and excessive in all their motions, are prone ofttimes not to a religious onely, but to a civil kinde of Idolatry in idolizing their Kings' (III, 343). It seems clear that, for Milton, the sweep of events during the 1640s laid bare the surreptitious workings of tyrannical custom and sensual idolatry throughout the Church, the home, the mind and the state.

The English Revolution, then, produced among its most perspicacious advocates a fairly sophisticated theory of false consciousness. As the above quotation indicates, however, the 'People' straggled some way behind the intellectual vanguard. The ultimate failure of the Revolution would force the issue of systematic error into philosophical prominence. Milton's preoccupation with the Fall and its consequences, exemplified in *Paradise Lost*, was one way of accounting for the tenacity of popular misconception. But, by applying concepts such as 'idolatry' and 'superstition' beyond the religious sphere, Milton had already prepared the way for a thoroughly secularized investigation of ideology.

HOBBES, LOCKE, SMITH AND ENGLISH EMPIRICISM

Milton and the other radical 'puritans' of the early modern period insisted that the spiritual dimension of consciousness must be kept free from any taint of materiality, whether this took the form of visible church decoration or ceremony, the dead weight of tradition and custom or the coercive intervention of the sovereign. The intention behind this argument was to reserve for religion a privileged status which would lie beyond the jurisdiction of the civil power. But this radical separation of material and spiritual competencies was susceptible to a very different interpretation. In Thomas Hobbes's *Leviathan* [1651] (1985), the rift between the kingdoms of God and Caesar is presented in such a way as to reduce the religious sphere to practical irrelevance.

Hobbes begins his book by establishing the fundamental difference between objects in the material world, and the ways in which these objects are represented in the human mind. The 'motion' of the external objects 'presseth our organs' so as to produce sense impressions of such qualities as colour and sound. However, these qualities are not inherent in the objects themselves, but are produced by our own sensory perceptions. It therefore follows that 'the object is one thing, the image or fancy is another'. The Platonic incommensurability of spirit and matter is here refracted into an irreconcilable division between the physical world and the concepts which human beings can have of that world. Perception, according to Hobbes, must always be a representation of an object which is not fully knowable in itself. The final section of *Leviathan*, entitled 'Of the Kingdom of Darknesse', suggests that the tendency to fetishize these purely subjective representations is the cause of religious idolatry:

> Before our Saviour preached, it was the general Religion of the Gentiles, to worship for Gods, those Appearances that remain in the Brain from the impression of external Bodies upon the organs of their Senses, which are commonly called *Ideas, Idols, Phantasmes, Conceits*, as being Representations of those external Bodies, which cause them, and have nothing in them of reality, no more than the things which seem to stand before us in a Dream.
>
> (665)

Here we can perceive how the theological concept of idolatry mutated into the secular notion of ideology. The idolatry of the Gentiles, says Hobbes, consisted in the worship of their own ideas. This worship was possible only because the benighted heathens did not perceive that their ideas were not self-sufficient, but were caused by external objects and mediated through the faculty of representation. (With his customary tact, Hobbes refrains from stating the obvious inference that it is idolatrous for *any* society to make fetishes of its ideas by regarding them as absolute or eternal.) The antidote to such error would be to point out that all ideas are determined by material phenomena, and are therefore contingent upon external circumstances. Hobbes thus advocates a sceptical materialism calculated to demolish any impious claim to transcendent truth.

The fact that religion makes just such a claim led Hobbes conclusively to distinguish theology from philosophy. 'The Scripture', he declares, 'was written to shew unto men the kingdome of God . . . leaving the world, and the Philosophy thereof, to the disputation of men, for the exercising of their naturall Reason' (145). Like Bacon, Hobbes believed that only this 'reason', which would operate according to the principles of empirical investigation, was capable of giving insight into the material world. Metaphysics, including theology, is ignominiously relegated to 'the Kingdom of Fairies' (370). This latter field of investigation is harmless enough, if rather irrelevant, unless it presumes to interfere with the civil power, in which case Hobbes believes it enters into 'the Kingdome of Darknesse'. To attempt to obtrude religious notions into the theory of state policy is not just mistaken, it is an act of moral turpitude which is designed to serve the selfish interests of the clerical party.

We are faced here with what later philosophers would refer to as the 'instrumentalization' of reason. Before Hobbes, reason had been directed to an end beyond itself; its purpose had been to know, serve or praise God. Even Bacon and Milton, who did advocate empirical research, conceived of science as a way to 'repair the ruins of our first parents' and regain the perfect knowledge which was lost after the Fall. In *Leviathan*, on the contrary, reason must strictly limit itself to the material world if it is not to be led astray by the nebulous fancies of mere ideas. Reason thus ceases to have any metaphysical purpose, but is to be exclusively concerned with the investigation of data which can be sensually apprehended.

One way of understanding the difference between Hobbes and Milton would be to look at the ways in which they state the opposition between reason and custom. Milton denigrates custom and advocates reason in order to make knowledge *historical*; he envisages truth as being in 'perpetual progression' once it is freed from the restrictive grip of customary assumptions. Hobbes, on the other hand, appeals to reason over custom in order to make truth trans-historical. 'Adherence to Custome', he claims, springs from plain 'Ignorance of the nature of Right and Wrong' (165). Social practices and institutions must thus be judged by rational, rather than historical, criteria. For example, Hobbes refuses to concede that precedent is sufficient warrant for a legal code. In order to be legitimate, the law must be formally set down in a constitution:

> we are not to understand that such Customes have their force, onely from Length of Time; but that they were antiently Lawes written, or otherwise made known, for the Constitutions, and Statutes of their Soveraigns; and are now Lawes, not by vertue of the Praescription of time, but by the Constitutions of their present Soveraigns.

> (315)

This sovereignty was first established, according to *Leviathan*, by means of a contract, or 'covenant' between the members of society. Originally, at least hypothetically, the power of the state draws its legitimacy from a rational agreement. Though Hobbes was a political conservative, his theory implicitly contains an assumption which could, in different hands, be used to justify a revolutionary reordering of habitual behaviour. If power originates in a rational contract, rather than acquiring authority through tradition or custom, then everything we do and believe can be re-evaluated according to the standard of reasonable enquiry, without regard for historical precedent. 'If we will reverence the Age', says Hobbes, 'the Present is the Oldest' (727).

As Hobbes sees it, the false apparitions of metaphysics, which have been inculcated to serve the interests of a priestly caste, are not empirically verifiable, and so can be disregarded by serious secular thinkers. He connects religion and custom to the impulse to worship the imaginations of our own minds. Today we might describe them as 'ideological' modes of thought. However, given the uncompromisingly sceptical attitude Hobbes adopts towards the possibility of objective knowledge, might it not be the case that reason itself has ideological elements? Why might not reason also serve the selfish, biased interests of a particular section of society? Hobbes's empiricism also leaves him vulnerable to the charge that he derives allegedly eternal verities about human nature from the specific, observable behaviour of people in his own particular society.

Most notably, in a doctrine still beloved by bourgeois economists, he assumes that the predatory individualism of nascent capitalism reflects an unavoidable 'state of nature'.

Nevertheless, the potential of rational analysis and empirical investigation for exposing and eliminating customary falsehood gave them great appeal for progressive thinkers for centuries after Hobbes. Most significantly for the history of ideology, *Leviathan* made it seem important to study the ways in which ideas are formed, and to investigate the relation of this process to material circumstances. John Locke's *Essay Concerning Human Understanding* [1689] (1867) takes a radically empiricist view of the issue. That is to say, Locke holds that there are no innate ideas, but that all knowledge derives from experience. He divides this latter category into 'sensation' of objective, physical things, and 'reflection' on the subjective workings of our minds:

> Our observation, employed either about external sensible objects, or about the internal operations of our minds, perceived and reflected on by ourselves, is that which supplies our understandings with all the materials of thinking.

(59)

It is, therefore, possible to examine and account for the formation of ideas in a fairly precise fashion. It is also possible to judge our theories and concepts according to an absolute standard: any ideas which are not demonstrably derived from experience must be regarded as irrational. A particular concern of Locke's is to expel 'faith' from philosophical discussion, for 'If the boundaries be not set between faith and reason, no enthusiasm or extravagancy in religion can be contradicted' (589). Locke alludes here to the radical sects which rose to prominence in the army and among the lower classes during the Civil War and the Interregnum, and which he wants to be able to refute. Their utopian and millenarian ideas were clearly unreasonable, since they did not appeal to empirical evidence, but expressed their hopes and desires in largely metaphysical terms. Locke bundles together all these 'strange opinions and extravagant practices' (589) under the rubric of 'enthusiasm', which he claims abandons reason in favour of 'the ungrounded fancies of a man's own brain' (590).

Locke thus excludes from philosophical discussion a great many of the ideas which were, in fact, held by his contemporaries. English empiricism originates as an aggressive, debunking mode of thought, which is concerned to make a polemical intervention in an urgent debate. Locke's *Essay* appeared in the aftermath of the 'glorious and bloodless revolution' of 1688, which forged a compromise between moderate monarchists and parliamentarians, and his apparently unbiased criteria actually militate strongly in favour of the terms of that settlement.

Once again, then, false consciousness consists in the fetishization of mere ideas. This error can be avoided, according to Locke, by accepting only those ideas which can be derived from empirical circumstances, and judged according to 'that standard of reason which is common to us with all men' (597). Reason is a universal natural principle by which we can learn the correct way to behave. It remains only to explain why many – or even most – people hold opinions which Locke regards as unreasonable. Several obstacles to the free exercise of reason are identified in the *Essay*. People may be 'hindered from inquiry', either by the demands of labour, or deliberately by 'those whose interest it is to keep them ignorant' (599). They may simply not be clever enough to think rationally, or they may 'fear that an impartial inquiry would not favour those opinions which best suit their prejudices, lives, and designs' (600). Incorrect assumptions may be 'riveted' in the mind 'by long custom and education' (601), which lead the unwary 'to reverence them as sacred things' (602). 'Received hypothesis' (602) and 'predominant passions' (603) may also prevent people from following the dictates of reason. Finally, 'authority', or 'the giving up our assent to the common received opinions, either of our friends or party, neighbourhood or country' (606) is the most powerful force which keeps people in error.

Like Bacon's 'idols', some of these obstacles to true perception are produced by the internal workings of the mind, while others are imposed on it by external forces. This corresponds to Locke's division of 'experience' into two categories: 'reflection' and 'sensation'. We can have experience of things outside us, and we can also experience the operations of our minds. Thus Locke still maintains an 'ideal' dimension of internal experience which is to be regarded as distinct from the sensual or 'material' encounter with the world around us. This raises the two questions which dominate the subsequent history of ideology: does one of these kinds of experience determine the other, and if so, which is which? To under-stand how this debate develops, we must first return to Hobbes, and particularly to his treatment of what today we would call 'the economy'.

Hobbes's approach is mechanistic and micrological. His analysis of society focuses on the smallest available unit: the individual human being. Furthermore, he thinks of human beings as purely material creatures whose actions are motivated by the effort to fulfil their 'appetites' or eschew their 'aversions', so that 'of all Voluntary Acts, the Object is to every man his own Good' (1985, 209). Hobbes's argument exhibits the germinal stage of today's market ideology, with its materialist, objectified conception of human nature. In a market economy, people must conceive of their subjective activity as 'labour'; that is to say, as a thing which can be bought and sold. As Hobbes puts it: 'A man's Labour also, is a commodity exchangeable for benefit, as well as any other thing' (295). Our 'labour' is *alienated* from us, it exists outside us in the objective form of the money for which we exchange it. To the degree that this happens, our identities cease to be essential and become relational, defined not by any intrinsic qualities but by their position in the market:

> The Value, or Worth of a man, is as of all other things, his Price; that is to say, so much as would be given for the use of his Power: and therefore is not absolute; but a thing dependent on the need and judgment of another.
>
> (151–2)

Hobbes pours scorn on psychological essentialism, mocking the notion of 'the Essence of a Man, which (they say) is his Soule' (692) and boasting of his disbelief in 'the Existence of an Incorporall Soule, Separated from the Body' (693).

This objectification of the subject is an unavoidable consequence of a market economy, as Adam Smith makes clear in *The Wealth of Nations* [1776] (1994). Once labour becomes a commodity, people must market their labour by becoming specialists in a particular kind of activity. Thus Smith observes that the 'division of labor . . . is the necessary, though very slow and gradual consequence, of a certain propensity in human nature . . . the propensity to truck, barter and exchange one thing for another' (14). The labourer must treat his 'labour' (which is really to say his subjective activity, his *self*) in the same way as a merchant treats his commodities: 'When the division of labour has been once thoroughly established. . . . Every man thus lives by exchanging, or becomes in some measure a merchant, and the society itself grows to be what is properly called a commercial society' (24). Like any other commodity, says Smith, labour has two kinds of value:

> The one may be called 'value in use'; the other, 'value in exchange'. The things which have the greatest value in use have frequently little or no value in exchange; on the contrary, those which have the greatest value in exchange have frequently little or no value in use. Nothing is more valuable than water: but it will purchase scarce any thing; scarce any thing can be had in exchange for it. A diamond, on the contrary, has scarce any value in use; but a very great quantity of other goods may frequently be had in exchange for it.
>
> (31–2)

Smith here translates into the technical vocabulary of what came to be called 'economics' an insight which had been clear to non-specialist observers of the market for decades. In *Centuries of Meditation* [1668–73] (1985), Thomas Traherne recalls a similar revelation:

> I began to enquire what things were most Common: Air, Light, Heaven and Earth, Water, the Sun, Trees, Men and Women, Cities Temples &c. These I found Common and Obvious to all: Rubies Perls Diamonds Gold and Silver, these I found scarce, and to the most Denied. Then began I to consider and compare the value of them, which I measured by their Serviceableness, and by the Excellencies which would be found in them, should they be taken away. And in Conclusion I saw clearly, that there was a Real Valuableness in all the Common things; in the Scarce, a feigned.
>
> (I, 142)

For Traherne as for Smith, an object's use value is 'real', while its exchange value is 'feigned'. Smith extends the scope of commodification further than Traherne, including 'Men and Women', or rather that portion of their activity which they alienate in the form of 'labour', under the category of things that have a 'feigned' value. For Smith, in fact, labour plays the role of a universal commodity. The various objects that are exchanged on the market have in common the fact that they are products of labour, and labour thus provides the common denominator in which the exchange values of other commodities are measured, as Smith declares: 'Labour is the real measure of exchange value' (33).

Labour may be the *real* measure of exchange value, but our experience tells us something quite different. Our experience, according to Smith, is systematically false. Large-scale commodity exchange demands that we express exchange value not in terms of labour but in terms of a *symbol* of labour. Representation elbows aside reality, and we call this representation 'money':

> But value is not commonly estimated by labour, because labour is difficult to measure, and commodities are more frequently exchanged for other commodities, especially money, which is therefore most frequently used in estimating value.
>
> (34–5)

The illusion that money literally *is* value thus quickly takes hold among the populace. This is a false, or ideological, consciousness brought about by empiricist habits of thought:

> The greater part of the people too understand better what is meant by a quantity of a particular commodity, than by a quantity of labour. The one is a plain palpable object; the other an abstract notion, which, though it can be made sufficiently intelligible, is not altogether so natural and obvious.
>
> (35)

Smith thus sees a systematic disjunction between appearance and reality as an inevitable consequence of a market economy. 'Labour', he repeatedly stresses, 'is alone the ultimate and real standard by which the value of all commodities can at all times and places be estimated and compared. It is their real price; money is their nominal price only' (36–7). According to this criterion, it would seem that in our society the nominal has replaced the real. This is what postmodernists mean when they claim to be living in a 'hyper-reality'.

THE FRENCH CONNECTION: CONDILLAC, HELVETIUS AND HOLBACH

The most interesting responses to the issues raised by English empiricism came from a loosely associated group of eighteenth-century French thinkers who are usually referred to as the *philosophes*, and whose ideas form the basis of the movement known to history as the Enlightenment. This is not to say that this movement was confined to France; on the contrary, its major exponents looked to England for political example and philosophical inspiration. But because the Reformation and the revolutions of the seventeenth century had rid England of many practical obstacles to free empirical enquiry, the later English empiricists did not approach their task with the same sense of practical urgency as animated the *philosophes*. The French connection of philosophical enquiry with political reform established a link between theory and practice which pervades all subsequent discussions of ideology.

Whereas Locke's empiricism could be used as a weapon against the 'enthusiasm' of radical Protestant sects, the *philosophes* identified the Catholic Church as the enemy of truth. To counter the claims of the Church, thinkers such as Condillac, Helvetius and Holbach had recourse to a 'sensationalist' reading of Locke. This means that they thought Locke's 'sensation' determined his 'reflection' and that all ideas thus had their source in material experience. This kind of philosophy has therefore become known as materialism. In his *Treatise on the Sensations* [1754] (2001), Condillac asks his readers to put themselves in the place of a marble statue, to which he then ascribes, one by one, the various senses. By this means he claims to trace human thought processes to their roots in physical sensation. Elsewhere, Condillac says that his method 'consists in re-ascending to the origin of ideas, in tracing their genealogy'. He argues, in short, that our ideas are always produced by material forces, and he evaluates ideas on the basis of their correspondence with material reality. Thus the soul, for example, has no real (because no material) existence, and all subjective human consciousness is nothing but 'transformed sensation'.

As we saw in our discussion of Hobbes, this approach involves a secularized version of the religious critique of idolatry. If an idea is empirically groundless, if it has no material referent, it is considered ethically harmful to treat it as though it were 'real'. We may note in passing that this kind of materialism seems rather naive today: it takes no account, for example, of the fact that the media of representation, in which our ideas must necessarily be expressed, themselves have a material dimension. Nevertheless, in the France of the *ancien régime*, this 'sensationalism' had a radical influence and a practical impact which philosophy did not attain again until the twentieth century. Following Condillac's injunction to search for the origin of ideas in the material world, Claude Helvetius developed a sociological dimension to the critique of 'prejudices'. Helvetius saw that the proposition that non-material ideas had a real existence served the interests of particular social groups, primarily the clergy, whose power depended on their ability to convince the rest of the population of the objective reality of certain metaphysical concepts. Sensationalism thus became closely associated with anti-clericalism, and the *philosophes* went about their work with Helvetius's injunction to 'pull off their masks' ringing in their ears.

Those most assiduous in this enterprise included Voltaire, whose motto 'Ecrasez l'infâme' ('Crush infamy') became the battle-cry of the anti-clerical movement, and Holbach, who took Condillac's materialism to its logical conclusion. One of the first overtly atheist philosophers, Holbach viewed false consciousness as the product of a conspiracy. He was sure that the priests were deliberately and cynically inducing people to believe things which were simply not true. In *The System of Nature* [1770] (1970) Holbach declares that all error can be traced to the human tendency to 'deceive themselves by abandoning experience to follow imaginary systems'. The tenacity of Aristotle's description of custom as a second nature is clear in Holbach's assertion that people naturally assume the truth of 'prejudices in which they have been instructed from their infancy; with which habit has familiarized them; and which authority has obliged them to conserve' (84).

It seemed to these men that the grip of systematic illusion could only be weakened through a Baconian re-education of the people, which would be conducted on an empirical basis. Helvetius's slogan 'L'éducation peut tout' neatly expresses the *philosophes*' desire to tear down inherited and customary ideas and reconstruct consciousness on the basis of rational enquiry. However, this faith in the redemptive power of empirical investigation and rational education contradicts the radical sensationalism which the *philosophes* also espoused. When Holbach claims that 'Man's mode of thinking is necessarily determined by his manner of being; it must therefore depend on his natural organization and the modification his system receives independently of his will' (93), he supposes that our thoughts and beliefs are determined by external circumstances, which operate on us 'independently' of our conscious intentions. This assumption contradicts his claim that false ideas are consciously inculcated by scheming priests, rather than automatically assimilated from experience. Furthermore, it is hard to see how Holbach can account for the fact that he and his contemporaries managed to identify false consciousness at all. He at once says that thought is determined by sensation and that thought can develop independently through education – that is, without corresponding changes in the material environment. In fact, the *philosophes* in general tend to assume that a project of re-education would be enough to bring about changes in society. Such a position is incompatible with their own materialism. It took a real, material cataclysm which surpassed their most ardent hopes and their worst fears to reveal this contradiction in their ideas.

ROUSSEAU, REVOLUTION, REFLECTION

The materialism of the *philosophes* offered a rather bleak and monochromatic view of the world. Many found the ideas of Condillac, Helvetius and Holbach to be, quite literally, soul-destroying. Fortunately, eighteenth-century France offered an alternative mode of thought to which such people could turn. Jean-Jacques Rousseau is often grouped among the *philosophes* and he associated and collaborated with many of them. But his own ideas were in sharp contrast to the cold empiricism of their projects. As Nietzsche remarked, Rousseau set the Enlightenment on its head. Another way of putting it would be to say that Rousseau takes the critical method of the Enlightenment and turns it against itself. As we have seen, thinkers from Hobbes on had judged existing social institutions and practices according to the standard of reason. The capacity for rational thought was held to be innate, or 'natural', to the human race. It is this proposition that Rousseau challenges as a 'metaphysical principle'. In an outflanking, radicalizing gesture, Rousseau subjects reason itself to the kind of critique which the *philosophes* carried out in its name.

What he discovered, as he says in the *Discourse on the Origin of Inequality* [1755] (1992), was that reason is actually completely *un*natural. He deduces this from an examination of human 'nature'. Due to the distorting effects of civilization, he suggests, our true nature now exists only inside our minds. Rousseau thus rejects the methodology of the *philosophes*, who claimed that it is the external world which forms our consciousness. 'Let us therefore begin', he says, 'by putting aside all the facts, for they have no bearing on the question' (17). The empirical, materialist approach, which treats the mind as an object, is itself part of the problem it purports to remedy: 'it is by dint of studying man that we have rendered ourselves incapable of knowing him' (11). By examining his own subjective nature, Rousseau evolves the hypothetical concept of the 'state of nature', which he uses as a standard against which to judge contemporary society. Taking issue with Hobbes's description of this condition as ethically inferior to civilization, Rousseau claims that moral categories do not apply to pre-social beings: 'savages are not evil precisely because they do not know what it is to be good' (36). Hobbes has 'wrongly injected into the savage man's concern for self-preservation the need to satisfy a multitude of passions which are the product of society' (35).

In the late eighteenth century, Rousseau's ideas spawned the philosophical and literary movement known as Romanticism. The Romantics revolted against the social and aesthetic consequences of burgeoning industrial capitalism, and advocated a return to what they imagined had been more 'natural' ways of living and thinking. In William Wordsworth's preface to the *Lyrical Ballads* [1800], the poet explains his choice of mainly rural themes in Rousseau-esque tones:

> Humble and rustic life was generally chosen, because in that condition, the essential passions of the heart find a better soil in which they can attain their maturity, are under less restraint and speak a plainer and more emphatic language . . . in that condition the passions of men are incorporated with the beautiful and permanent forms of nature.
>
> (1988, 282)

Along with this advocacy of the pastoral goes an appeal to 'passion', and a mistrust and denigration of 'reason' as an unnatural mode of thought. Reason, for Rousseau, is the faculty which has tempted man to abandon the state of nature and become civilized. It is thus a decidedly dubious quality:

> I almost dare to affirm that the state of reflection is a state contrary to nature and that the man who meditates is a depraved animal. . . . Reason is what engenders egocentrism and reflection strengthens it. Reason is what turns man in upon himself. Reason is what separates him from all that troubles and afflicts him.
>
> (1992, 37)

This latter freedom from animalistic fears, while apparently comforting, is not achieved without cost. In Rousseau's words, people are led 'to buy imaginary repose at the price of real felicity' (17). As human beings begin to combine in societies, their natural differences in strength and ability become perverted into inequality (53). Private property is the foundation of all inequality (44), and is the most unnatural institution of all. Once the principle of social hierarchy has been established, moreover, people will distort and deny their true natures in order to enhance their social status, so that 'Being something and appearing to be something become two completely different things' (54). The result is that people are no longer able to perceive the natural equality which lies behind the surface inequalities of civilization. Rousseau's major contribution to the history of ideology was to realize that this pervasive ignorance was instituted to protect the interests of property holders:

> the rich, pressed by necessity, finally conceived the most thought-out project which ever entered the human mind. It was to use in his favor the very strength of those who attacked him, to turn his adversaries into his defenders, to instill in them other maxims, and to give them other institutions which were as favorable to him as natural right was unfavorable to him.
>
> (56)

Thus the whole apparatus of civilized society has the purpose of maintaining an eminently unnatural division of wealth. An appeal to reason as a way of judging social institutions, such as was made by the empiricist *philosophes*, fails to recognize that reason is itself an unnatural, or social, phenomenon, and that it is thus part of the problem to which it purports to be a solution. In place of this artificial standard, Rousseau proposes a new one: the 'state of nature'. As with Hobbes, it must be stressed that this is not intended as more than a hypothetical postulate which can be used to reveal the arbitrary status of present social relations. In fact, Rousseau's appeal to nature amounts, in practice, to an appeal to history:

> In discovering and following thus the forgotten and lost routes that must have led man from the natural state to the civil state . . . no attentive leader can fail to be struck by the immense space that separates these two states. It is in this slow succession of things that he will see the solution to an infinity of moral and political problems which the philosophers are unable to resolve . . . he will explain how the soul and human passions are imperceptibly altered and, as it were, change their nature; why, in the long run, our needs and passions change their objects; why, with original man gradually disappearing, society no longer offers to the eyes of the wise man anything but an assemblage of artificial men and factitious passions which are the work of these new relations and have no true foundation in nature.

> (69)

Here the originally religious injunction against fetishizing our own 'works' is used to expose the 'artificial men' of civilized society. The empiricists had rejected any metaphysical concepts on the grounds that they were not 'real', but rather human inventions. Rousseau goes a step further, pointing out that *all* social practices, including reason itself, are human inventions. In the hands of his followers Rousseau's Romanticism frequently involves an open revolt against rationality and an appeal for humanity to return to a more 'natural' mode of inner experience. This tendency culminates in such irrationalist expostulations as John Keats's demand in 1817, 'for a Life of Sensations rather than of Thoughts!' (1958, 185). Because all rational social conventions and traditions are man-made, there is a sense in which they are not 'real': there is nothing natural, eternal or inevitable about them. Everything, therefore, can be changed.

The empiricist *philosophes* also wanted to change things. But they envisaged a gradual, Baconian process of re-education, which would tactfully remove the idols and install reason in their place. Despite the obstruction of the *ancien régime* in Church and state, this philosophical project was making modest but significant progress in Enlightenment France. Rousseau's iconoclasm was much more radical; in fact, it was revolutionary. It is hardly surprising that it was Rousseau rather than Condillac who was heralded as a prophet by the radical Jacobins, or that Robespierre insisted that a cult of the Rousseauian 'Supreme Being' replace what he called the 'ridiculous farces' celebrating deified Reason. Rather than implying rational reform, Rousseau's theories suggested the possibility of wiping away the entire structure of social organization and starting anew. As the French revolutionary constitution declared, 'there is no longer any nobility nor peerage nor hereditary distinctions of orders nor feudal regime nor patrimonial justice nor any title, denomination or prerogative' (cit. Schama, 1989, 574).

The Constituent Assembly thus established the formal equality of all men. Even before the constitution was completed, however, this notion had been the subject of a devastating critique by the Anglo-Irish politician Edmund Burke. In his *Reflections on the Revolution in France* [1790] (1965), Burke claimed that the revolutionaries had misread their purported mentor. 'I believe', he declared, 'that were Rousseau alive, and in one of his lucid intervals, he would be shocked at the practical phrenzy of his scholars' (211). In Burke's opinion, Rousseau had been making essentially philosophical arguments and did not intend that anyone should attempt to put them into practice, for the very good reason that this was impossible. Social institutions, in Burke's view, are historically determined, and it is therefore the ultimate in 'presumption' to regard society as a *carte blanche*, to be restructured at will: 'as the liberties and the restrictions vary with times and circumstances, and admit of infinite modifications, they cannot be settled upon any abstract rule; and nothing is so foolish as to discuss them upon that principle' (72).

The revolutionaries' error was to have assumed that Rousseau's 'state of nature' was an empirically attainable condition rather than a hypothetical postulate designed to make us evaluate our customs historically. Rousseau says that people are by nature equal, and the revolutionaries are thereby led to assert something that is manifestly empirically not the case: that all men are equal *here and now*. This, as Burke saw, is a purely formal equality, with no material reality:

> Believe me, Sir, those who attempt to level, never equalize. They only
> change and pervert the natural order of things, they load the edifice of
> society, by setting up in the air what the solidity of the structure requires
> to be on the ground.
>
> (57–8)

What Burke calls the 'metaphysic rights' of man (73) are, in reality, not
universal at all: rather, they are a mask (we might say an ideology)
disguising sectional interests:

> The whole of the power obtained by this revolution will settle in the
> towns among the burghers and the monied directors who lead them.
> . . . Here end all the deceitful dreams and visions of the equality and
> rights of men. In 'the Serbonian bog' of this base oligarchy they are all
> absorbed, sunk, and lost for ever.
>
> (240, 242)

The mere assertion that men are, in the abstract, 'equal', unaccompanied
by any attempt to make them equal in fact, is identified by Burke as
bourgeois ideology. The 'monied interest' requires this formal equality –
the removal of all obstacles to the free pursuit of wealth and power – for
its own ends, but it cunningly claims to be following a universal principle
and restoring society to a 'natural' condition. With admirable perspicuity,
Burke foresaw the consequences of this desire to erase the work of history,
and to cut away the 'wise' accoutrements of culture and tradition. Any
attempt to realize Rousseau's 'state of nature' in practice could only
reduce humanity to the condition of Tom O'Bedlam:

> All the super-added ideas, furnished from the wardrobe of a moral
> imagination which the heart owns, and the understanding ratifies, as
> necessary to cover the defects of our naked shivering nature, and to
> raise it to dignity in our own estimation are to be exploded as a
> ridiculous, absurd, and antiquated fashion. . . . On this scheme of
> things, a king is but a man; a queen is but a woman; a woman is but an
> animal; and an animal not of the highest order.
>
> (92–3)

As Shakespeare puts it in *King Lear*, 'Allow not nature more than nature needs / Man's life is cheap as beast's' (II, iv, 266–7). The 'natural' state to which the revolutionaries wanted to restore France would, as Burke foresaw, resemble that of Hobbes far more closely than that of Rousseau. After the dust of the revolution had settled, however, important achievements remained. One was the elevation of the universalizing, naturalizing, equalizing ideology of the bourgeoisie to something approaching orthodoxy, in which position it remains, by and large, to this day. Another, which is perhaps a result of the former, was the establishment in a prominent place among the human sciences of the study of 'ideology'.

DESTUTT DE TRACY AND THE INVENTION OF IDEOLOGY

One of the many replies to Burke's attack on the French Revolution came from a renegade aristocrat and member of the revolutionary Constituent Assembly named Destutt de Tracy. In a fifteen-page pamphlet written in 1790, Destutt took issue with Burke's advocacy of the moderate, compromising English settlement of 1688 as a model for France. This was no time for half measures, he claimed, what was needed was a 'complete revolution'. Six years later, as a member of the Institut de France, Destutt invented the term 'ideology', and sixteen years after that, Napoleon Bonaparte did him the honour of blaming him for the retreat from Moscow, as well as for the revolutionary Terror:

> We must lay the blame for the ills which our fair France has suffered on ideology, that shadowy metaphysics which subtly searches for first causes on which to base the legislation of peoples, rather than making use of the laws known to the human heart and of the lessons of history. These errors must inevitably and did in fact lead to the rule of bloodthirsty men.
>
> (cit. Kennedy, 1978, 215)

On a personal level, the accusation was most unfair; Destutt had actually been imprisoned under the Terror, and only Thermidor saved him from the guillotine. But Napoleon was correct to ascribe a dangerous, radical and destructive tendency to the science of 'ideology' which Destutt invented.

Bonaparte pointed out that Destutt's 'ideology' neglects to examine 'the laws known to the human heart and of the lessons of history'. As he says, this science reacts against both the idealist notion of *a priori* concepts, and the possibility of historical determinism. These reactions bespeak the legacy of Locke and Condillac, the two most important influences on Destutt's thought. His reading of these thinkers led him to believe, as he says in the *Elémens d'Idéologie* [1804–15] (1986–7), that there were no innate ideas, all thought being derived from sensation. On the other hand, he also thought that 'Nothing exists for us except by the ideas we have of it, because our ideas are our whole being, our existence itself.' As with Hobbes, things create ideas, but these ideas can never be fully adequate to the things. The only way to avoid the sceptical position that true knowledge is impossible, so it seemed to Destutt, would be to analyse the process by which our minds translate material things into ideal forms. This area of study had already been opened up by Condillac; under the leadership of Destutt it was institutionalized in the section of the Institut de France which dealt with moral and political sciences, and it was given the name 'Idéologie': the science of ideas.

Ideology thus originates as a 'meta-science', a science of science. It claims to be able to explain where the other sciences come from and to give a scientific genealogy of thought. As Napoleon came to recognize, this amounted to a claim to epistemological superiority over all other disciplines, and by his vigorous suppression of the *idéologues* after 1803 he acknowledged the threat posed by this hubristic science to his own despotic ambition. Napoleon's plans called for the imposition of an ideology in the repressive, derogatory sense of the term: he thought, for example, that Christianity could ensure 'public order'. The project of the *idéologues* threatened to 'destroy all illusions' and thus unmask the base designs behind the Emperor's embrace of the Vatican.

Destutt de Tracy's 'ideology', then, traces ideas, through sensations, to their roots in matter. But this science moves beyond Condillac's reductive materialism by emphasizing more strongly the movement, the process through which human beings interact with their material surroundings. Destutt was thus able to claim that 'Idéologie' achieves a momentous philosophical breakthrough, by transcending the ancient oppositions between matter and spirit, things and concepts. He is therefore led, as Emmet Kennedy observes, 'in two opposite directions – towards an idealist conception of error and a sensationalist conception of truth'. That is to say, while the sensations we get from external objects are reliable and accurate, the ideas which these sensations produce in our minds may be wrongly arranged, and so lead us to false conclusions. By observing the movement by which sensations are transformed into ideas, it ought to be possible to understand, and so to avoid, the ways in which such erroneous patterns of ideas come into being.

The new discipline of 'ideology' thus claimed to be nothing less than the science to explain all sciences. It had ambitions, as Maine de Biran put it, to establish 'a grammar and language modelled after mathematics . . . in which each idea was assigned its corresponding linguistic sign' (cit. Kennedy, 1978, 100). This system might then be used to study the relations between ideas, as well as to identify their origins. As Napoleon understood, however, the practical implications of such a science meant that it could not itself be disinterested. To 'unmask' the source of ideas was to deny them absolute validity. If this was to be done to all ideas, it was easy to see how Destutt's ambition to change the face of the earth might seem plausible enough. Unfortunately for him, Destutt de Tracy was not the only man in France with such ambitions. Napoleon recognized a threat when he saw one; he was also shrewd enough to perceive that 'Idéologie' involved a thoroughgoing scepticism towards all authoritative knowledge, which must issue in continual chaos and 'lead to the rule of bloodthirsty men'.

It would thus be wrong to see, in the unequal struggle between the *idéologues* and Bonaparte, a symbol of the contradictory demands of theory and practice. When he attacked Destutt and his followers as 'dreamers' and 'windbags', Napoleon did not suggest that their theories were purely 'ideal', with no bearing on political reality. On the contrary, he knew that their theories were all too relevant to political issues. If the *idéologues* were allowed to pursue their millennial aims, he foresaw a permanent revolution, a maelstrom in which ideas were continually being unmasked, invalidated and replaced by new ones. The subsequent history of ideology and its relations with practical politics would seem to bear him out.

3

IDEALISM

What you call the Spirit of the Age
Is in reality the spirit of those men
In which their time's reflected.
(Johann Wolfgang von Goethe, *Faust*, ll. 577–9)

THE CARTESIAN SELF

During the seventeenth and eighteenth centuries, empiricism and materialism provided a rational basis for the study of consciousness. This allowed 'Idéologie' to take its place among the sciences of the Enlightenment. But in the process of analysing the formation of ideas, the *idéologues* deprived this process of the dignity and reverence to which it had previously seemed entitled. In particular, the concept of the soul had no place in the materialism of the *philosophes*. Destutt de Tracy's remark that 'Idéologie' was a branch of zoology evinced a rather cavalier attitude to the cherished notion that there is some kind of supernatural, quasi-divine essence within the mind which elevates humanity above the animals. Rousseau provided one escape route for those whose sensibilities were too delicate to countenance studying the mind like any other object of science. But Rousseau wrote in direct reaction to the doctrines of materialism, and his glorification of the autonomous, individual self is merely the reverse side, the antithesis, of Condillac and Destutt's dour sensationalism. For a more rational and coherent account of the mind's freedom from matter, it is necessary to return to the seventeenth century, to the work of René Descartes.

When, in *The Sufferings of Young Werther* [1774] (1957), Goethe has his protagonist announce that 'I return into myself, and find a world!' (21), he protests against the 'sensationalist' doctrine that all mental processes can be traced to external stimuli. Descartes also finds a superior ground for certainty within the individual self, or subject. In his early tract *Rules for the Direction of our Intelligence* [1628] (1911), Descartes unequivocally declares that 'the human mind has something within it that we may call divine, wherein are scattered the first germs of useful modes of thought' (10). This assumption is radically at odds with the materialist project of tracing the origin of human ideas to causes in the external world. Descartes notes that our senses, through which we inevitably experience material things, can often deceive us. A tower which appears round when viewed from one angle may appear square from another; when dreaming or in a delusional condition we may think we see objects which are not there, and so on. Descartes thus believes that 'prejudices' arise from putting too much credence in what we naively assume to be our experience of the world outside us, which is in fact mediated through our notoriously unreliable senses. In the *Meditations on First Philosophy* [1641] (1911), Descartes notes the problematic status of sense-perception, and consequently advocates 'doubt about all things and especially about material things' (140). Such a systematic doubt is useful 'inasmuch as it delivers us from every kind of prejudice, and sets out for us a very simple way by which the mind may detach itself from the senses'. In fact, the only thing of which the mind can be absolutely certain is the existence of its own activity. Descartes expressed this claim in the famous aphorism *cogito ergo sum*, 'I think therefore I am.'

Descartes intends this as a self-confirming proposition. That is, he believes that its truth is established in the very act of conceiving it. However, on closer examination we can see that this is not quite so. The so-called '*cogito*' certainly proves that *thought* exists. But Descartes draws from this the unwarranted conclusion that there also exists an individual, unified subject – an 'I' – which is doing the thinking. From this presupposition Descartes proposes to deduce the rest of his theory. The originary, unitary, transcendent Cartesian ego thus provides an alternative standard of certainty and coherence for a world in which the traditional conception of God as the source of all truth was rapidly being diminished.

Since he will admit the certainty only of his own self and its thought-processes, Descartes assumes an irreconcilable divergence, or dualism, between the material world and the ideas we have about that world. This is the most important difference between Descartes and the materialists. Descartes does not believe that thought derives from sensation – that it is, as Condillac was to put it, 'transformed sensation'. Rather, he insists on the separation between the ideal and material spheres. Because he believes that our innate rational capacities determine and make possible our experience of the world, Descartes is usually referred to as a rationalist. In the third *Meditation*, Descartes claims that we do not really perceive the external world at all:

> I have before received and admitted many things to be very certain and manifest, which yet I afterwards recognized as being dubious. What then were these things? They were the earth, sky, stars and all other objects which I apprehended by means of the senses. But what did I clearly and distinctly perceive in them? Nothing more than that the ideas or thoughts of these things were presented to my mind. And not even now do I deny that these ideas are met with in me. But there was yet another thing which I affirmed, and which, owing to the habit which I had formed of believing it, I thought I perceived very clearly, although in truth I did not perceive it at all, to wit, that there were objects outside of me from which these ideas proceeded, and to which they were entirely similar.

> (158)

When we think we are seeing objects in the material world, we are really seeing only our ideas, or concepts, of objects which may or may not exist outside us. Ignorance of this fact is the prime cause of false consciousness: 'the principal error and the commonest . . . consists in my judging that the ideas which are in me are similar or conformable to the things outside me' (160). As we saw in the previous chapter, empiricists such as Hobbes also argue that the material world is incommensurable with our ideas of it. For Hobbes, however, this means that we should strive all the harder to verify our concepts with reference to material reality, even in the knowledge that the one can never be fully adequate to the other. When an idea becomes so divorced from the empirical that it has no material referent whatsoever, it is liable to be exiled to Hobbes's 'Kingdom of Fairies'. In contrast, Descartes does not believe that ideas must aspire to correspondence with anything 'outside' themselves in order to be valid. Rather than being simply nonsensical, ideas which cannot be traced to empirical things must have another cause, which is not the less real for not being material:

> For if we imagine that something is found in an idea which is not found in the cause, it must then have been derived from nought; but however imperfect may be this mode of being by which a thing is objectively or by representation in the understanding by its idea, we cannot certainly say that this mode of being is nothing, nor, consequently, that the idea derives its origin from nothing.
>
> (163)

Our concepts, which are all that we can know, are not necessarily prompted by anything material, but can have a perfectly legitimate ideal origin. Descartes would thus disagree with Locke's comparison of non-material ideas to religious idols. On the contrary, he is of the opinion that our knowledge of ideas is prior to, and more certain than, any knowledge we can have of things in themselves.

'RAVING WITH REASON': KANT AND ENLIGHTENMENT

Descartes's relevance to an account of ideology lies in his claim that our sense-perceptions represent the material world to us in a way that is comprehensively false. There is thus an absolute divergence between reality and our ideas, the 'object' and the 'subject'. We should note that this opposition is mutually defining: the category of 'subject' would have no content without the category of 'object', and vice versa. Nevertheless, the Cartesian dualism provides the basis for the terminology which is conventionally applied to philosophical history. Very broadly, those thinkers, such as Hobbes, who believe that the external world determines our ideas, are known as 'empiricists', and those, like Descartes, who believe that our innate ideas form the basis of our experience of reality, are called 'rationalists'. Those, such as Plato, who consider the realm of ideas to be the only true reality are termed 'idealists', and those, like Condillac, who claim that the physical world is more authentic than human concepts are known as 'materialists'. In fact, however, the most interesting philosophers of the three centuries following Descartes are those who tried to overcome or reconcile these fundamental oppositions.

The empiricist approach to this problem was taken to divergent, but equally startling, extremes by two philosophers from the 'Celtic Fringe' of Europe: George Berkeley and David Hume. In *The Dialogue of Hylas and Philonous* [1713], the Irishman Berkeley suggested that we do not have any innate ideas. The only knowledge we can have of the material world comes from our sense-impressions. But we have no reason to believe that these impressions give us an accurate representation of whatever, if anything, may cause them. It follows that, for all practical purposes, the true nature of the external world is unknowable, and things only exist insofar as they are perceived. In fact, objects would cease to exist when unobserved by human beings, were it not for the omnipresence of an observing divinity.

For the Scottish philosopher David Hume, Berkeley's theory led to the conclusion that our ideas do not correspond to any objective reality, but are merely faint and blurred representations of our physical sense-impressions. Complex ideas are merely combinations of these representations. In his *Treatise of Human Nature* [1739–40], Hume went so far as to claim that, since we have no sensual impression of our own unified self – of what we would today call the 'subject' – we have no knowable internal personality, and are in fact nothing but a bundle of random perceptions, on which we arbitrarily impose an ideal order and label it our 'self'.

The implications of Hume's ideas were extremely radical and disconcerting. Among other things, he neatly eliminated the soul from philosophical consideration: to all intents and purposes it could be regarded as a fiction. Even the consolation of Descartes's unified thinking subject was denied. Moreover, Hume suggested that accurate knowledge of the external world was impossible. The inference could be drawn that we have no reliable criteria for distinguishing truth from falsehood. Even the relation of cause-and-effect was held to be an artificial imposition on a recalcitrant reality. As we shall see, these doctrines of Hume anticipate to a remarkable degree many of the axioms of the twentieth-century postmodernists.

Among those who found these doctrines intolerable was Immanuel Kant, who famously remarked that reading Hume awoke him from his 'dogmatic slumbers' – that is to say, from his uncritical rationalism. In *The Critique of Pure Reason* [1781] (1934), Kant takes upon himself the task of establishing beyond all doubt the existence of a transcendent human subject. In other words, he is concerned to demonstrate that we possess a continuous and coherent self, which transcends the random blur of representation. Kant does this by challenging the dualism between rationalism and empiricism. As he says in the introduction:

> though all our knowledge begins with experience, it by no means follows, that all arises out of experience. For, on the contrary, it is quite possible that our empirical knowledge is a compound of that which we receive through impressions, and that which the faculty of cognition supplies from itself.

(1)

We are intuitively aware of the objective world outside ourselves, but we can only become truly conscious of that world by unifying these intuitions in the form of concepts. When, for instance, I subsume this objective piece of lead and wood under the ideal, general category of 'pencil', I impose a human concept on a material object, and thus arrive at a properly human knowledge of it. This ability to conceptualize is an innate property of the human understanding.

In place of the rigid Cartesian opposition, Kant thus proposes a unity, whereby knowledge is produced by experience and reason working together. He calls the part of our knowledge which derives from experience '*a posteriori*' knowledge, and he refers to knowledge which is logically prior to experience as '*a priori*'. This latter field is further divided into 'analytic' and 'synthetic' propositions. The first of these are state-ments of which the truth is guaranteed by virtue of the predicate being contained in the subject, such as 'the big house is a house'. The second describes statements in which the predicate goes beyond, or adds something to, the subject, such as 'the big house is empty'. In the empiricist view of things, all synthetic judgements must be *a posteriori*, or derived from experience. Kant, on the other hand, believed that there are certain synthetic judgements which are true *a priori*, and precede any possible experience. Newtonian science and geometry appeared to offer examples of this kind of judgement. Because their axioms would necessarily be true for any conceivable human experience, they cannot be derived from experience, but must be prior to it. The question which empiricism cannot answer, and which Kant undertakes to answer himself, is thus: how are these synthetic *a priori* judgements possible?

His answer was that there are, inherent in the human mind, certain 'categories' or ideas which are not empirical, but which make experience possible. Without such concepts as substance and causality, for example, it would simply be impossible to have any kind of recognizably human experience. These categories are therefore not derived from experience, but must spring from some subject which transcends the material. In a sense, Kant is saying that our experience of the material world is made possible, and that the material world is thus, in effect, created 'for us', by this transcendent subject. This is Kant's 'Copernican revolution'; he suggests that our knowledge need not conform to external objects but that, insofar as we can know them, these objects must conform to our capacity for knowledge. If, as Hume suggests, we do not perceive the object in itself but only as it is mediated through our faculty of intuition then, claims Kant, the object can be known by studying that faculty. The study of the subject can reveal the nature of the object, insofar as it has a nature 'for us'.

Kant agrees that, as Hume argued, we do not perceive the material world as it really is 'in itself'. But by rescuing the subject from Hume's scepticism, Kant shows that it is nevertheless possible to perceive an objective, determinate representation of things. The transcendent subject guarantees our access to absolute truth, even though this truth is only absolute 'for us': that is, from a particular perspective within space and time. Kant thus posits a radical disjunction between the object as it appears to us and the 'thing-in-itself', of which we can have no knowledge. The realm of our experience is that of 'phenomena', and it has its own coherence and objectivity. This does not mean, however, that it pretends to discover perspectiveless or 'unconditioned' truths about objects in themselves: these belong to the sphere of 'noumena', which exists beyond the ken of human perception. There is a sense in which, as an abstract ideal, this 'noumenal' sphere enables and determines the phenomenal, but we cannot gain access to it through either empirical observation or rational analysis.

It is important to remember that the distinction between the appearance of the thing and the thing-in-itself refers not to different objects, but to the same object viewed from different perspectives. As appearance, or 'for us', the thing is knowable; but the same thing has another existence 'in itself', of which we can do no more than deduce the possibility. Kant thus theorizes and schematizes to an unsurpassed degree the belief that what we perceive in the world is systematically distinct from the world as it 'really' is. He therefore denounces any hubristic attempt to pronounce on things-in-themselves by removing them from their empirical situation, a pernicious but tenacious tendency which is labelled 'hypostatization'. This tendency, Kant feels, is the primary source of false consciousness. However, the human mind is ineluctably drawn to such futile speculation about noumena. The most we can do to avoid this pitfall is to remember always that our knowledge emanates from our perspective: it is inextricably situated in time and space, and we must try to resist the temptation to view our own ideas as though they were absolute or eternal. In this proscription, then, we can make out the echoes of the theological denunciations of idolatry which we discussed in previous chapters.

THE IDEOLOGY OF THE AESTHETIC

The Kantian reaction against empiricism had especially exciting implications for aesthetic theory. In England, Condillac's position that thoughts were simply the result of material, mechanical processes had been espoused and modified by David Hartley who held that thinking was the result of an original physical stimulus, followed by an automatic process of association of ideas. The Romantic poets William Wordsworth and Samuel Taylor Coleridge were at first impressed with Hartley's theory, but Coleridge later came to find it too soulless and mechanistic for his taste. He circumvented this problem by differentiating, in the *Biographia Literaria* [1817] (1969), between two separate mental faculties, which he called the Fancy and the Imagination. The former corresponds to Hartley's account of mental processes, which have 'no other counters to play with but fixities and definites' (202). The latter, subdivided into an originary 'primary' and a consequent 'secondary' form, is by contrast an active, creative agency through which the subject imposes itself on the objective world around it.

We can understand the philosophical differences between materialist empiricism and subjective idealism by examining two poetic approaches to the same issue: the difficulty of ageing, with its concurrent loss of the passion and inspiration of youth. In the ode entitled 'Intimations of Immortality', Wordsworth laments 'That there hath past away a glory from the earth' (1984, 298), and that he no longer experiences the same 'visionary gleam' which illuminated his younger days. The problem is here conceived as resulting from an inevitable process: as one gets older, the intensity of experience which is spontaneously felt by children gradually fades, until 'At length the Man perceives it die away, / And fade into the light of common day' (ll. 75–6). Inspiration is a one-way street, flowing from external nature into the self. At first, this is a tremendously thrilling and wonderful experience, but it loses its lustre as one grows accustomed to it. In 'Dejection: An Ode' (1912, 365), his answer to Wordsworth's poem, Coleridge takes issue with his friend's diagnosis of this melancholia:

> I may not hope from outward forms to win
> The passion and the life, whose fountains are within.
>
> O Wordsworth! we receive but what we give,
> And in our life alone does Nature live.

(ll. 45–8)

Courageously, Coleridge refuses himself the Wordsworthian consolation that the incremental loss of wonder is an ineluctable consequence of a growing familiarity with the external world. Rather, the source of the problem is located within the subject itself. In fact, the 'glory and the dream' whose departure is lamented by Wordsworth were always located within the subject, rather than in our objective surroundings, and their loss must therefore indicate an interior problem with the self. We could thus say that the philosophical positions espoused in Wordsworth's and Coleridge's odes are materialist and idealist, respectively.

Kant also addressed the issue of aesthetics in his late work, the *Critique of Judgment* [1790] (1987). In the introduction to this text, Kant announces that he is unhappy with the duality, which informs his earlier work, between the phenomenal, or 'sensible', and the 'supersensible' noumenal spheres:

> an immense gulf is fixed between the domain of the concept of nature, the sensible, and the domain of the concept of freedom, the super-sensible, so that no transition from the sensible to the supersensible . . . is possible, just as if they were two different worlds, the first of which cannot have any influence on the second; and yet the second *is* to have an influence on the first, i.e. the concept of freedom is to actualize in the world of sense the purpose enjoined by its laws. . . . So there must after all be a basis *uniting* the supersensible that underlies nature and the supersensible that the concept of freedom contains practically.
> (14–15)

The first kind of 'supersensible' is the noumenon, or thing-in-itself; the second is the 'categorical imperative', or abstract rule which determines ethical behaviour and which, in the *Critique of Practical Reason* [1786], Kant derives from the biblical injunction to do unto others as you would have them do unto you. Because it will result in action, this latter supersensible commandment will transform the material world, or 'actualize in the world of sense the purpose enjoined by its laws' (1987). Thus, there clearly must be some point of connection between the material and the supersensible spheres. The faculty which Kant believes can mediate between these two is that of aesthetic judgement. Kant states the complex relations between the various mental faculties under discussion as follows: 'between the cognitive power and the power of desire lies the feeling of pleasure, just as judgment lies between understanding and reason' (17). What is pleasurable in the contemplation of beauty is the judgement's perception in the object of a 'purposiveness' which is analogous to its own ability to impose concepts on intuitions. This feeling of pleasure is entirely subjective. On the other hand, it is also universally experienced and communicable. This subjective universality is produced, according to Kant, by the interaction or 'free play' of the imagination and the understanding, which can be presumed to operate in all humans, and which is set in motion by the pleasurable object:

> the cognitive powers brought into play by this presentation are in free play, because no determinate concept restricts them to a particular rule of cognition. Hence the mental state in this presentation must be a feeling, accompanying the given presentation, of a free play of the presentational powers directed to cognition in general . . . hence this subjective universal communicability can be nothing but [that of] the mental state in which we are when imagination and understanding are in free play [insofar as they harmonize with each other as required for *cognition in general*].
>
> (62)

So the faculty which Kant intends to mediate between his ethics and his epistemology turns out to be nothing but the 'free play' of the mind when confronted by the 'abyss' (115) of a pleasurable representation. It is hardly an entity in itself, but consists in an oscillation between understanding and imagination. What is more, the experience of what Kant calls the 'sublime' further emphasizes the gulf between pure and practical reason: that is, between the ability to conceptualize objects and the ability to act ethically in the world. For Kant, however, the point is not so much the existence of this gulf as the desire to bridge it, which is also provoked by the contemplation of the sublime. Once again, this quality is conceived as existing only within the mind:

> nothing that can be an object of the senses is to be called sublime. [What happens is that] our imagination strives to progress toward infinity, while our reason demands absolute totality as a real idea, and so [the imagination,] our power of estimating the magnitude of things in the world of sense, is inadequate to that idea. Yet this inadequacy itself is the arousal in us of the feeling that we have within us a supersensible power. . . . *Sublime is what even to be able to think proves that the mind has a power surpassing any standard of sense.*
>
> (106)

By bringing home to us the gap between our phenomenal perception and the noumenal reality which underlies appearances, the sublime provokes the desire (which must, however, remain unfulfilled) to achieve access to this 'supersensible' dimension. The effect of the sublime is to drive us towards the two elements of reality we can never grasp: the thing-in-itself, and the totality of existence. The striving after these two unreachable targets is the experience of the sublime:

> to be able even to think the infinite *as a whole* indicates a mental power that surpasses any standard of sense. . . . If the human mind is nonetheless to *be able even to think* the given infinite without contradiction, it must have within itself a power that is supersensible, whose idea of a noumenon cannot be intuited but can yet be regarded as the substrate underlying what is mere appearance, namely, our intuition of the world.
>
> (111)

It is a notable feature of *The Critique of Judgment* that Kant suggests that the impulse towards the noumenal is simultaneously a striving after 'totality'. It is not hard to discern a quasi-religious motive behind this desire for an ultimate, unified reality lying beneath the disparate surface appearances of things. Kant is heavily influenced here by the Protestant proscription of idolatry, and the biblical injunction to eschew the worship of 'the works of men's hands'. The sublime is that desire which refuses to be satisfied by anything material. Kant is perfectly explicit about the potential of the sublime as an iconoclastic force:

> Perhaps the most sublime passage in the Jewish law is the command-ment: Thou shalt not make unto thee any graven image, or any likeness of any thing that is in heaven or on earth or under the earth, etc. This commandment alone can explain the enthusiasm that the Jewish people in its civilized era felt for its religion when it compared itself with other peoples, or can explain the pride which Islam inspires.
>
> (135)

Most germane for our purposes is Kant's connection of idolatry with political oppression. Continuing his discussion of graven images, he declares:

That is also why governments have gladly permitted religion to be amply furnished with such accessories: they were trying to relieve every subject of the trouble, yet also of the ability, to expand his soul's forces beyond the barriers that one can set for him so as to reduce him to mere passivity and make him more pliable.

(135)

Thus the sublime does indeed, as Kant had said it would, mediate between our conceptual and our ethical capacities. Our awareness that we cannot give a conceptual account of the sublime drives us beyond the appearance of the object in search of its supersensible substrate, which is also a quest for the totality: the ultimate ground and source of the noumena. This quest is a moral good, and to obstruct it by fixating on material appearances is ethically wrong. Hence Kant's distinction between 'superstition' and 'enlightenment':

A propensity to a passive reason . . . is called *prejudice*; and the greatest prejudice of all is *superstition*, which consists in thinking of nature as not subject to rules which the understanding through its own essential law lays down as the basis of nature. Liberation from superstition is called *enlightenment*; for although liberation from prejudices generally may be called enlightenment, still superstition deserves to be called a prejudice pre-eminently, since the blindness that superstition creates in a person, which indeed it seems to demand as an obligation, reveals especially well the person's need to be guided by others, and hence his state of passive reason.

(161)

While many postmodern thinkers find much to admire in the Kantian notions of 'free play' and the 'abyss', this advocacy of 'enlightenment' is frequently chastised as reprehensible. It is easily presented as a will to dominate the material world by forcing it to fit our own ideas, and as equally implicated in false consciousness as the 'superstition' it seeks to eradicate. In a suggestive phrase of Kant's, the enlightenment philosopher can be seen as 'raving with reason': so utterly convinced of the power and goodness of rationality as to countenance imposing its benefits on the 'superstitious' by force. Against such criticisms it might be argued that idolatry and superstition do yet greater violence to both the objective world and the subjective observer. In order to adjudicate, it will be necessary to examine the modifications to which the Kantian system was subjected by subsequent philosophers.

HEGEL AND THE DIALECTIC

Kant's *Critique of Pure Reason* succeeds in establishing the existence of a transcendental subject. But this subject is placed in such a frustrating and contradictory position that some have wondered why he bothered to defend it. In all three *Critiques* we are made painfully aware that we can achieve only a perspectival understanding of our surroundings, whose true nature and purpose must always remain hidden from us. And yet the very awareness that we perceive the world from a particular point of view itself implies the possibility of a world viewed from no particular point of view. We are thus in a tragic predicament: constantly impelled to chase after an unconditioned knowledge which is by definition unattainable. In fact, as soon as we do try to lift our knowledge out of experience, we run straight into irreconcilable contradictions. Kant called these contradictions 'antinomies'. To take one example, the concept of causality is easily proved to be true 'for us'. In any particular experience we could have, the law of cause-and-effect will pertain. However, if we depart from the realm of experience and try to apply our concept of causality to the totality of the universe, we run into an antinomy: that is, a contradiction both sides of which are equally true for us. It makes an equal amount of sense to claim that something caused the entire universe as it does to argue that the universe has no ultimate cause. In other words, antinomies arise from the attempt to apply perspectival knowledge to the totality, which is also an attempt to shift our perceptions of phenomena on to things-in-themselves. According to Kant, we can only avoid running into antinomies if we resist the temptation to fetishize our own ideas by claiming knowledge of the absolute, eternal nature of things.

This idea that the subject is unable to achieve any absolutely true knowledge can easily be interpreted as an affront to human dignity. It seems a trifle absurd, as well as unbearably tragic, that there should exist a being which is condemned ceaselessly to aspire towards this truth, while knowing that its best attempts are always already doomed to failure. It seems doubly intolerable that *we* should be this unhappy being. By claiming that the mind imposes its categories on the world, and that these categories produce what we can know of reality, Kant at once bestowed an unprecedented freedom on the subject and firmly limited the scope of what that subject might aspire to know. We are given our independence from material constraints at the price of eschewing any complete knowledge of our surroundings. Many subsequent thinkers took Kant's description of our predicament as a challenge; some, such as G.W.F. Hegel, took it as a provocation.

Hegel wanted to retain the subjective freedom we glean from Kant, while eliminating the supposedly insurmountable obstacles to absolute knowledge. The thing-in-itself appeared to him as a pernicious absurdity. For what is the point of retaining as a philosophical concept something of which we can never have any knowledge? Indeed, if we can know nothing of the thing-in-itself, how can we know that it exists? What is to prevent us from claiming that the appearance of things, the reality which is posited for us by the mind, is in fact the only reality?

There are actually many reasons why such a claim is hard to sustain. In the first place, our concepts are continually changing, and there must be some reason for this. Human history shows that the most treasured beliefs of one age have very often been regarded as utter delusions by later epochs. The sheer inaccessibility of the thing-in-itself provides one explanation for this tendency of human beings to get things 'wrong'. But Hegel refused to accept this solution. Instead, in *Phenomenology of Spirit* [1807] (1977) he advanced the radical notion that truth is by definition, historical:

> The bud disappears in the bursting-forth of the blossom, and one might say that the former is refuted by the latter; similarly, when the fruit appears, the blossom is shown up in its turn as a false manifestation of the plant, and the fruit now emerges as the truth of it instead.

(2)

Clearly, it does not make sense to say that the appearance of the fruit means that the blossom was 'wrong'. The fruit grows out of the blossom, and could not have come into existence without it. And yet the fruit is somehow 'truer' than the blossom or, put another way, the fruit is the truth *of* the blossom. Hegel believes that human thought progresses in an analogous fashion. Its history forms an organic unity, in which each individual moment can only be understood in its relation to the whole. In the *Phenomenology of Spirit* Hegel gives to this whole the name *Geist*, which can be translated as either 'Mind' or 'Spirit'. This entity is closely related to earlier manifestations of the 'absolute subject', such as Descartes's 'I' and Kant's transcendental subject, but Hegel is determined that, unlike the works of the two earlier philosophers, his *Phenomenology* will leave nothing outside the scope of Spirit.

Hegel's method in this book is often referred to as 'dialectical'. Although this term goes back to Plato, Hegel gives it its characteristic modern application. The Hegelian dialectic denies the existence of self-identical entities. That is to say, Hegel assumes that nothing just is, that nothing exists 'in itself'. Rather, all identity is relational, being formed out of, or determined by its relations to other identities. This is true from a temporal perspective; for example, the identity of the blossom is dependent on the bud and the fruit. It is also true from a logical perspective. For example, the notion of 'master' can only be established by virtue of its relation to the notion of 'servant'. There is thus a sense in which the notion of 'servant' is constitutive of the notion of 'master', its ostensible opposite. This doctrine, which is referred to as the 'inter-penetration of opposites', is of the utmost importance for future theories of false consciousness.

Hegel did not invent the notion that the opposing poles of a dichotomy define each other, and are thus constitutive of one another's identity. This idea crops up with some regularity in Western literature. When, in 'Crazy Jane Talks With the Bishop' [1932] (1989), W.B. Yeats's eponymous heroine declares that 'Fair and foul are near of kin / And fair needs foul' (ll. 7–8), she echoes the prophetic revelation of Shakespeare's witches, over three centuries earlier, that 'Fair is foul, and foul is fair' (*Macbeth* I, i, 11). The poetic books of William Blake, such as *Songs of Innocence and Experience* and *The Marriage of Heaven and Hell*, are extended ruminations on the mutually definitive nature of the concepts juxtaposed in their titles. But Hegel was the first to schematize the theory of relational identity into a completely coherent philosophical system, within which he gave it the most crucial role, making it nothing less than the motor of all human history and knowledge.

In order to become conscious of its own existence, says Hegel, the Absolute Spirit must create an opposite, an other, against which it can define itself. Since Spirit is *ipso facto* spiritual, this other can only be material. In fact, the objective world of matter is this self-alienation of Spirit. Kant had discerned this situation when he understood that the transcendental subject creates the grounds of its experience out of its own *a priori* categories. But because his thought was 'formalist' rather than 'historicist', Kant thought of the subject's inability to know the thing-in-itself as an eternal, inevitable state of affairs. As Hegel sees it, however, this is merely the condition which pertains while Spirit remains unaware that the material world is its own objectified form. The history of thought represents the progressive realization by Spirit of this fact. Once Spirit has achieved full self-consciousness, once it has learnt to recognize the external world as its own alienated and objectified form, the opposition between subject and object will be abolished and human history will have achieved its purpose.

The problem with Kant's notion of the unknowable thing-in-itself, according to Hegel, is that 'it takes for granted certain ideas about cognition as an instrument and as a medium, and assumes that there is a difference between ourselves and this cognition' (47). Given these assumptions of Kant's, it is possible to claim that human cognition is a faulty tool, necessarily inadequate to the thing-in-itself. If, however, as Hegel believes, there is no meaningful distinction to be drawn between ourselves and our cognition, then it makes no sense to suggest that there is something of which we can know the existence but not the qualities. Our lack of knowledge of its qualities simply means that 'for us' it has no qualities, and therefore no existence. The Kantian disjunction between 'for us' and 'in-itself' thus evaporates. The 'in-itself', as Hegel puts it, 'was only an in-itself *for consciousness*' (54).

One possible inference from this would be that we do indeed perceive objects as they really are. But Hegel goes on to demonstrate that our sense-perceptions, far from offering transparent access to the world, actually prove to be mediated emanations from the Absolute Subject. All sense-perceptions, he remarks, depend upon the concepts 'Here' and 'Now'. But these concepts do not designate anything that actually exists. We say and think that we live in the 'now', in the present. But in fact, perception takes time. We do not, therefore, perceive the present, we only

see the past. And the past, by definition, does not exist. Similarly, the
concept 'here' is merely a formal category which can be filled with an
entirely different content simply by turning around. The ideas of 'here'
and 'now', without which no sense-perception would be possible, are
simply 'universal' concepts, and 'it is the universal that is the true content
of sense-certainty' (60).

So the empirical road to truth is closed, because experience is produced
out of universal concepts. Kant had come to a similar conclusion. But like
Descartes, he had retained within the individual a transcendental ego,
which could function as the ultimate guarantor of truth 'for us'. Hegel
considers the option of grounding knowledge in such an individual
subject:

> the vanishing of the single Now and Here that we mean is prevented
> by the fact that I hold them fast. 'Now' is day because I see it; 'Here' is a
> tree for the same reason. But in this relationship sense-certainty
> experiences the same dialectic acting upon itself as in the previous one.
> I, *this* 'I', see the tree and assert that 'Here' is a tree; but another 'I' sees
> the house and maintains the 'Here' is not a tree but a house instead.
>
> (61)

So the concept 'I' is also a 'universal' which is imposed upon a fluid and
nebulous series of impressions. We may recall here that Hume reached
much the same conclusion. But Hegel has no intention of relapsing into
Humean scepticism. On the contrary, he believes that by demolishing all
possible grounds for immediate truth, he has established the potential for
humanity to uncover the real, ultimate truth which underlies these
deceiving illusions. In Hegel's thought, the characteristics of Kant's
individual transcendent subject are magnified into the Absolute Subject:
the universal Spirit which both creates and is the material universe, and
which works through the material agency of discrete, individual human
subjects.

In the *Phenomenology*, Hegel famously declares that 'the True is the
whole' (11). He means that we can only make proper sense of individual
ideas when we think of them in relation to the Absolute Subject. We may
recall that for Kant, this was precisely what we must *not* do. Kant had
argued that when we try to reason about the totality, we founder upon

irreconcilable contradictions, or antinomies. Hegel retorted that in fact every concept is made up of a unity of opposite moments. To mould an abstract concept out of the flux of sensual perception, we must force these chaotic data into a determinate form, which will involve a temporary and artificial reconciliation of real conflicts. Our ideas are formed out of this 'interpenetration of opposites'. But the contradictions within the concept can be revealed by what Hegel calls a 'dialectical' analysis. Better yet, these contradictions are resolved in the course of time, giving rise to a synthesis, which in turn contains a new contradiction, and so on.

Hegel's declaration that 'the True is the whole' thus refers us to a historical perspective. As he goes on to say, 'the whole is nothing other than the essence consummating itself through its development. Of the Absolute it must be said that it is essentially a *result*, that only in the *end* is it what it truly is' (11). What Hegel has done here is to integrate the epistemology of Kant's individual subject with the Judaeo-Christian idea of a Providential history. He adheres to the ancient idea that history has a meaning which is progressively revealed to those who live it. This means, among other things, that the truth will change and develop along with history. For Hegel, ignorance of this fact produces a systematically false consciousness: '*Dogmatism* as a way of thinking, whether in ordinary knowing or in the study of philosophy, is nothing else but the opinion that the True consists in a proposition which is a fixed result or which is immediately known' (23).

What Hegel's followers would soon be calling 'ideology' emerges here as a critique of abstract rationalism. It is, as Hegel puts it, 'dogmatic' to assume that human reason can attain fixed truths which will not develop and be superseded with the forward march of history. It is also 'dogmatic' to claim that a concept is 'immediate': to assert that it has an independent, or 'essential' existence, free from the influence of other concepts and from internal contradiction. Twentieth-century philosophers would refer to these two erroneous tendencies as 'ahistoricism' and 'essentialism' respectively. In Hegel, this kind of mistaken thinking produces a 'bad insight', which allows religious superstition and political repression to flourish. This does not happen automatically or by accident, but is the result of

> an evil intention by which the general mass of the people is befooled.
> The masses are the victims of the deception of a *priesthood* which, in its

envious conceit, holds itself to be the sole possessor of insight and pursues its other selfish ends as well. At the same time it conspires with *despotism* which . . . stands above the bad insight of the multitude and the bad intentions of the priests, and yet unites both within itself.

(330)

So Hegel, like most of the thinkers we have been analysing, shows how tyrannical rulers deliberately inculcate false consciousness in their subjects. In an allusion to the French Revolution, Hegel notes that 'these three aspects of the enemy' – false consciousness, priestcraft and tyranny – are under attack by the force which, following Kant, he calls 'Enlightenment'. However, Hegel's theory of the dialectical interpenetration of opposites leads him to the conclusion that Enlightenment is itself determined by the very forces it strives to overthrow:

If all prejudice and superstition have been banished, the question arises, *What Next? What is the truth Enlightenment has propagated in their stead?* It has already declared that this positive content is in its extirpation of error. . . . In its approach to what, for faith, is absolute Spirit, it interprets any *determinateness* it discovers there as wood, stone, etc., as particular, real things. Since in this way it grasps in general *every determinateness*, i.e. all content and filling, as a *human entity* and *(mere) idea*, absolute Being becomes for it a *vacuum* to which no determinateness, no predicates, can be attributed.

(340)

Enlightenment provides the critical tools to demolish superstition and idolatry. It follows that its own nature is defined by the prejudices it attacks, just as Rousseau's exaltation of the individual subject, reacting against the *philosophes'* degradation of the subject to the sum of its objective experiences, is determined by the very doctrines it criticized. In Hegel, the criticism of false consciousness once again consists in the revelation that the idols of superstition are merely 'human entit[ies]'. However, since it is a purely negative, critical mode of thought, Enlightenment cannot propose alternative qualities for the Absolute which the idolaters have made anthropomorphic. As a result, Enlightenment perceives itself, quite wrongly, as completely independent of the superstition it attacks: 'it does not recognize that what it condemns in faith is directly its own thought' (344). The danger to which Hegel points here, which is amply borne out by subsequent history, is that the method we use to criticize ideology can easily turn into an ideology itself.

THE YOUNG HEGELIANS

Hegel ended his life as a respectably conservative, officially sanctioned pillar of the Prussian establishment. But the spectacularly radical potential of his ideas intoxicated a whole generation of acolytes who flourished in the Berlin of the 1840s. This group, which included the young Karl Marx and Friedrich Engels, was known as the 'Free Ones', and is now referred to as the 'Young Hegelians'. These youthful radicals, few of whom were out of their twenties when they published their most important work, seized on the historicizing aspect of Hegel's thought, and developed it into a theory of political revolution.

Hegel's *Phenomenology* is at root a theology. Christianity believes in a spiritual God, who objectifies Himself in the Incarnation, and whose Providence guides human history towards an ultimate reconciliation with Himself. Hegel uses much the same narrative, but transposes it into philosophical terminology. But this in itself seemed blasphemous to many, as was revealed by the publication of David Strauss's *Life of Jesus* [1835]. To the horror of the Prussian academies, Strauss announced that the Gospels were not supposed to be read as literal descriptions of historical events, but as 'mythical' or symbolic accounts of truths which were nonetheless 'real' for not being empirically accurate. Strauss's purpose was not to attack but to defend Christianity from the mocking assaults of Voltaire and the rationalist *philosophes*:

> For as both the natural explanations of the Rationalists, and the jesting expositions of the Deists, belong to that form of opinion which, whilst it sacrifices all divine meaning in the historical record, still upholds its historical character; the mythical mode of interpretation agrees with the allegorical, in relinquishing the historical reality of the sacred narratives, in order to preserve to them an absolute inherent truth.
>
> (Stepelevich, 1983, 25)

Strauss attempts to establish the legitimacy of his own 'mythical' method by comparing it to ancient 'allegorical' interpretative modes. In fact, though, his work has little in common with the Patristic commentators. As he goes on to admit, 'The . . . essential distinction therefore between these two modes of explanation is, that according to the allegorical this higher [spirit] is the immediate divine agency; according to the mythical, it is the spirit of a people or a community' (26). In the Prussia of 1835, this was an astonishing confession. Strauss was claiming that the Gospels were not direct expressions of the divinity, but were mediated through the 'spirit of a people'. He was asserting, in other words, that the source of biblical inspiration was mortal.

This was the first eruption of the radicalized Hegelianism which dominates the subsequent history of philosophy. Strauss's claim was plausible because it invoked Hegel's concept of *Geist*, the universal spirit which works through human agency. The combined effect of Kant and Hegel had been to establish, through a purely rational and logical process, the existence of an Absolute Subject which determines human thought and history, and which manifests itself objectively in the material world. Strauss thought that the truth of Christianity could be established far more certainly through this philosophy than by relying on the dubious veracity of historical evidence. In fact, Strauss deduced the historical reality of Jesus Christ from the doctrines of Hegel:

> That which is rational is also real; the idea is not merely the moral imperative of Kant, but also an actuality. Proved to be an Idea of the reason, the unity of the divine and human nature must also have an historical existence.
>
> (46)

To the Prussian clerical and academic establishment this was getting things backwards, to put it mildly, and the 27-year-old Strauss was banished for ever from the academic profession. But his book had a tremendous impact. It began to dawn on people that Hegel, of late the august and austere sage of Berlin, had actually been the most dangerous iconoclast since Luther.

However, it took a critical reinterpretation of Hegel to bring out the revolutionary implications of his ideas. Just as Strauss brought the 'spiritual' source of Christianity down to earth in the 'spirit of a people', so other young Hegelians busied themselves in showing the relevance of the master's doctrines to practical affairs. In a newspaper article of 1842, Arnold Ruge announced that 'Our times are political, and our politics intend the freedom of this world. . . . This application of theory to existence is lacking in Hegel's political thought' (in Stepelevich, 1983, 211, 227). 'Hegel's turn to theory' (230), in Ruge's view, led him to the quasi-religious conclusion that we can do nothing of our own volition to hasten the stately progress of Spirit towards self-consciousness. Ruge, on the contrary, saw no reason why Spirit's alienation should not be overcome through human agency: 'the dissolution of the abstract theoretical Spirit . . . is to be brought about by involving it in political life' (256). Ruge thus proposes to abolish the age-old distinction between the material and the ideal by integrating Hegelian theory with political practice.

Apart from Marx and Engels, the young Hegelian whose influence was most important and long lasting was undoubtedly Ludwig Feuerbach. It has often been said that Marx turned Hegel on his head; in fact that description better fits the work of Feuerbach. In *The Essence of Christianity* [1841] (1957), Feuerbach takes Strauss's revision of Hegel to its logical conclusion. He will, as he declares in the preface, carry out 'a faithful, correct translation of the Christian religion out of the Oriental language of imagery into plain speech' (xxxiii). Like Strauss, then, Feuerbach proposes to reveal the true meaning of Christianity. But unlike Strauss, he wants to do this by using the methods of materialism: 'I do not generate the object from the thought, but the thought from the object' (xxxiv). For Feuerbach, religion is an ideal reflection which corresponds to certain causal factors in the material world:

> Religion is the dream of the human mind. But even in dreams we do not find ourselves in emptiness or in heaven, but on earth, in the realm of reality; we only see real things in the entrancing splendour of the imagination and caprice, instead of in the simple daylight of reality and necessity.
>
> (xxxix)

This is precisely the reverse of the methods of Kant and Hegel, and Feuerbach's work thus represents a radical departure in German philosophy: the turn away from idealism and towards materialism. He refuses to locate the truth about the world in any extraterrestrial being, whether it be God or the various philosophical substitutes which have been proposed by his precursors:

> This philosophy has for its principle, not the Substance of Spinoza, not the *ego* of Kant and Fichte, not the Absolute Identity of Schelling, not the Absolute Mind of Hegel, in short, no abstract, merely conceptual being, but a real being, the true *Ens realissimum* – man.
>
> (xxxv)

To the question of the origin of religion, Feuerbach thus gives the answer to the riddle of the Sphinx: it is man. The contention that ideology always fetishizes human qualities or activities is exemplified by the work of Feuerbach. Man is distinguished from the animals, he argues, in that we are able to achieve self-consciousness, that is, to become aware that we are a species. We can clearly see the influence of Kant here. Feuerbach is saying that human beings are defined by their ability to conceptualize, to subsume the particular beneath the general. When we do this to ourselves, we come up with the concept of 'man' as 'species-being'. It is this notion of 'man' as a generalized concept that is to replace the more nebulous entities such as Descartes's ego, Kant's subject or Hegel's Spirit as the guiding principle of the world.

God, according to Feuerbach, is merely an 'alienation' (today we might say a 'projection') of the infinite capacities of 'man' considered in general, as a 'species-being'. This is the truth which Christianity represents through the symbol of the Incarnation:

> And it is our task to show that the antithesis of divine and human is altogether illusory, that it is nothing else than the antithesis between the human nature in general and the human individual. . . . The divine being is nothing else than the human being.
>
> (13–14)

Feuerbach claims that the history of religion is a continual revelation of this fact:

> Hence the historical progress of religion consists in this: that what by an earlier religion was regarded as objective, is now regarded as subjective; that is, what was formerly contemplated and worshipped as God is now perceived to be something *human*. What was at first religion becomes at a later period idolatry; man is seen to have adored his own nature. Man has given objectivity to himself, but has not recognized the object as his own nature: a later religion takes this forward step; every advance in religion is therefore a deeper self-knowledge.
>
> (13)

Feuerbach believed that he had achieved this task for religion in general, by finally demonstrating that God was merely the alienated concept of the human species. We should note here that he has simply reversed the terms used by Hegel. Where Hegel saw the objective world as the self-alienation of the Absolute Spirit, Feuerbach sees the Absolute Spirit as the self-alienation of mortal man. Because he has merely reversed Hegel, however, Feuerbach does not depart from the fundamental conceptual apparatus which he found already in place. Thus he, too, retains the notion of an Absolute Subject, only he identifies this entity with the generalized concept of humanity, its species-being. He then asserts that the material, in the form of mankind, generates and determines the ideal, in the form of God. Feuerbach, that is to say, is a materialist determinist.

We must also bear in mind that this position is quite incompatible with Hegel's dialectic. The dialectic views all binary oppositions as illusory, since they are produced and upheld by the interpenetration of opposites. It is thus undialectical to assert that one pole of the opposition (say, the material) 'determines' the other (say, the ideal), because all oppositions are mutually determining. In Hegel for example, the objectification of Spirit is a necessary pre-condition of Spirit's own self-consciousness. Feuerbach's confident claim that his work 'generates thought from the *opposite* of thought, from matter, from existence, from the senses' (xxxv) indicates an unfortunate relapse away from the full rigour of Hegel, back towards the naive 'sensationalism' of Condillac and

Destutt de Tracy. This error, which inaugurated an extremely powerful and resilient 'materialist Hegelianism', was to prove perhaps the most costly and tragic mistake in the history of philosophy. To see why, we will have to turn to the work of Feuerbach's most perspicacious follower, Karl Marx.

4

MARXISM

Our Works are the mirror wherein the spirit first sees its natural lineaments.

(Thomas Carlyle, *Sartor Resartus*)

MARX AND MATERIALISM

Marxism has become indelibly associated with materialism. Many Marxists have believed, and have thought that Marx himself believed, that ideas are mechanistically determined by the material environment. This proposition had already been advanced by 'metaphysical' materialists such as Condillac and Destutt de Tracy. However, the followers of Marx allied this materialism with an emphasis on the historical process, originally inspired by Hegel. This led them to assert that both our objective circumstances and our subjective ideas inevitably change and develop through history, and that this process is driven by the material engine of the economy. The kind of economic system under which a person lived, and the position that person occupied within that system, were thus held to determine his or her consciousness.

However, this interpretation of Marx is erroneous, and the fact that it gained widespread currency is regrettable. It is based largely on *The German Ideology* [1845–6], a work composed as a polemical intervention in a topical debate, in which Marx's opponents were the idealist young Hegelians discussed in the previous chapter. To refute them, Marx makes several statements that do indeed read like materialist manifestos. For example, announcing his departure from idealist Hegelianism, Marx declares:

> In direct contrast to German philosophy which descends from heaven to earth, here it is a matter of ascending from earth to heaven. . . . The phantoms formed in the brains of men are also, necessarily, sublimates of their material life-process. . . . Morality, religion, metaphysics, and all the rest of ideology as well as the forms of consciousness corresponding to these, thus no longer retain the semblance of independence. . . . It is not consciousness that determines life, but life that determines consciousness.
>
> (Marx and Engels, 1975, V, 36–7)

Together with Marx's focus on the economy in his later work, statements such as these have misled many thinkers into a crude materialism, in which ideological phenomena are simply explained away by being referred to economic developments. In the Soviet Union, this kind of reading was institutionalized and provided with the political power to maintain and propagate itself. There has, however, always been an alternative current within Marxism which has seen the relationship between ideas and the objective world in more sophisticated terms, and which has thus remained truer to the dialectical approach of Marx himself. For instance, in the *Theses on Feuerbach* [1845], Marx goes out of his way to criticize the reductive materialism of his predecessor:

> The chief defect of all previous materialism (that of Feuerbach included) is that things, reality, sensuousness, are conceived only in the form of the *object*, or *of contemplation*, but not as *sensuous human practice*, not subjectively. Hence, in contradistinction to materialism, the *active* side was set forth abstractly by idealism – which, of course, does not know real, sensuous activity as such. Feuerbach wants sensuous objects, really distinct from conceptual objects, but he does not conceive human activity itself as *objective* activity.
>
> (Marx and Engels, 1975, V, 3)

Marx thus challenges Feuerbach's oppositions between the subject and the object, the ideal and the material. He suggests that the dichotomy between these spheres is superseded in human activity, or praxis. Since it involves the translation of mental ideas into physical effects, praxis is simultaneously material and ideal, at once subjective and objective. Feuerbach, like the eighteenth-century French materialists, remains trapped within a false polarity:

> The materialist doctrine concerning the changing of circumstances and upbringing forgets that circumstances are changed by men and that the educator must himself be educated. This doctrine must, therefore, divide society into two parts, one of which is superior to society.

(V, 4)

It is a logical error, according to Marx, to reduce ideas to mere reflections of material conditions. By isolating one factor as primary or determining, Feuerbach ignores the interpenetration of opposites, and loses sight of the social totality. In the *Economic and Philosophical Manuscripts* [1844], Marx declares that 'Thinking and being are thus certainly distinct, but at the same time they are in unity with each other' (Marx and Engels, 1975, III, 299). Clearly, we could not even form the concept of an 'ideal' sphere unless we also conceived of a 'material' realm. The poles of the opposition create and define each other, and this fact is revealed in human life, which combines thought and material activity.

Referring to his own method, Marx announces that 'consistent naturalism or humanism is distinct from both idealism and materialism, and constitutes at the same time the unifying truth of both' (III, 336). Marx intends his method to be a synthesis of idealism and materialism. The antinomy between these approaches is, in fact, definitive of false consciousness. It arises, according to Marx, because philosophers have imagined themselves as standing outside the historical process. Since history is driven by the dialectical interaction of the ideal with the material, the contradiction between these terms will be abolished once it is understood that philosophical ideas are themselves part of the material process which they describe:

> We see how subjectivity and objectivity, spirituality and materiality, activity and suffering, lose their antithetical character, and thus their

existence as such antitheses only within the framework of society; we see how the resolution of the *theoretical* antithesis *is only* possible in a *practical* way, by virtue of the practical energy of man. Their resolution is therefore by no means merely a problem of understanding, but a *real* problem of life, which *philosophy* could not solve precisely because it conceived this problem as *merely* a theoretical one.

(III, 302)

Here Marx applies Hegel's philosophical breakthrough to the theory of ideology. Previously, idealists had claimed that materialists had simply got it wrong, while materialists had found the source of illusion in idealism. But here, Marx suggests that false consciousness actually consists in the contradiction between these two schools of thought. Ideas and matter form a totality, which cannot be broken up into discrete elements without producing serious errors. Through the unity of philosophical theory with material practice, the age-old antithesis between subject and object could be resolved, and a higher truth might therefore be achieved.

However, Marx by no means implies that this opposition is illusory. On the contrary, it is entirely real, on both a theoretical and an empirical level. The subject / object relationship really has become distorted. The polarity is thus both real and false: it is an accurate description of the wrong state of affairs. Like many of his contemporaries, Marx was aware that the independent self was entering into an antagonistic relationship with its environment, and that the progress of instrumental reason was being achieved at the expense of ethical judgement. (As Tennyson puts it in 'Locksley Hall' [1842] (1969): 'Knowledge comes, but wisdom lingers, and I linger on the shore / And the individual withers, and the world is more and more' (697).) Since the subject / object antithesis is an accurate description of the existing situation, it can only be altered along with the situation it describes. It follows that, as Marx puts it in the *Theses on Feuerbach*, 'The question whether objective truth can be attributed to human thinking is not a question of theory but is a practical question' (III, 2). Like Hegel's progressive self-consciousness of Spirit, Marx's unity of the material and the ideal is a task to be performed, rather than a condition to be described.

Marx's most sustained analysis of the relationship between ideology and political change, *The Eighteenth Brumaire of Louis Napoleon* [1852], does not deal in abstract theory, but studies a particular series of historical events. In this text, Marx is concerned to explain how Louis, the feckless and disreputable nephew of Napoleon Bonaparte, had recently managed to bring off a *coup d'état* in France. What is striking for our purposes is the complex interplay – the dialectical interpenetration of opposites – between the influence Marx ascribes to ideas and the role he gives to material factors. He announces the complexity of this relationship right at the beginning:

> Men make their own history, but they do not make it just as they please; they do not make it under circumstances chosen by themselves, but under circumstances directly encountered, given and transmitted from the past. The tradition of all the dead generations weighs like a nightmare on the brain of the living.
>
> (Marx and Engels, 1975, XI, 103)

There is thus a mutual determination between the inherited objective circumstances in which people unavoidably find themselves, and their ability to impose their subjective will on this material environment and alter it. In Hegelian terms, Marx abolishes the opposition between the ideal and the material, by insisting that these spheres form a totality. Once again, the emphasis on the totality identifies false consciousness with the illusion that either ideas or matter is logically prior to, or causally determining of, the other. In *The Eighteenth Brumaire*, Marx turns his attention to representation, the faculty which mediates between the poles of this opposition.

Marx begins his study of Louis Napoleon with a look at the great revolutionaries of earlier eras: Luther, Cromwell, Robespierre. He points out that each of them dressed up his cause with imagery and symbols drawn from the past. In these representations they 'found the ideals and the art forms, the self-deceptions they needed to conceal from themselves the bourgeois limitations of the content of their struggles' (XI, 104). They 'needed' to deceive themselves by the use of representation, because they had to believe that their cause was absolutely righteous and true. In fact, from a later historical perspective, their struggles can be seen to have advanced the interests of nascent capitalism, and thus to have served a particular class of people in the name of all humanity. Because they were not really serving the interests of all humanity, but needed to believe that they were, they had recourse to symbols and representations to persuade themselves and others of the universality of their cause. We can thus see that, for Marx, representation has at times exercised a determining influence on history. But this has been necessary only because the people who used it have been deluded, and have deluded others, about what they were doing. Marx warns that this is a persistent tendency:

> And as in private life one differentiates between what a man thinks and says of himself and what he really is and does, so in historical struggles one must still more distinguish the language and the imaginary aspirations of parties from their real organism and their real interests, their conception of themselves from their reality.

> (XI, 128)

Although these 'imaginary' representations are not 'real', and in fact conceal 'real', material interests and motives, they nevertheless really exert a determining influence on the way people think and behave. This is an example of how representation can actively determine material conditions, rather than emerging out of them as a mere 'reflection'. In fact Marx goes out of his way to point out that, in the situation he is describing, the political representatives of the people cannot be identified by class or economic interest. Representation has become independent, and this autonomy of representation is necessary to the project of falsely presenting the particular interest of a class as if it were the general interest of humanity:

> Only one must not form the narrow-minded opinion that the petty bourgeoisie, on principle, wishes to enforce an egoistic class interest. Rather, it believes that the *special* conditions of its emancipation are the *general* conditions within which alone modern society can be saved and the class struggle avoided. Just as little must one imagine that the democratic representatives are indeed all shopkeepers or enthusiastic supporters of shopkeepers. In their education and their individual position they may be as far apart from them as heaven from earth. What makes them representatives of the petty bourgeoisie is the fact that in their minds they do not get beyond the limits which the latter do not get beyond in life.

> (XI, 130)

To use Hegelian language again, when the particular is falsely subsumed within the general, representation is forced to assume a determining role which does not naturally belong to it. We recall that in Kant and Hegel, the process of conceptualization involved the subsumption of the particular intuition beneath the general concept. Here, the petty bourgeoisie has formed a false concept of itself as the universal class. Because of this concept's falsity, the normal relationship of representation to reality is distorted and people can only see the representation, which they therefore mistake for reality. We find ourselves once more in Plato's cave.

Marx regards the delusion that representation is material and substantive as ideological. A representation is a product of the human brain, and humanity is under a constant temptation to idolize these representations, and treat them as though they were real. This temptation serves the interests of political tyranny, as in the case of Louis Napoleon, whose power depends on his ability to represent himself as his illustrious uncle. Marx is describing here the beginnings of the aestheticization of politics, which culminates in the consuming concern of postmodern politics with 'image' and 'perception'. He scornfully refers to Louis's

> expedition to Strasbourg, where a trained Swiss vulture had played the part of the Napoleonic eagle. For his irruption into Boulogne he puts some London lackeys into French uniforms. They represent the army. In his Society of December 10, he assembles 10,000 rogues who are to play the part of the people, as Nick Bottom that of the lion.
>
> (XI, 149)

Louis's power thus depends on the spurious autonomy of representation. Or rather, it depends on his ability to persuade the French people of this autonomy. He is, according to Marx, able to succeed in this only among the most ignorant and parochial elements:

> Bonaparte represents a class, and the most numerous class of French society at that, the *small-holding* peasantry. . . . Historical tradition gave rise to the belief of the French peasants in the miracle that a man named Napoleon would bring all the glory back to them. . . . The fixed idea of the Nephew was realized, because it coincided with the fixed idea of the most numerous class of the French people.
>
> (XI, 187–8)

Due to their ignorance and isolation, says Marx, the peasants 'cannot represent themselves, they must be represented' (XI, 187). Most of the French people (and the French were the most highly educated nation in the world) were unable clearly to distinguish representation from reality. This is why they lay mired in false consciousness, and were unable to resist, or even to desire to resist, the *coup d'état* and despotism of Louis Napoleon.

MONEY, ALIENATION AND REPRESENTATION

In the previous chapter, we saw how Kant attributed the subject's inability to perceive the thing-in-itself to the inherent capacities of the human mind. We also saw how Hegel historicized this obstacle to our knowledge by describing the objective world as the self-alienation of the Absolute Subject. Finally, Feuerbach suggests that this Subject is nothing else than 'man' himself, in the form of an idealist fantasy. Marx removes the last mythologizing element from this narrative. For him, Feuerbach's identification of 'man' with 'species-being' is simply another abstraction. Marx unites idealism and materialism through his recognition that the essence of 'man' which has become alienated is no abstraction, but is actually nothing more mysterious than our own activity, our labour.

Feuerbach had argued that the being we call 'God' is actually only a projection of the capacities of the human species. When we worship 'God', therefore, we really adore an alienated form of ourselves. Marx concurs, remarking of 'men' that 'The products of their brains have got out of their hands. They, the creators, have bowed down before their creations' (V, 23). The religious strictures against idolatry again loom large here. For Marx, however, this alienated form of human activity is incarnated in the material products of our labour: 'The product of labor is labor which has been embodied in an object, which has become material: it is the objectification of labor' (III, 272). This, rather than Feuerbach's abstract 'species-being', is the true objectification of mankind's essence.

In a capitalist economy, however, this objectified essence of our selves does not even belong to us. The product made by the worker belongs to the capitalist, who considers it as a commodity to be sold. This leads Marx to emphasize that capitalism involves an alienation of our selves, as well as an objectification. What is more, under the system of wage-labour the worker's own labour power becomes a commodity, which he or she sells for money. As we have seen, Adam Smith concluded from this that money represents human labour in objectified form. As such it functions as the 'universal commodity', against which everything can be measured, which can be exchanged for anything, and which makes universal exchange possible. When we alienate our activity (which is to say our lives, our selves) in the form of commodities and then allow these commodities, in the abstract shapes of finance and the market, to dictate and command our lives, we therefore commit a secular form of idolatry. We fetishize 'the works of men's hands', and allow alienated human activity to exert a determining influence over human life. Our objectified labour dominates our subjective labour. As Marx puts it in *On the Jewish Question* [1843], 'Money is the estranged essence of man's work and man's existence, and this alien essence dominates him and he worships it' (Marx and Engels, 1975, III, 172).

In the *Economic and Philosophical Manuscripts*, Marx points out that Adam Smith has repeated once again the critical response to all kinds of superstition since Luther; he has unmasked it as the fetishization of human activity, which transforms the subject into an object:

> To this enlightened political economy, which has discovered – within private property – the *subjective essence* of wealth, the adherents of the monetary and mercantile system, who look upon private property only as an *objective* substance confronting men, seem therefore to be *fetishists, Catholics. Engels* was therefore right to call *Adam Smith* the *Luther of Political Economy.*

> (Marx and Engels, 1975, III, 290)

The false consciousness of earlier economists had been the result, once again, of a mistaken attitude to representation. Money is originally merely a symbol, which mediates between various objects, acting as a common denominator so as to facilitate exchange. However, when we sell our own lives for money, we lose sight of its merely symbolic role. As Marx puts it in *Comments on James Mill* [1844]:

> It is clear that this *mediator* thus becomes a *real God*, for the mediator is the *real power* over what it mediates to me. Its cult becomes an end in

itself. Objects separated from this mediator have lost their value. Hence the objects only have value insofar as they *represent* the mediator, whereas originally it seemed that the mediator had value only insofar as it represented *them*.

(Marx and Engels, 1975, III, 212)

The problem of false consciousness, then, is for Marx a problem of representation. Ideology consists in an inability to recognize the mediating function of representation, in assuming that it is an autonomous sphere, and thus mistaking the appearance for the thing-in-itself. Marx's thought is clearly Kantian here. But Marx mingles this influence with the Hegelian view that identity is relational and historical. Ideology also involves a blindness to the fact that our concepts are mediated through their relations to other concepts. Describing the process of 'ideological subdivision' in *The German Ideology* [1846], Marx observes that 'In consciousness – in jurisprudence, politics, etc. – relations become concepts; since they do not go beyond these relations, the concepts of the relations also become fixed concepts in their mind' (Marx and Engels, 1975, V, 92).

We have thus identified three main elements in Marx's notion of ideology: the idolatry of human activity, the mistaking of the sign for the thing and the conversion of 'relations' into 'fixed concepts'. Thus far, he seems quite 'idealist'. However, Marx's aim was to transcend the opposition between idealism and materialism, which he saw as itself a symptom of false consciousness. In accordance with this purpose, he connects these ideal errors with a particular kind of economic system. In order to investigate the nature of this connection, we must turn to Marx's most detailed criticism of ideology: *Capital* [1867] (1976).

Marx founds this work on a minute analysis of the commodity, which he undertakes in the first chapter. Following Aristotle, he points out that an object can be regarded in two ways: as something to be used (in which case one is concerned with its 'use-value') and as something to be exchanged (in which case one thinks of its 'exchange-value'). If two objects with different use-values (say a desk and a chair) are to be exchanged, some way must be found to render them equivalent. We must find a way to say 'x desks = y chairs'. In fact, for the purposes of exchange, we must be able to perceive the ideal value of the desk in the material object which is the chair. But since the desk is not materially the same as the chair, this equivalence can only be figurative. We must, that is, impose an alien and ideal representation, or 'form of value', on the material objects. We therefore no longer see the thing-in-itself, we see only the 'commodity form' – our own idea or concept – which we have imposed upon it.

As with Hegel's adaptation of the idea that opposites are mutually definitive, Marx's notion of the 'form of value' involves a newly systematic application of a venerable intuition. The knowledge that exchange-value and use-value imply two completely different ways of conceiving objects goes back to Aristotle, and it recurs frequently in literary history. By the sixteenth century, the phenomenon of 'commodification' (whereby the essential nature of an object is distorted by its financial representation) was widely remarked upon. In Shakespeare's *King John* (1595), Philip the Bastard complains about the growing influence of:

> That smooth-fac'd gentleman, tickling commodity,
> Commodity, the bias of the world –
> The world, who of itself is peized well,
> Made to run even upon even ground,
> Till this advantage, this vile-drawing bias,
> This sway of motion, this commodity,
> Makes it take head from all indifferency,
> From all direction, purpose, course, intent –
> And this same bias, this commodity,
> This bawd, this broker, this all-changing word,
> Clapp'd on the outward eye of fickle France,
> Hath drawn him from his own determined aid . . .

> (II, i, 573–84)

The word 'commodity' here means both 'self-interest' and 'unnatural value'. Shakespeare, Adam Smith and Marx agree that financial value is a fetishized and illusory representation of real human activity. But there is one vital difference between Adam Smith's labour theory of value and Marx's adaptation of Smith's work. Smith argues that the particular, concrete acts of labour carried out by the individual worker are the true source of a commodity's value. This assertion is hard to sustain in practice, because other factors, such as the degree of demand for a specific commodity, obviously play a practical role in determining its value. But the multiple determination of value in particular cases poses no threat to Marx's labour theory of value, because he regards financial value as the objectified form, not of any particular acts of labour, but of human labour *in general*. Financial value is brought into existence by an act of abstraction from concrete labour:

> the labour that forms the substance of value is equal human labour, the expenditure of identical human labour-power. The total labour-power of society, which is manifested in the value of the world of commodities, counts here as one homogenous mass of human labour-power, although composed of innumerable units of labour-power. . . . The value of a commodity represents human labour pure and simple, the expenditure of human labour in general.
>
> (Marx, 1976, 129, 135)

In the *Grundrisse*, Marx argues that this abstraction of labour becomes more pronounced to the degree that capital becomes a global power. The world market depends upon an 'indifference towards any specific kind of labour', and conceives of labour as 'the means of creating wealth in general . . . [labour] has ceased to be organically linked with particular individuals in any specific form' (1973, 104).

The function of financial value is to be a common denominator, a term in which the value of anything can be expressed. It must therefore be a generalization, an abstraction from concrete, particular objects. A concrete, particular act of labour cannot fulfil the function of value; this function can only be fulfilled by labour conceived of as a whole, in general. Financial value is the objectified representation of human labour *per se*. Furthermore, the terms 'labour' and even 'labour power' are inadequate to describe what value represents. Because labour is commodified, we tend to equate it with those portions of our life that we literally sell: our 'labour' is whatever we do during the forty or so hours a week in which we exchange our time for money. But labour conceived in general is not so restricted. What we really sell for money is not our labour, but our time, our lives, and by the term 'labour power' Marx intends human life in general. Money, in short, is the objectified and alienated form of life itself. We see here the full extent of Hegel's influence on Marx. Marx presents the contradiction between capital and labour as the latest form taken by the Hegelian contradiction between Spirit and its self-alienation. It is the ultimate, seminal and essential contradiction of human history, the contemporary manifestation of a conflict that other epochs have described as taking place between the flesh and the spirit, between God and the Devil, between life and death.

So, rather than discovering the concept of financial value, Marx simply relocates it within an over-arching philosophical tradition. Specifically, Marx uses the notion of value as an explanation for our inability, noted by Kant, to perceive the thing-in-itself. As a result of 'the fetishism of the commodity', we no longer see the 'real' thing, but only its 'form of appearance'. In keeping with his Hegelian background, however, Marx also offers us a way out of this frustrating situation. Just as, for Hegel, alienation would be transcended when Spirit recognized matter as its own alienated self, so for Marx alienation will be abolished when human beings understand that the 'market forces' which shape their lives are nothing but representations of their own alienated activity.

We may note here that Marx's solution to the central problem of philosophy is 'materialist' in the sense that he connects it to the economy. On the other hand, the capitalist economy is itself made possible by a gigantic and purely ideal delusion. There is no material difference between a rose regarded as an object of beauty, and a rose regarded as a commodity for sale. The difference – which is none the less real for not being material – exists only in the mind of the beholder. Like the spurious symbols used by Louis Napoleon, the commodity form is a representation which falsely assumes a material appearance, and thereby comes to exert a pernicious determining influence on material circumstances. It is, in other words, a purely ideological phenomenon. Marx illustrates the ideological effects of exchange-value with a quotation from Shakespeare's *Timon of Athens*:

> What is here?
> Gold? Yellow, glittering, precious gold!
> No, gods, I am no idle votarist:
> . . . Thus much of this will make
> Black white, foul fair, wrong right,
> Base noble, old young, coward valiant.

> . . . This yellow slave
> Will knit and break religions, bless th'accursed,
> Make the hoar leprosy adored, place thieves
> And give them title, knee, and approbation
> With senators on the bench.
>
> (IV, iii, 25–38)

In his commentary on this speech, Marx points out that to see something as a commodity is to view it as what it is not: to perceive the ideal representation of some other thing within the material body of the object. Money, the generalized commodity-form, spreads this illusory perception throughout society, dissolving all previous identities and distinctions, and remoulding human consciousness in its own image. In the fully developed form of capital, money achieves an active, self-generating power through which it shapes the lives of concrete individuals. It is therefore, says Marx, a 'visible god' (III, 324). Timon also perceives in the gold an invitation to idolatry; he refuses to worship it as an 'idle votarist'. For Shakespeare as for Marx, the material medium of representation known as money at once expresses, embodies and produces an idolatrous consciousness.

In the twentieth century, the alien significance which exchange-value imposes upon the thing-in-itself was often explored by analogy with humanity's alienation from the world of objects. In Jean-Paul Sartre's *Nausea* [1938] (1957), for instance, the protagonist Roquetin is afflicted by a feeling that material things have become possessed with an unnatural, sickening, active power:

> Objects should not touch because they are not alive. You use them, put them back in place, you live among them: they are useful, nothing more. But they touch me, it is unbearable. I am afraid of being in contact with them as though they were living beasts.
>
> (10)

How do objects achieve this power of subjective agency? Marx's theory would ascribe it to the fact that commodities are the repositories of fetishized human activity. Georg Simmel's *The Philosophy of Money* [1900] (1978) reaches a similar conclusion by a quite different route. Simmel argues that the value we attach to an object cannot, by definition, be objective. Nothing is valuable in itself; the value of an object is created by the subject's desire for it. Just as for Kant the human mind creates the objects of its experience, so for Simmel it is subjective desire which creates the value of those objects. But this does not mean that value is purely subjective, either. If it were not incarnated in an object, value could have no existence. In fact, value mediates between subject and object. It is 'a third category, which cannot be derived from either subject or object, but which stands, so to speak, between us and the objects' (68). Value is representation; it is created when we represent our subjective desire in material form.

In order to exchange one object for another, however, we must conceive of them as equivalent in value. This means that we need a common denominator in which the values of the two objects can be expressed. This common denominator is thus the objectified form of value, as Simmel points out: 'The value of an object becomes objectified by exchanging it for another object' (81). Value thus takes on an existence which is independent of the objects being exchanged, and this objectified value is represented in the form of money:

> Money is the representative of abstract value. . . . All other objects have a specific content from which they derive their value. Money derives its content from its value; it is value turned into a substance, the value of things without the things themselves.
>
> (120–1)

Money is thus the material representation of abstract value. It is the 'third term', the 'mediator' between subject and object, which has been given a purely objective form. It is clear, then, that Simmel agrees with Marx that money involves an objectification of subjective activity: it occludes the subjective element in the creation of value, rendering value completely objective. It thus also involves a distortion of the relationship between ideas, matter and representation, conflating the third term of this trinity with the second. To the extent to which this objectified mediator dominates social life – the degree to which we live in a 'money economy' – we might therefore expect that all forms of representation would come to seem autonomous and aspire to exert a determining influence over human life. This is one way of characterizing the ideology of the 'postmodern condition'. However, for the first half of the twentieth century Marxists generally conceived of ideology in materialist fashion, as empty ideas whose true determination could be found in the material world. How did this misinterpretation of Marx gain such widespread currency?

THE MATERIALIST FALLACY

Clearly, the relationship in Marx's work between the ideal, the material and the representational is extremely complex, and it would be a gross simplification to claim that false consciousness is 'caused' by one of these factors alone. Unfortunately, the most immediately influential of Marx's followers, his friend and collaborator Friedrich Engels, sometimes commits precisely this error. At times, Engels seems to agree with Marx that false consciousness consists in rigid, 'metaphysical' antitheses, such as the one between ideas and matter. Thus, in the *Anti-Dühring* [1877–8], he gives the following description of false consciousness, or 'metaphysics':

> To the metaphysician, things and their mental reflexes, ideas, are isolated, are to be considered one after the other and apart from each other, are objects of investigation fixed, rigid, given once and for all. He thinks in absolutely irreconcilable antitheses. . . . For him a thing either exists or does not exist; a thing cannot at the same time be itself and something else. Positive and negative absolutely exclude one another; cause and effect stand in a rigid antithesis one to the other.
>
> (Marx and Engels, 1975, XXV, 22)

The 'metaphysician', in other words, commits the two cardinal sins against Hegel: ahistoricism and essentialism. He sees things as eternal, self-identical essences, and he remains unaware of either the historical process by which they come into being, or of their mediation and determination by other things. This account of ideology corresponds to the tendency Marx identifies in *Capital* whereby we impose an alienated, fetishistic image upon an object, thus obscuring the labour which produced it and its relation to other objects. However, Engels does not apply these strictures to his own 'scientific' methodology, which conse-quently comes to seem rather 'metaphysical' itself. For example, Engels constructs just such a 'rigid antithesis' between materialism and idealism. He claims that 'Marx and I were pretty well the only people to rescue conscious dialectics from German idealist philosophy and apply it in the materialist conception of nature and history' (XXV, 11). This was necessary, he says, because 'Hegel was an idealist. . . . This way of thinking turned everything upside down, and completely reversed the actual connection of things in the world' (XXV, 25). Engels has evidently forgotten here about the interpenetration of opposites, and the mutual definition of the poles of dichotomies. As a result, he lapses into the most brutally simplistic kind of materialist determinism. Due to his and Marx's efforts, claims Engels:

> it was seen that *all* past history was the history of class struggles; that these warring classes of society are always the products of the modes of production and of exchange – in a word, of the *economic* conditions of their time; that the economic structure of society always furnishes the real basis, starting from which we can alone work out the ultimate explanation of the whole superstructure of juridical and political institutions as well as of the religious, philosophical, and other ideas of a given historical period. But now idealism was driven from its last refuge, the philosophy of history; now a materialistic treatment of history was propounded, and a method found of explaining man's 'knowing' by his 'being', instead of, as heretofore, his 'being' by his 'knowing'.
>
> (XXV, 26–7)

The unequivocal absolutism of Engels's opposition, together with his assertion that a particular relation of cause-and-effect always remains constant in human history, is about as far away from Marx's historical dialectics as it is possible to be. The whole tenor of Marx's *oeuvre* suggests that to claim that one side of an opposition necessarily determines the other is itself an ideological error, which can be traced to a particular historical configuration of ideal and material forces. Engels commits this error in the *Anti-Dühring*. However, the proposition that the economic structure of society always determines every idea anyone ever has is difficult to defend for long, and Engels was forced to retreat somewhat from this position. In a letter to Bloch, composed in 1890, Engels takes a more conciliatory tone:

> According to the materialist conception of history the determining
> element in history is *ultimately* the production and reproduction of real
> life. More than this neither Marx nor I have ever asserted. . . . The
> economic system is the basis, but . . . the reflexes of all these actual
> struggles in the brains of the combatants: political, legal, philosophical
> theories, religious ideas and their further developments into systems of
> dogma – also exercise their influence upon the course of the historical
> struggles and in many cases may preponderate in determining their
> form.
>
> (Engels, 1942, 475–6)

We should notice here that Engels is backing off only from the empirical claim that the economy is *always* the *only* determining factor. He still does not recognize the theoretical objection that, according to the dialectics of Hegel and Marx, it is logically impossible to separate the material sphere from the ideal. Consequently, he is left in the position of asserting that the economy merely determines people's ideas quite a lot, and quite often. The difference is only one of degree, and the contradiction with his own dialectical method remains intact. As we shall see, this is an error which crops up with disturbing regularity in the history of Marxist thought.

Ironically enough, one of the first alarms about the dangers of economic determinism was sounded by George Plekhanov, the Russian Marxist who was to become the major theoretical influence on Lenin, and thus on the ultra-materialist theory which came to dominate institutional Communism in the twentieth century. In *The Materialist Conception of History* [1897] (1940) Plekhanov differentiates between 'economic materialists' and 'dialectical materialists'. The former group, he says, remain trapped within the 'theory of factors'. That is, they do not think of society as a 'totality', but instead try to isolate a 'factor' (in this case the economy) and claim for it a determining influence. As Plekhanov points out, this way of thinking is precisely what Hegel and Marx criticized: 'A historico-social factor is an abstraction, and the idea of it originates as the result of a process of abstraction' (15–16). That is to say, economic determinism 'dismembers the activity of social man and converts its various aspects and manifestations into separate forces, which are supposed to determine the historical movement of society' (17).

Tragically for the subsequent history of institutional Marxism, Plekhanov's thought is not so clear when he comes to discuss the method of the so-called 'dialectical materialists'. Plekhanov claims that, instead of identifying abstract 'factors', this takes a 'synthetic' approach to society, viewing it in its 'totality' (18). But when he begins to describe exactly what this involves, Plekhanov can only talk of 'explaining the activity of social man by his needs and by the means and methods of satisfying them prevailing at the given time' (20). Incisive and pertinent when identifying the errors of the 'economists', Plekhanov is hard pressed to suggest a significantly different, alternative kind of 'materialism'. In fact, his most cogent statement of his own opinion only avoids relapsing into a 'theory of factors' by reducing all 'social relations' to the level of material 'productive forces':

> The history of ideologies is to a large extent to be explained by the rise, modification and breakdown of associations of ideas under the influence of the rise, modification and breakdown of definite combinations of social forces . . . men do not make several distinct histories – the history of law, the history of morals, the history of philosophy, etc. – but only one history, the history of their own social relations, which are determined by the state of the productive forces in each particular period. What is known as ideologies is nothing but a multiform reflection in the minds of men of this single and indivisible history.
>
> (44)

Plekhanov's work is thus materialist, not only in the sense that he believes the ideal is *caused* by the material, but also in the sense that he believes the ideal actually *is* material. Human ideas are simultaneously 'reflections' of productive forces and a part of the 'one history' of material 'social relations'. This view would become extremely influential in the twentieth century, when thinkers such as Gramsci and Althusser sought for alternatives to the causal, determinist materialism espoused by Plekhanov's most famous disciple, V.I. Lenin.

In *Materialism and Empirio-Criticism* [1908] (1927) Lenin does his utmost to enlist Marxism under Plekhanov's banner of 'dialectical materialism', which he quite wrongly claims was Marx's own term for his ideas. In the course of this effort he forgets that Plekhanov's approach emphasized the dialectical, rather than the materialist, element of this phrase. Lenin therefore abandons Plekhanov's concept of the totality, and lapses definitively back into a 'theory of factors'. The 'empirio-criticism' of the book's title refers to a theory recently advanced by one of Lenin's political rivals, Bogdanov. Using recent discoveries in physics, which suggested that atoms were not solid matter but were made up of relations between electrons, Bogdanov had proposed that there was no intrinsic difference between physical and mental phenomena. Rather, these were merely different ways of organizing the same experiences. Appalled at what seemed to him an infernal mixture of Berkelean idealism and Humean scepticism, Lenin vehemently defended two main propositions: that there is a material world which exists outside the subject, and that this world causes the mental activity of that subject:

> All knowledge comes from experience, from sensation, from perception. That is true. But the question arises, does *objective reality* 'belong to perception', i.e., is it the source of perception? If you answer yes, you are a materialist. If you answer no, you are inconsistent, and will inevitably arrive at subjectivism.

(125–6)

Lenin thus insists on the most rigid opposition between the ideal and the material. Although his later work evinces some softening of his position, here he propagandizes furiously in favour of materialist causality, and perceives only deception and turpitude in idealist 'subjectivism'. The centralized organization of the Bolshevik party, the repressive methods to which the party found itself impelled after the revolution, and the rise to power after Lenin's death of the theoretically unsophisticated Josef Stalin, all contributed to the establishment of this naively reductive materialism as the official philosophy of the Marxist world. This was a tragedy in two senses. Most importantly, it gave a crude plausibility to the megalo-maniacal ambitions of such 'engineers of the soul' as Stalin and Mao. But more relevantly for our purposes here, it reintroduced the use of the term 'ideology' in the Napoleonic sense: as designating vague, nebulous ideas which spuriously claim independence from material circumstances. The resulting confusion has plagued the theory of ideology ever since.

THE RETREAT FROM MOSCOW: GEORG LUKÁCS

The first theorist to make a significant advance on Marx's theory of ideology while remaining true to the dialectical approach of Marx himself was the Hungarian Communist leader, theoretician and literary critic, Georg Lukács. His *History and Class-consciousness* [1922] (1971) bases its entire theory on the first chapter of *Capital*, which Lukács says 'contains within itself the whole of historical materialism' (170). At first glance, this seems a rather surprising claim because, as we have seen, *Capital*'s first chapter is concerned with the fetishism of the commodity – that is to say, with an ideological rather than a material problem. And yet Lukács's book does succeed in convincingly demonstrating that commodity fetishism is the central, definitive characteristic of capitalist society.

We should recall here that in *Capital*'s first chapter, entitled 'The Commodity', Marx shows how exchange-value emerges out of the relationship between two commodities by means of a process of figuration, so that, for instance, when a coat is exchanged for a piece of linen: 'The linen expresses its value in the coat; the coat serves as the material in which that value is expressed . . . the physical body of commodity B becomes a mirror for the value of commodity A' (1976, 139, 144). Commodity exchange presupposes the real presence of the value of one object in the physical body of another. This value is not, of course, materially present, but it is nevertheless actually present. Thus commodity exchange depends on the ability of a figure, a symbol, to become real. It depends, that is to say, on the power of ideas to impose themselves on material reality – the Kantian 'appearance' must supersede the 'thing-in-itself'. This is achieved by introducing a common denominator, which will express the value of materially distinct objects as though they were the same. The medium through which this illusory equivalence is achieved is human labour: not any particular act of labour, but human labour considered in general, in the abstract form for which the universally recognized symbol is money. But to objectify and abstract human labour (that is to say, human activity, human life itself) demands a specific kind of false consciousness. Lukács will term this ideological phenomenon 'reification', which means 'to turn into a thing'. In *Capital*, Marx describes its effects as follows:

the commodity-form . . . is nothing but the definite social relation between men themselves which assumes here, for them, the fantastic form of a relation between things. In order, therefore, to find an analogy we must take flight into the misty realm of religion. There the products of the human brain appear as autonomous figures endowed with a life of their own, which enter into relations both with each other and with the human race. So it is in the world of commodities with the products of men's hands. I call this the fetishism which attaches itself to the products of labor as soon as they are produced as commodities, and is therefore inseparable from the production of commodities.

(1976, 765)

Lukács's achievement is to show how this commodity fetishism, and its concomitant 'reified consciousness', have permeated every aspect of capitalist society. He insists, repeatedly, on the total nature of this phenomenon – 'Reification requires that society should learn to satisfy all its needs in terms of commodity exchange' (91); 'the basic structure of reification can be found in all the social forms of modern capitalism' (171); 'Reification is, then, the necessary, immediate reality of every person living in capitalist society' (197). This ubiquitous and evil tendency freezes relations and processes, so that they appear as immutable, self-identical things. It erases mediation and history, making the actually fluid phenomena of society appear to be 'supra-historical essences' (14). It obscures the fact that identity is relational, and thus makes it hard to consider society as a 'totality'. In the form of 'the market', it transforms relations between people into relations between the products of their labour. In short, reification is the tendency to fetishize our own activity, when that tendency has grown into a universal and determining influence over every aspect of our lives.

In this description of a thoroughgoing false consciousness, Lukács has recourse to the Aristotelian concept of 'second nature'. Aristotle's notion referred to 'custom': when we have done things a certain way for a long time, we assume this is the 'natural' way to do them. Lukács gives this concept a more materialist inflection. The commodity is a product of human labour. For it to be possible 'for the commodity structure to penetrate society in all its aspects and to remold it in its own image' (85), we must endow these products with an autonomous existence. 'Men', says Lukács, 'erect around themselves in the reality they have created and "made", a kind of second nature which evolves with exactly the same inexorable necessity as was the case earlier on with irrational forces of nature' (128). Once again, false consciousness consists in allowing this 'second nature', which is only 'the works of men's hands', to exert a fetishistic dominance over our lives.

Lukács regards the philosophical tendency to separate the ideal from the material as another result of reification. Because the workers must sell their labour power as a commodity (they must objectify their own activity), the duality between subject and object enters into the subject itself. Just as, for Hegel, Spirit alienates itself in the material world, so for Lukács the human subject objectifies its own activity. This gives rise to what Lukács calls 'reflection theories', which try to reduce one pole of the subject / object dichotomy to a mere 'reflection' of the other:

> In the theory of 'reflection' we find the theoretical embodiment of the duality of thought and existence, consciousness and reality, that is so intractable to the reified consciousness. And from *that point of view* it is immaterial whether things are to be regarded as reflections of concepts or whether concepts are reflections of things. In both cases the duality is firmly established.
>
> (200)

It follows that materialism is merely an 'inverted Platonism' (202), a 'mythology' which is produced by the reification of what is actually a *relation* into two separate *things*. On a theoretical plane, then, the way out of false consciousness demands that '*things should be shown to be aspects of processes*' (179), because 'the *developing tendencies of history constitute a higher reality than the empirical "facts"*' (181). This is why Lukács declares, in a statement which is in direct contradiction to Leninist orthodoxy, that 'It is not the primacy of economic motives in historical explanation that constitutes the decisive difference between Marxism and bourgeois thought, but the point of view of the totality' (27). Earlier modes of thought had reached the same conclusion regarding the importance of the totality, as Lukács admits: 'God, the soul, etc. . . . are nothing but mythological expressions to denote the unified subject or, alternatively, the unified object of the totality of the objects of knowledge considered as perfect (and wholly known)' (115).

However, this totality had previously been doomed to remain a philosophical abstraction, since there had not existed any material means to realize it in the real world. Lukács believes that Marx discovered this practical instrument in 'the standpoint of the Proletariat'. The 'proletariat' was another word for the 'working class'. It referred to people whose income was derived from selling their labour power for wages. (It is important to note that, by this definition, almost everyone today is a proletarian, and that Marx's theories are thus not rendered obsolete by the recent numerical decline of the industrial working classes.) When Marx and Lukács wrote, however, there were many other social classes in Europe: a landowning aristocracy, a smallholding peasantry and a capitalist or 'bourgeois' class which owned the factories and mines in which the proletarians worked. Of these, only the proletariat was able to achieve consciousness of the process of reification. It was able to do this because, by selling their labour power, its members objectified themselves, turning themselves into commodities. In Hegel, history works towards an end, or *telos*, in which Spirit recognizes the material world as its own alienated condition. In Marx and Lukács, history functions so as to reveal to the proletariat that capital, the force which dominates and controls their lives, is nothing more than their own objectified labour. This knowledge of the interpenetration of object and subject is what Lukács means by the proletariat's 'class-consciousness'.

As a result of this revelation, there will no longer be a need for ideology. The antinomies between subject and object, ideas and matter, will dissolve, and the totality will become visible. For the moment, then, philosophy's task is to show the proletarians that the reified, fragmentary and contradictory world in which they live is simply the product of their own objectified activity: 'to deduce the unity – which is not given – of this disintegrating creation and to prove that it is the product of a creating subject. In the final analysis, then: to create the subject of the "creator"' (140). The problems which plagued Kant and Hegel will then evaporate, as Lukács rhapsodically anticipates: 'The genesis, the creation of the creator of knowledge, the dissolution of the irrationality of the thing-in-itself, the resurrection of man from his grave' (141).

Using a similar line of reasoning, Engels had once declared that 'the German proletariat is the heir of classical German philosophy'. We can, perhaps, imagine the reaction of a German proletarian on being informed of this illustrious lineage. Marxism as a whole takes a large gamble when it bestows the task of reconciling all philosophical contradictions on a group of fallible and very busy human beings. In its materialist manifestations, Marxism has assumed that the proletarian revolution is an inevitable event. Since material circumstances determine ideas, the theory runs, it will be possible to deduce the point at which the workers will rebel simply by analysing the progress of the economy. However, a dialectical view of the relations between ideology and material activity cannot share this confidence. Lukács chooses to end *History and Class-consciousness* on a pessimistic note:

> History is at its least automatic when it is the consciousness of the proletariat that is at issue. The truth that the old intuitive, mechanistic materialism could not grasp turns out to be doubly true for the proletariat, namely that it can be transformed and liberated only by its own actions, and that the 'educator must himself be educated'. The objective economic evolution could do no more than create the position of the proletariat in the production process. It was this position that determined its point of view. But the objective evolution could only give the proletariat the opportunity and the necessity to change society. Any transformation can only come about as the product of the – free – action of the proletariat itself.
>
> (208–9)

So it is perfectly possible that the proletariat will choose not to take this action. Once capitalism has achieved a certain level of prosperity for practically all of its denizens, the charms of the commodity may come to seem preferable to the arduous and dangerous quest for revolution. The fact that one's consciousness is reified, that one sees only appearances and representations rather than the things-in-themselves, may come to seem rather unimportant. As we know, this is what did in fact occur. There were no successful proletarian revolutions in Western Europe, and the proletariat settled down in front of the television to enjoy its commodified world in peace. The task of philosophy from this point on is the critical negation of this virtually universal false consciousness.

GRAMSCI AND HEGEMONY

Antonio Gramsci's *Prison Notebooks* [1929–34] (1971) represent the first theoretical attempt to come to terms with the defeat of the proletarian revolution. Following the failure of the Italian workers to seize power after the First World War, Gramsci, the leader of the Italian Communist Party, was imprisoned by Mussolini's Fascist government. Ironically enough, this confinement gave him a unique freedom to re-evaluate many of the doctrines which Moscow forcibly imposed on politically active Communists. Like Lukács, Gramsci jettisoned any kind of materialist determinism. Given his situation, it was obvious that there was nothing inevitable about the triumph of the proletariat. The revolution had failed, despite the fact that the 'objective', material conditions for its success had been in place. Gramsci therefore sought the reasons for this defeat in the subjective, ideological control which the capitalist state exercised over its inhabitants.

Gramsci's view of ideology is best approached through two passages from Marx, to which he returns repeatedly in the *Prison Notebooks*. Discussing the question of revolutions, Marx writes:

> In considering such transformations a distinction should always be made between the material transformation of the economic conditions of production, which can be determined with the precision of natural science, and the legal, political, religious, aesthetic or philosophic – in short, ideological forms in which men become conscious of this conflict and fight it out.
>
> (cit. Gramsci, 1971, 365n54)

Gramsci glosses this passage as saying that 'men acquire consciousness of structural conflicts on the level of ideologies' (365), and goes on to maintain that it 'should be considered as an affirmation of epistemological and not simply psychological and moral value' (164). That is to say, Gramsci believes that revolutions, while they may be facilitated by shifts in the economic structure, are also fought out, and their outcomes are decided, on the level of 'ideologies'. Consequently, he devotes an enormous amount of attention to conflicts between different systems of ideas. The other major source for Gramsci's conception of the relationship between ideology and political power is Marx and Engels's *Communist Manifesto* [1848] (1975), where it is announced that 'the ruling ideas of each age have ever been the ideas of its ruling class' (VI, 503). This is the so-called 'dominant ideology thesis', which suggests that the class which is economically dominant will try to impose its own peculiar way of seeing the world on society as a whole. The realm of ideology thus becomes a field of class conflict, and it is this battle which Gramsci sets out to study using the concept of 'hegemony'.

By this term, Gramsci means the nexus of material *and* ideological instruments through which the ruling class maintains its power. Hegemony is thus a form of praxis. This allows Gramsci to reserve the term 'ideology' for pure consciousness, and he proposes to 'distinguish between historically organic ideologies, those, that is, which are necessary to a given structure, and ideologies that are arbitrary, rationalistic, or "willed"' (376–7). The former may be specific to a particular class, or 'group', but they are an accurate expression of that group's material interests. Interestingly, Gramsci identifies the latter kind of ideology with the mechanistic mode of thought exemplified by Destutt de Tracy's 'science' of 'Idéologie'. Because it traces the formation of ideas to material sensations, this kind of approach is, in Gramsci's view, utterly mistaken. He claims that Marxism

> represents a distinct advance and historically is precisely in opposition to Ideology. Indeed the meaning which the term 'ideology' has assumed in Marxist philosophy implicitly contains a negative value judgment and excludes the possibility that for its founders [i.e. Marx and Engels] the origin of ideas should be sought for in sensations, and therefore, in the last analysis, in Physiology.
>
> (376)

The theory that ideologies are merely pale reflections of material influences is, according to Gramsci, unable to account for the existence of 'organic' ideologies, which are necessary and in a sense true. Materialism wrongly presupposes an essential distinction between matter and ideas. The result of this tendency in Destutt, and also in Marxist 'economistic superstition' (164), has been a three-fold error:

1   ideology is defined as distinct from the structure, and it is asserted
    that it is not ideology that changes the structures but vice versa;
2   it is asserted that a given political situation is 'ideological' – i.e.
    that it is not sufficient to change the structure, although it thinks
    that it can do so; it is asserted that it is useless, stupid, etc.;
3   one then passes to the assertion that every ideology is 'pure'
    appearance, useless, stupid, etc.

(376)

So Gramsci reacts against the notion of ideology as false consciousness, asserting that 'all systems have an historical validity, and are necessary' (138). This also involves a reaction against the belief that ideology is a mere reflection of material circumstances. The effect of these advances is to thrust an immense importance on to the sphere of ideas. In fact, Gramsci points out that material factors are only ever expressed and understood through consciousness, and that developments in the history of consciousness can thus be more significant than economic changes: 'it may be ruled out that immediate economic crises of themselves produce fundamental historical events; they can simply create a terrain more favourable to the dissemination of certain modes of thought' (184). Because '"popular beliefs" and similar ideas are themselves material forces' (165), any revolutionary theory must deal with class conflict on the level of ideas at least as much as in the economic arena. In fact, Gramsci is unwilling to distinguish between these two levels, preferring his notion of 'hegemony', which constitutes a '"historical bloc", i.e. unity between nature and spirit (structure and superstructure), unity of opposites and of distincts' (137).

Gramsci thus pointedly declines the metaphor, drawn from Marx but popularized by Engels and Lenin, of the economic 'base' on which is founded an ideological 'superstructure'. For him, the material sphere is itself a 'structure', which may be allied with and analogous to, but does not 'support', a 'superstructure' of ideas. These ideas, Gramsci notes, are institutionalized in 'civil society': the law courts, the bureaucracy, the religious and educational systems and the mass media. In Western Europe (as opposed to Russia) these 'ideological' institutions are more important in upholding the hegemony of the ruling class than any 'purely' economic factors:

> The superstructures of civil society are like the trench-systems of modern warfare. . . . In Russia the State was everything, civil society was primordial and gelatinous; in the West there was a proper relation between State and civil society, and when the State trembled, a sturdy structure of civil society was at once revealed.
>
> (235, 238)

Thus we can see how Gramsci's theory of hegemony could explain the failure of the revolution in Western Europe. Although the years following the First World War produced unprecedented economic crises, which rocked states like Germany and Italy to their foundations, the solidity of 'civil society' ensured that people's ideas remained in thrall to the ruling powers. The pressing need, as Gramsci saw it, was to determine how this had been possible, and this would entail a careful analysis of the institutions which transmitted ideology to the people. From his prison cell, Gramsci was able to do no more than suggest where such a study might begin:

> The school as a positive educative function, and the courts as a repressive and negative educative function, are the most important State activities in this sense: but, in reality, a multitude of other so-called private initiatives and activities tend to the same end – initiatives and activities which form the apparatus of the political and cultural hegemony of the ruling classes.
>
> (258)

Because Gramsci's view of the relative autonomy of ideology was in such direct contrast to the official position of the rest of the European Communist leadership, these suggestive insights were not followed up for over thirty years. They do, however, form the major inspiration behind the work of Louis Althusser, which in turn became the most significant influence on post-war debates about ideology.

5

POST-MARXISM

> There can't be any doubt about it any longer: the struggle against
> ideology has become a new ideology.
>
> (Bertolt Brecht, cit. Taylor, 1977, 97)

ALTHUSSER AND MATERIALISM

The work of Louis Althusser espouses a materialism which is deeply collusive with the process of objectification that it purports to criticize. It is thus significant that Althusser's ideas, often filtered through the works of his pupil Michel Foucault, have become the decisive influence on postmodern critiques of ideology. In particular, the anti-Hegelian aspects of Althusser's thought – his emphasis on the materiality of ideas, his opposition to 'totalizing' systems of thought, his attack on the subject – have won an appreciative audience, and spawned a vogue for vulgar materialism which is only now beginning to subside.

In *Lenin and Philosophy* [1969] (1971), Althusser explores Gramsci's burgeoning but unfulfilled interest in the material institutions which administer ideology to the masses. This book's most influential chapter, 'Ideology and Ideological State Apparatuses', pursues Gramsci's reference to capitalism's 'need to elaborate a new type of man suited to the new type of work and productive process' (Gramsci, 1971, 286). The first task of any economic system, according to Althusser, is to reproduce its own conditions of production. This involves reproducing the kinds of people who will be able to participate in the process of production. The power of the modern capitalist state to do this is dependent on two types of institutions: the 'Repressive State Apparatuses', such as the police, law courts and army, and the 'Ideological State Apparatuses', which include the Church, the family, political parties, the media and, most importantly, the education system. As we might expect, the difference between the 'RSAs' and the 'ISAs' is that 'the Repressive State Apparatus functions "by violence", whereas the Ideological State Apparatuses function "by ideology"'.

'Ideology' is therefore embodied in material practice. Althusser notes that 'an ideology always exists in an apparatus, and its practice, or practices. This existence is material' (166). We saw in the last chapter that Gramsci had said much the same. But Althusser proceeds from this to the peculiar claim that 'Ideas have disappeared as such' (168). Althusser reaches the unwarranted conclusion that, due to the fact that ideas are expressed and transmitted by material institutions, ideas are themselves material. To assert otherwise, he claims, is 'ideology':

> the ideal and spiritual existence of 'ideas' arises exclusively in an ideology of the 'idea' and of ideology, and let me add, in an ideology of what seems to have 'founded' this conception since the emergence of the sciences, i.e. what the practices of the sciences represent to themselves in their spontaneous ideology as 'ideas', true or false. Of course, presented in affirmative form, this thesis is unproven. I simply ask that the reader be favorably disposed towards it, say, in the name of materialism. A long series of arguments would be necessary to prove it.
> (165–6)

It would indeed require a long series of arguments to prove that ideas are material. The fact that Althusser asks his readers to accept this as a matter of faith is a signal that we have returned to a species of that 'metaphysical' materialism which typified the French Enlightenment. The polemical commitment to materialism which characterizes his work enables Althusser to slide from the presupposition that matter determines ideas into an assumption that ideas do not exist:

> the existence of the ideas of [the subject's] belief is material in that *his*
> *ideas are his material actions inserted into material practices governed by*
> *material rituals which are themselves defined by the material ideological*
> *apparatus from which derive the ideas of that subject.*
>
> (169)

If ideas are material then the subject which has ideas must, in fact, be an object. The very notion of an autonomous subject, like the concept of non-material ideas, is described by Althusser as ideological: 'the category of the "subject" is constitutive of ideology, which only exists by constituting concrete subjects as subjects. . . . The existence of ideology and the hailing or interpellation of individuals as subjects are one and the same thing' (173, 175).

Here we have the origin of the dispersed, objectified subject celebrated by the postmodernists. Ideology, says Althusser, exists before the individual. When the concrete individual comes along, ideology has 'always already' determined a specific set of roles, a particular subjectivity, into which the individual will be slotted. This occurs through a process of 'interpellation', which basically means that a person will be systematically addressed, or 'hailed', in such a way as to force him or her into this pre-allocated 'subject-position'. Nor is this process unique to twentieth-century capitalism, for 'the formal structure of all ideology is always the same' (177). Ideology is not a historical phenomenon, but is rather an inherent tendency within the human mind which, it seems, cannot bear very much reality. The paradigmatic example of an ideological 'structure' is Christianity, which, as Althusser sees it, interpellates its followers as individual subjects by 'reflecting' such an image back to them through the Absolute Subject, which is God:

> We observe that the structure of all ideology, interpellating individuals
> as subjects in the name of a Unique and Absolute Subject is *speculary*,
> i.e. a mirror-structure, and *doubly* speculary: this mirror duplication is
> constitutive of ideology and ensures its functioning. Which means that
> all ideology is *centred*, that the Absolute Subject occupies the unique
> place of the Centre, and interpellates around it the infinity of individuals
> into subjects in a double mirror-connexion such that it *subjects* the
> subjects to the Subject, while giving them in the Subject in which each

subject can contemplate its own image (present and future) the *guarantee* that this really concerns them.

(180)

It is interesting to note that Althusser actually concurs with Christianity, and with post-Christian philosophers such as Hegel, that individual subjects are derived from the Absolute Subject. However, because Althusser assumes that anything which is not material is not real, he presupposes that such a Creator must produce purely illusory creatures, so that the human individual becomes merely an ideological bourgeois fantasy. Or rather, since he cannot deny that the individual subject does apparently enjoy a real existence, he emphasizes the 'artificial' nature of the creative process, and insinuates that there is something repressive and underhand about it.

In Althusser's defence, it should be noted that the objectified subject he describes does correspond to Marx's and Lukács's diagnoses of capitalism's dehumanizing effects. But whereas Marx and Lukács lament this loss of unified subjectivity as the most horrible of capitalism's evils, Althusser blithely accepts it as the correct and inevitable state of affairs. It remains only for him to scratch his head at the befuddlement of previous millennia and to deride their idealist mythologies. Especially among literary critics and 'posthumanist' philosophers such as Donna Haraway, the doctrine that the subject is purely material remains very popular, and its potential for politically progressive purposes is frequently asserted. This continued influence of the Althusserian theory of ideology testifies to the extent to which reification has penetrated the minds of even capitalism's declared adversaries.

Any attempt to identify ideology with material practice is Quixotic because the ideal / material opposition is a mutually defining dichotomy; that is to say, the very notions of 'ideal' and 'material' would be meaningless without each other. It is one thing to argue that this polarity is at root illusory and pernicious: Hegel and Marx both thought so, and they suggested ways in which it might be possible to transcend it, and thus overcome alienation. But Althusser does not do this; rather he simply collapses one pole of the opposition into the other, and announces that ideas have 'disappeared'. He means by this that ideas do not exist 'in the mind'. Instead, they only exist in material practice, in which case, of course, they are not ideal but material. Althusser misses the point that just because ideas are manifested in praxis (which is precisely the unity of ideas and concrete activity), they are not therefore reducible to it. What is more, if there are no ideas there can be no subject to 'have' ideas. Althusser therefore claims that the subject is itself formed by and composed of material practice, in which case it is not logically a subject at all: it is an object. Once again, a mutually defining opposition has been reduced to one of its terms. In order to sustain this reductionism, Althusser is forced to take up some original positions, which have come to form the basis of many postmodern theoretical assumptions.

As a loyal member of the French Communist Party, Althusser was concerned to establish that his materialism accorded with Marx's own teachings, and this is the task he undertook in his radically innovative *For Marx* [1965] (1969). As we saw in the last chapter, many of Marx's texts are explicitly opposed to materialism. To circumvent this fact, Althusser argues that there are actually *two* Marxes, separated by a yawning methodological chasm: 'This "epistemological break" divides Marx's thought into two long essential periods: the "ideological" period before, and the scientific period after, the break in 1845' (34). This 'break', then, occurs with the composition of *The German Ideology* – that is, with the only one of Marx's texts which is susceptible to a consistently materialist interpretation.

For Althusser, 'ideology' is the imaginary way in which people experience their real lives, the ideal representation of a material process. Despite his sometimes tortuous formulations of the term, it is not too crude to say that Althusser ultimately equates ideology with 'idealism', by which he means the tendency to attribute a real existence to purely ideal phenomena, and to the individual human subject in particular. 'Science', which Althusser calls the 'knowledge of' ideology, is generally used as an approximate term for a 'materialism' whose task it is to explain the source of these ideas, and so reveal their role in maintaining the power of the capitalist class, or 'bourgeoisie'. Althusser lays heavy stress on this opposition, warning of the need to preserve 'science' from 'the threats and taints of idealism, that is, of the *ideologies* which besiege it' (170), and calling for 'a continuous struggle against ideology itself, that is, against idealism' (ibid.).

By this definition, Hegel is clearly an 'ideological' thinker, and even the proto-materialist Feuerbach still relies on the non-material concept of 'species-being', thus falling prey to 'an idealist *anthropology*' (89). The early Marx succumbs to a similar 'humanism' when he makes alienated labour his central concern. This is because Marx perceives alienation as the objectification of human life, and thus as a negation of the human subject. For Althusser, of course, there is no human essence which is not always already material, and thus no subject which could be alienated by being made into an object. As a result, he must conclude that 'in Marxism, *negativity* and *alienation* are *ideological concepts* that can only designate their own *ideological* content' (214–15).

Althusser is determined to rid Marx of all traces of idealism. The major problem with this is the looming presence of Hegel throughout Marx's work. If one reads Marx as a materialist, this troublesome Hegelian heritage can be disposed of by a simple inversion, which transfers its metaphysical baggage into the material realm:

> Hegel explains the material life, the concrete history of all peoples by a dialectic of consciousness (the people's consciousness of itself: its ideology). For Marx, on the other hand, the material life of men explains their history; their consciousness, their ideologies are then merely the phenomena of their material life. This opposition certainly unites all the appearances of an 'inversion'.
>
> (107)

A further problem arises here, however. In Hegel, one seminal contradiction – the objectification of Spirit – produces all the others. What is more, the founding unity which is Spirit is also the ultimate destination and purpose – the 'end' – of history. This is why Hegel's thought is frequently called totalizing and teleological. Now, if one were to argue that Marx had simply 'inverted' Hegel, turning the ideal elements of his system into material equivalents, one would need to find a material substitute for this founding unity of Spirit. But the real world and the process of material history appear on a purely empirical level to be so complex and discontinuous that no such original force can be identified. Thus, says Althusser, 'Marxism . . . rejects the theoretical presupposition of the Hegelian model: the presupposition of an original simple unity. . . . This presupposition has not been "inverted", it has been eliminated' (198).

Althusser's determination to read Marx as a materialist thus leads him to reject the notion that Marx founds his theory on a single, original contradiction. For example, the neo-Hegelian concept of alienated labour cannot be the basis of Marxism for Althusser, since it partakes of 'the ideological myth of a philosophy of origins' (ibid.). Since Marxism is a 'science' and Hegelianism an 'ideology', and since 'a science is not obtained by inverting an ideology' (192), Marx must be made to depart from the position that the problems of the world can ultimately be traced to one all-encompassing contradiction. Here Althusser is forced to read strenuously against the grain. There is, in fact, one fundamental contradiction which runs through all of Marx's work: the opposition between labour power and capital or, as it is expressed in the early works, between human activity and the alienated form of human activity. As Lukács shows, this single opposition informs and determines every aspect of life under capitalism, moulding people's consciousness as well as dictating their economic activity. But the notion of alienation is too 'ideological' for Althusser to tolerate. He thus dismisses 'the Hegelian model and its faith in the resolving "power" of the abstract contradiction as such: in particular, the "beautiful" contradiction between Capital and Labour' (104), and so he is led inexorably to the conclusion that 'the apparently simple contradiction is always overdetermined' (106).

This use of the term 'overdetermination' is Althusser's major contribution to the theory of ideology. It means that every situation has more than one determining factor. For example, the forms taken by oppression in twentieth-century France cannot be reduced to merely economic factors. At a glance, one can see that other, ideal forces, such as conceptions of race, sexuality or gender, are at work. Althusser is thus willing to concede a 'relative autonomy of the superstructures' (111). The ideas we have about the world, in other words, are not only produced by our material lives, but also attain a certain degree of independence, and can come to play a partially determining role in history. This line of reasoning is often portrayed as Althusser's departure from crude materialism. But, as we have seen, he is forced to elaborate the concept of overdetermination precisely as a result of his own ultramaterialist determinism. To reiterate: Althusser wants to eliminate all traces of Hegelian idealism, or 'ideology', from Marx. This means that he refuses to accept the validity of Marx's notion of alienated labour, which merely 'inverts' Hegel's description of alienated Spirit. He thus cannot read Marx as employing the Hegelian notion of a single, informing contradiction: the material world is visibly more complex than that. He is therefore driven, despite himself, to allow ideas to have a certain determining influence on the material world.

However, this conclusion is diametrically opposed to Althusser's materialist agenda. There are two possible ways out of this contradiction. As we saw in our discussion of *Lenin and Philosophy*, one solution, albeit a very paradoxical one, is simply to declare that ideas are in fact material. In *For Marx*, Althusser stresses instead the '*determination in the last instance by the (economic) mode of production*' (111). Although ideas may attain a 'relative autonomy', and so appear, in certain circumstances, to be independent of the material base, we are asked to retain our faith that the economy is actually the hidden, ultimate cause of ideological phenomena. As he readily admits, Althusser derives this notion from Engels's letter to Bloch, which we discussed in Chapter 4. Like that letter, it amounts to little more than a ritualistic declaration of faith in a debased and diluted materialism, which is given no empirical or logical justification.

Althusser's influence on contemporary thought has been as profound as it has been malign. In particular, as a result of Althusser's emphasis on the constitutive role of ideology, significant doubt has been cast on the concept of 'false consciousness'. All forms of idealism, he argues, are ideological. And yet it is impossible to imagine a society which did not think to some degree in idealist terms (due to the fact, which Althusser does not recognize, that the ideal and the material are mutually definitive concepts). It follows that 'ideology is not an aberration or a contingent excrescence of History: it is a structure essential to the historical life of societies' (232). This is, surely, to stretch the term 'ideology' until it is emptied of significant content. But there is yet a further problem with Althusser's model. If 'ideology' is an illusory consciousness, and if 'science' is the 'truth of' ideology, how – given the inevitability of ideology – does one make the transition from one to the other? Here we come upon what is perhaps Althusser's most enduring legacy to postmodernism: the central role played in his theory by the aesthetic dimension.

A MATERIALIST AESTHETIC?

The problem of art is a particularly thorny one for any theory which is concerned to identify and account for false consciousness. Aesthetic statements cannot accurately be called false, but neither do they make any claim to be true. As Sir Philip Sidney pointed out in *The Defence of Poesy* [1595], 'for the poet, he nothing affirms, and therefore never lieth'. In Chapter 3 we saw how Kant used the category of aesthetic judgement to mediate between his epistemology and his ethics: that is, between his theory and its practical effects. Art performs a similar function in Althusser's work. In *Lenin and Philosophy* he declares

> I do not rank real art among the ideologies, although art does have a quite particular and specific relationship with ideology. . . . What art makes us see, and therefore gives to us in the form of 'seeing', 'perceiving' and 'feeling' (which is not the form of knowing), is the ideology from which it is born, in which it bathes, from which it detaches itself as art, and to which it alludes.

> (221–2)

It seems that 'art' (which term remains suspiciously undefined) occupies an area midway between 'science' and 'ideology'. It also seems as though art provides a conduit by which one may pass from ideology to the 'knowledge' which is science. It does this by unmasking the contradictions within ideology, making them visible by imposing upon it a predetermined aesthetic form. This is the argument pursued by Althusser's friend Pierre Macherey, in *A Theory of Literary Production* (1966). Macherey begins from the proposition that 'literary' language is essentially different from other modes of expression. It 'does not concern itself with distinctions between the true and the false, in so far as it establishes . . . its own truth'. Literature takes up a position in between truth and falsehood; it twists and distorts 'the everyday language which is the language of ideology' (59), thus distancing the reader from this language, drawing attention to its ideological nature, and so making possible a later transition to a scientific 'knowledge' of ideology:

> We could offer a provisional definition of literature as being charac-terized by this power of parody. Mingling the real uses of language in an

> endless confrontation, it concludes by *revealing* their truth. Experimenting with language rather than inventing it, the literary work is both the analogy of a knowledge and a caricature of customary ideology.
>
> (ibid.)

Because literary language must mould ideology into a form dictated by pre-existent literary convention, the astute critic will be able to perceive the contradictions in ideology within the literary text. According to the Althusserian framework, these contradictions will not be visible in everyday life, where ideology is successfully able to smooth them over:

> there can be no ideological contradiction, except if we put ideology into contradiction with itself. . . . By definition, ideology can sustain a contradictory debate, for ideology exists precisely in order to efface all trace of contradiction. Thus, an ideology, as such, breaks down only in the face of the real questions. . . . Ideology's essential weakness is that it can never recognize for itself its own real limits: at best it can learn of these limits from elsewhere, in the action of a radical criticism.
>
> (130–1)

These limits, so the argument runs, are made visible when ideology is forced into a form not of its choosing, as when it must conform to the generic requirements of a particular literary mode. Ideology's limits can be exposed through a two-fold method of analysis. Critics must first study the 'conditions of possibility' of the aesthetic work. These are to be sought outside the text, in the historical circumstances which produced it. Second, they must examine 'the conditions of those conditions' – the ideology which upheld and legitimated the historical situation – and these can be discerned within the text itself. Thus, in the example Macherey gives, the late works of Tolstoy emerged out of the dilemma felt by liberal Russian intellectuals between the revolutions of 1905 and 1917. This situation, in which the necessity of revolution was recognized but its feasibility was denied, gave rise to a resigned pacifism which acknowledged the existence of oppression but precluded any resistance to it. This, according to Macherey, is the ideology which Tolstoy expresses, and it is possible to discern the limitations of this ideology through a close reading of his books.

There are many difficulties with Macherey's book, not the least of which is the lack of an adequate definition of 'literature'. He attempts to remedy this in a later essay co-authored with Etienne Balibar, 'On Literature as Ideological Form' (1981). Nowhere are the limitations of the Althusserian approach to ideology more clearly displayed. The authors are scrupulously materialist, declaring that 'The objective existence of literature is . . . inseparable from given social practices in given ISAs.' This means that literature must be studied in the context of the education system, and particularly in the light of the French division of schools into 'primary-technical' institutions for training the working classes, and a 'secondary-advanced' level which produces the bourgeoisie. In the first kind of school only basic language skills are taught, in the second these are augmented with the ability to manipulate language stylistically, in 'literary' ways. Macherey and Balibar claim that, since literary texts contain both these kinds of language, '*Literary language is itself formed by the effects of an ideological class contradiction*' (51). However, literary works subordinate the straightforward, denotative language of the workers to the ornate, connotative mode of the bourgeoisie: this is in fact the definitive characteristic of literature. It follows that 'The effect of domination realized by literary production presupposes the presence of the dominated ideology within the dominant ideology itself' (58), and thus that for the proletariat, 'reading is nothing but the confirmation of their inferiority . . . domination and repression by literary discourse of a discourse deemed "inarticulate," "faulty" and inadequate for the expression of complex ideas and feelings' (57).

This is the bleak but logical conclusion of Althusserian materialism, which cannot conceive of representation or ideas other than as they are embodied in material practice. A more sophisticated consideration of literature's relationship to ideology can be found in the critical controversy over German Expressionism which took place during the 1930s. Expressionism was an avant-garde school of poetry, music and the visual arts, roughly comparable to surrealism in France, or to modernism in Britain. It aimed to produce a shock-effect by presenting a discontinuous, jarring and fractured view of the world. A good example of the kind of technique labelled 'Expressionist' is the cinematic device of montage, in which meaning is conveyed through the rapid juxtaposition of apparently unconnected images. In English literature, expressionistic

techniques were pioneered by writers such as T.S. Eliot, in poems like
'The Waste Land' [1921] (1970):

> 'On Margate Sands.
> I can connect
> Nothing with nothing.
> The broken fingernails of dirty hands.
> My people humble people who expect
> Nothing.'
>   la la
> To Carthage then I came
>
> Burning burning burning burning
> O Lord Thou pluckest me out
> O Lord Thou pluckest
>
> burning

(ll. 300–11)

The form as well as the content of works like this was supposed to
reflect the fragmentary and disconnected experience of life in capitalist
modernity. In the 1930s, the ideological implications of this kind of art
became the subject of a heated debate among European Marxists. Georg
Lukács, as might be expected from the Hegelian author of *History and
Class-consciousness*, attacked Expressionism on the grounds that its
fragmentary style obscured society's true interconnections, which actually
formed a 'totality'. In response, Ernst Bloch noted that the subjective
experience of capitalism's commodified world was itself confused and
diffuse, and suggested that Expressionism might be an accurate reflection
of the way things are: 'What if authentic reality is also discontinuous?'
(cit. Taylor, 1977, 22). Lukács, in turn, readily conceded that the world
seems chaotic and disordered. But he argued that this is an ideological
illusion, which conceals the underlying unity of the coherent totality:

> Bloch's mistake lies merely in the fact that he identifies this state of
> mind directly and unreservedly with reality itself. He equates the highly

> distorted image created in this state of mind with the thing itself,
> instead of objectively unravelling the essence, the origins and media-
> tions of the distortion by comparing it with reality.
>
> (cit. Taylor, 1977, 34)

In Lukács's view, modernist writers like Joyce or Beckett limit themselves to evoking the ideological appearance of life under capitalism, whereas realist authors such as Balzac or Thomas Mann penetrate beneath this distorted surface to illustrate the real, though hidden, unity of social relations. It is thus clear that Lukács has given the totality a 'metaphysical' status. He is ready to admit that no one experiences the capitalist world as a totality. But this does not mean that it is not, in fact, a totality; it just means that false consciousness has become universal. As Lukács's opponents were quick to point out, however, there is a sense in which a universal consciousness is real, if not necessarily true. The reification which Lukács himself diagnosed in *History and Class-consciousness* cannot simply be ignored or dismissed as an illusion. Rather, as Theodor Adorno stresses, it must be accepted as the actual, objective condition of the world. When a work of art expresses this reified consciousness through devices of distortion and discontinuity, it is therefore more realistic than the traditional, coherent, unifying 'realism' which Lukács finds in Balzac and Mann. According to Adorno, avant-garde art faithfully reflects the subjective consequences of reification, and thus offers an ironic, critical perspective on the commodified world:

> in the form of an image the object is absorbed into the subject instead
> of following the bidding of the alienated world and persisting
> obdurately in a state of reification. The contradiction between the object
> reconciled in the subject, i.e. spontaneously absorbed in the subject,
> and the actual unreconciled object in the outside world, confers on the
> work of art a vantage-point from which it can criticize actuality. Art is
> the negative knowledge of the actual world.
>
> (cit. Taylor, 1977, 160)

The most realistic modes of art, then, are those whose forms exhibit most clearly the reified condition of reality, which reproduces itself within the subject. As Adorno puts it elsewhere, 'The fetish character of the commodity is not a fact of consciousness; rather ... it produces consciousness' (cit. Taylor, 1977, 111). This idea, first expressed by Lukács, that the commodification of the external world is paralleled in every aspect of the individual's subjective, psychological activity, forms the basis of the account of ideology offered by the group of thinkers known as the Frankfurt School.

THE FRANKFURT SCHOOL

The philosophers associated with the Institute for Social Research (which was originally based in Frankfurt, Germany) accomplished the most profound insights into the impact of the commodity on consciousness. Members of this group, such as Theodor Adorno, Max Horkheimer and Herbert Marcuse, based their investigations on the analysis of commodification given by Marx in *Capital*'s opening chapter, and on Lukács's development of Marx's description into a comprehensive theory of reification. As Horkheimer notes in 'On the Problem of Truth' [1935], for Marxism 'every thesis necessarily follows from the first postulate, the concept of free exchange of commodities ... knowledge of all social processes in the economic, political and all other cultural fields will be mediated by that initial cognition' (cit. Arato and Gebhardt, 1978, 433). As we have seen, Marx argues that the process of exchange involves the mental imposition of a false, ideal equivalence on objects which are actually, materially different. In a society in which exchange is the dominant form of economic organization – in a 'market economy' – the principle of exchange comes to dominate people's consciousnesses. A false appearance obscures the thing-in-itself, as objects are regarded for their exchange-value rather than for their intrinsic uses, and representation consequently becomes autonomous. This process affects intellectual as well as economic life. As Horkheimer puts it, explaining the rise of nominalism in 'The End of Reason' [1941]:

> The objects could be regarded as an unqualified mass in philosophy because economic reality had levelled them, rendering all things equivalent to money as the common denominator. In the face of such levelling, the proper being of the object is no longer taken into account.
>
> (cit. Arato and Gebhardt, 1978, 31)

The main problem, as Horkheimer sees it, is not the 'objective' material conditions of production, to which materialist Marxists refer, but rather a distortion of the subject:

> The methods for the production of social wealth are available, the conditions for the production of useful natural effects are largely known, and the human will can bring them about. But this spirit and this will themselves exist in false and distorted form.
>
> (41)

Commodity fetishism involves the idolization of subjective human activity, so that the products of that activity, 'even though summoned up by men themselves, face them as incalculable forces of destiny' (ibid.). As in the Old Testament, false consciousness consists in idolizing 'the works of men's hands'. In a diabolical irony, these products then re-enter the subject in a distorted and distorting form which issues in what Adorno calls 'the displacement of feelings into exchange value' (cit. Arato and Gebhardt, 1978, 290). The process of objectification is not confined to the workplace, but becomes a habit of mind, so that people conceive of themselves and others as objects. Worse still, the completely commodified world does not permit one to opt out of this process. This leads Adorno to characterize liberal Western democracy as 'totalitarian': 'When the feelings seize on exchange-value. . . . It corresponds to the behavior of the prisoner who loves his cell because he has been left nothing else to love' (280).

The potential effects of this fetishism were forcefully impressed upon the members of the Institute when, as refugees from the Nazis, they arrived in the USA. The culture shock which these patrician, central European, Marxist intellectuals experienced on finding themselves in southern California was profound and productive in equal measure. They evidently found that their new environment provided ample confirmation of the philosophical theories they had developed in Germany. Adorno and Horkheimer's *Dialectic of Enlightenment* [1944] (1972) contains their most comprehensive account of the American experience. It is remarkable for its sustained tone of horrified fascination with the sheer power of the commodity. The potency of this force led them to the worrying conclusion that we are entering a new, surreal mode of consciousness in which 'Real life is becoming indistinguishable from the movies' (126).

It does not surprise Adorno and Horkheimer that 'the impotence and pliability of the masses grow with the quantitative increase in commodities allowed them' (xiv–xv), that 'public opinion has reached a state in which thought inevitably becomes a commodity, and language the means of promoting that commodity' (xi–xii), or that 'the economic apparatus . . . equips commodities with the values which decide human behavior' (28). What really shocks and disturbs them is the distorting effect of the representations imposed by commodification on the intellect: 'Representation is exchanged for the fungible – universal interchange-ability. . . . The identity of everything with everything else is paid for in that nothing may at the same time be identical with itself' (10–12). The intrinsic identity of things, their use-value, is occluded when they are viewed in terms of abstract, symbolic exchange-value. This 'levelling domination of abstraction' (11) dulls the critical faculties, ensuring that 'ideology expends itself in the idolization of given existence and of the power which controls technology' (xvi).

These two aspects of ideology – instinctive deferral to 'the facts' as they are immediately represented to us, and blind faith in instrumental science – are the most dangerous effects of commodity fetishism. In order for a thing to become a commodity, the coercive power of human reason must be exerted over the thing-in-itself: we must represent it as what it is not, and then take this representation for the reality. But this power of reason is purely formal, because it must be universally applicable without regard to the concrete materiality, the content, of the things it considers. It thus ultimately issues in the fetishization of abstract reason itself: 'Before, the fetishes were subject to the law of equivalence. Now equivalence itself has become a fetish' (17). The result is that the formal, abstract principles of reason, as manifested in the natural sciences, are held to be the only means to objective truth. In the words of Horkheimer, 'The tattered veil of money has given way to the veil of technology' (cit. Arato and Gebhardt, 1978, 45).

Having been fetishized as uniquely capable of producing true insight, the methods of the natural sciences are erroneously applied to the sphere of the human sciences, with disastrous results. Empirical facts are taken as 'given', that is, they are assumed to be automatically significant, without any 'mediation'. This Hegelian term alludes to the fact that everything that exists 'for us' is made possible by its relation to other things, so that nothing is self-identical. In order, therefore, to understand a brute fact, we must interpret it in the light of the other facts which give it significance by providing its context. In Hegelian terms, facts are only meaningful when they are 'mediated through the totality'.

Perhaps some examples may be useful here. Today, in the USA, statistics show that a disproportionate amount of crime is committed by young black men. This is a 'fact'. Taken in isolation, this fact might well be interpreted as indicating that young black men are predatory and dangerous people, in need of supervision and restraint. This is what Adorno and Horkheimer would regard as 'ideological' thinking. But if this fact is mediated through the totality, if it is interpreted in the context of slavery and segregation, policing tactics and media representation, the education and welfare systems, then one might well read this 'fact' as leading to the opposite conclusion: that young black men are oppressed and victimized people, in need of assistance and opportunity. At another level, in the realm of intellectual endeavour, the fetishization of pure facts gives rise to the privileging of natural science, and its indiscriminate application without regard for social consequences. The most conspicuous results of this process, for Adorno and Horkheimer, were the gas chambers and the atomic bomb. The commodification of consciousness, then, produces a way of seeing the world which is not merely false but actually evil:

> That the hygienic shop-floor and everything that goes with it, the Volkswagen or the sportsdrome, leads to an insensitive liquidation of metaphysics, would be irrelevant; but that in the social whole they themselves become a metaphysics, an ideological curtain behind which the real evil is concentrated, is not irrelevant.

> (1972, xv)

More recently, John Dupre has cogently criticized this kind of ideology, which he calls 'scientism'. He calls attention to the prevalent but illegitimate tendency to apply natural science to human society, citing as examples the rational choice theory of Gary Becker and the sociobiology of Richard Dawkins. According to Dupre, this tendency originates in the reified approach to human history which characterizes the philosophy of Hobbes and the economics of Adam Smith:

> Although there are important dissenting tendencies within the discipline of economics, there is also an overwhelmingly dominant hegemony. This is the conception of economics as the investigation of the consequences of individuals striving to maximize their selfish interests. And recently this selfish model of human life has increasingly been imported from its homeland in commodities markets and inflation rates, and offered as an insight into human life generally.
>
> (2001, 3)

Charles Darwin freely admitted that the competitive individualism of eighteenth-century economists like Smith and Malthus inspired his theory that evolution is driven exclusively by the competitive adaptation of individual organisms to their environment. Darwin's theory of evolution is thus a textbook example of the Marxist theory of ideology in practice. Smith's economic theory, although designed to advance the interests of a particular social class, claimed to be expressing a universal truth about human nature. Once accepted in the sphere of economics, its scope was expanded yet further, into the natural sciences, where it was drafted into the service of a doctrine that was accepted as authoritative by generations of believers. Only with the discovery that the most important events of evolutionary history are caused by the collision of the earth with asteroids, rather than by natural selection, did Darwin's theory begin to give way to what Thomas Kuhn would have called a new scientific 'paradigm'.

Adorno and Horkheimer describe this power of ideology to gain universal acceptance as 'totalitarian'. There is running through *Dialectic of Enlightenment* a disturbing analogy, which is sometimes overt but more often implicit, between the open dictatorship of Nazi Germany and the subtle totalitarianism of commodity-fixated California. The formally free American society compels a conformism which constrains every aspect of life, and which is the more insidious for being experienced as voluntary:

> But freedom to choose an ideology . . . everywhere proves to be freedom to choose what is always the same. The way in which a girl

accepts and keeps the obligatory date, the inflection on the telephone or in the most intimate situation, the choice of words in conversation, and the whole inner life . . . bear witness to man's attempt to make himself a proficient apparatus, similar (even in emotions) to the model served up by the culture industry. The most intimate reactions of human beings have been so thoroughly reified that the idea of anything specific to themselves now persists only as an utterly abstract notion: personality scarcely signifies anything more than shining white teeth and freedom from body odor and emotions. The triumph of advertising in the culture industry is that consumers feel compelled to buy and use its products even though they see through them.

(167)

Herbert Marcuse reached a similar conclusion in *One-dimensional Man* (1964):

The means of mass transportation and communication, the commodities of lodging, food and clothing, the irresistible output of the entertainment and information industry carry with them prescribed attitudes and habits, certain intellectual and emotional reactions which bind the consumers more or less pleasantly to the producers and, through the latter, to the whole. The products indoctrinate and manipulate; they promote a false consciousness which is immune against its falsehood.

(12)

This, according to the Frankfurt School, is the essence of commodity culture. Consciousness recognizes itself as false but it does not care, because a true consciousness would be either practically unattainable, intrinsically impossible, or – and here we reach the territory of postmodernism – actually undesirable.

ENLIGHTENMENT AND THE IDEOLOGY OF THE PRIMITIVE

The process of Enlightenment, which enables us to recognize ideology, thus seems to be a rather mixed blessing. As Hegel noted, the same reason which allowed Voltaire to expose religious 'infamy' can itself become a fetishistic object of superstitious veneration. What is more, the rationality of the Enlightenment has, in practice, furnished a pretext for all kinds of domination and exploitation: the rule of the commodity over humanity, the hegemony of mankind over the natural world, the intellectual triumph of instrumental science and empiricist philosophy, the assumed superiority of the present over the past, and the rule of the European possessors of reason over the 'primitive' inhabitants of the 'undeveloped' world. An uneasy sense that enlightened reason is somehow complicit with the primitive superstition against which it battles is expressed in numerous literary texts of the early twentieth century. In Joseph Conrad's *Heart of Darkness* (1902), for example, Kurtz, the European ivory-trader who writes reports for 'the International Society for the Suppression of Savage Customs', himself 'regresses' to a 'barbaric' condition as soon as he is removed from the artificial restraints of 'civilization'.

A strikingly perspicacious study of the arrogance of Western reason is provided by Max Weber, in *The Protestant Ethic and the Spirit of Capitalism* [1904] (1930). This work raises the question of why Protestant societies are particularly proficient at developing and exploiting a capitalist *ethos* which Weber defines as resting 'on the expectation of profit by the utilization of opportunities for exchange' (17). Rather than stressing the impact of commodification on consciousness, however, Weber is interested in the more general process of 'rationalization' which is necessary for the imposition of formal equivalence on objects, but which is also manifested in new ways of organizing human behaviour. In a capitalist society, the working of the labour-force and the morality of private life must be brought into line with the method of rational calculation on which an exchange-based economy depends. As Weber puts it, capitalism demands that all aspects of society must be made to correspond to 'the natural sciences based on mathematics and exact and rational experiment' (24).

Weber shows how Protestantism, and in particular the Calvinist concept of predestination, provided a system of ideas which encouraged and legitimated the growth of a capitalist economy. According to Calvin, the salvation or damnation of each human soul had already been decided before the creation of the world. It followed that nothing one might do in one's life could possibly affect one's status in the eyes of God. In a

Christian society, the effect of this doctrine would be to lay a heavy burden of anxiety on believers, who would naturally be curious about the nature of their eternal dwelling place. This concern could be allayed by searching one's life for evidence of God's favour, and this evidence seemed to be strikingly provided by material prosperity. There was thus, according to Weber, an intense psychological imperative on the Calvinist faithful to amass as much wealth as possible in their earthly lives, and this is the source of the 'Protestant work ethic'.

Weber notes that this 'spirit' of capitalism is frequently present before any glimmer of actual capitalist activity. Clearly, then, he rejects the materialist premise that a particular economic system produces a corresponding ideology. But, as he emphasizes, 'it is, of course, not my aim to substitute for a one-sided materialistic an equally one-sided spiritualistic causal interpretation of culture and of history' (183). Like Lukács and Adorno, Weber observes analogous developments in the realms of ideology and the economy, but he refuses to reduce one to the other. However, the real challenge of Weber's book is its implication that Enlightenment rationality is not intrinsically a truer or better way of thinking than those followed by historically or geographically distant societies. This kind of relativism was profoundly shocking in the Europe of 1904. It indicated that noble systems of thought could be used to justify the most base impulses. It also raised the question of whether any system of thought could be judged superior to another. If the great process begun by Protestantism and completed by the Enlightenment – the elimination of irrational superstition from the thought of the European intelligentsia – was simply a mask for some basically shabby economic motives, then how could the professors of Paris and Berlin feel superior to the natives of the Congo or of the Dakota territories? What, in other words, gave Europeans the right to rule the rest of the world?

Sigmund Freud's *Totem and Taboo* [1913] (1950) provides an interesting answer to this question, as well as a committed defence of Enlightenment reason. Like Althusser, Freud attacks idealism in the name of a materialism which is no less dogmatic and reductive than the beliefs it criticizes. In an earlier work, *Three Essays on the Theory of Sexuality* [1905] (1962), Freud noted, with regard to the fetishistic displacements he observes in the sexual development of children, 'Such substitutions are with some justice likened to the fetishes in which savages believe that their gods are embodied' (19). He assumes that human societies progress in a manner comparable to the maturation of an individual, so that 'primitives' are essentially child-like. This belief leads him, in *Totem and Taboo*, to discount the accounts of the 'savages' themselves of why they invest particular objects with supernatural powers. The 'primitives' say that these objects are inhabited by demons. Freud refuses this explanation on Feuerbachian grounds: 'It would be another matter if demons really existed. But we know that, like gods, they are the creations of the human mind: they were made by something and out of something' (1950, 32).

Freud thus begins from the assumption that the 'savages' cannot give an adequate account of their own ideas, and that he, as an enlightened man of science, understands their beliefs better than they do. He accounts for the fetishism of taboo objects in the same way that, according to Adorno and Horkheimer, enlightened reason always exposes superstition: by unmasking it as 'anthropomorphism, the projection onto nature of the subjective' (Adorno and Horkheimer, 1972, 6). Freud announces that what the 'savages' fear is fear itself – 'objectified fear' (1950, 33) – which they have projected on to an alien object. The 'savages' offer another example of the superstitious tendency to make idols out of human ideas. In Freud, this fetishistic displacement of subjective processes into the objective world is called 'projection', and it is the defining characteristic of both the 'savage' and the civilized 'neurotic':

> The projection outwards of internal perceptions is a primitive mechanism, to which, for instance, our sense perceptions are subject, and which therefore normally plays a very large part in determining the form taken by our external world . . . internal perceptions of emotional and intellective processes can be projected outwards in the same way as sense perceptions; they are thus employed in building up the external world, though they should by rights remain part of the internal world.
>
> (83)

As usual in ideology, this fetishism misconstrues the relation of subject and object. The 'savage' and 'neurotic' minds are characterized by an extreme idealism. They share the irrational belief that ideas alone can determine material events. The 'primitive' man mistreats an effigy of his enemy in the opinion that this will harm the real man; the 'neurotic' European feels compelled to perform a certain mechanical ritual to ward off misfortune. Each of them, according to Freud, mistakes 'an ideal connection for a real one' (104):

> Things become less important than ideas of things: whatever is done to the latter will inevitably also occur to the former. Relations which hold between the ideas of things are assumed to hold equally between the things themselves.
>
> (106)

The belief that ideas are present in the material world is characteristic of the primitive 'animism' which conceives of spirits inhabiting things. Freud provocatively adds that 'primitive peoples believe that human individuals are inhabited by similar spirits' (95), a notion which he scorns. As he was well aware, many people in Freud's own society still believed in such 'spirits' or 'souls'. But Freud puts his faith in the progress of human societies, from 'animism' through 'religion' to 'science' (110). This involves the progressive disengagement of ideas from the material world, until the scientific consciousness is able to analyse itself as just another object:

> primitive man transposed the structural conditions of his own mind into the external world; and we may attempt to reverse the process and put back into the human mind what animism teaches as to the nature of things.
>
> (114)

As Horkheimer and Adorno comment apropos of Freud's book, 'Animism spiritualized the object, whereas industrialism objectified the spirits of men' (1972, 28). We can thus see that, although they move in opposite directions, 'savage' superstition and Freud's scientific method both insist on an illegitimate collapse of the subject / object dichotomy. The savages believe that their ideas can influence the material world, while Freud assumes that material experience creates our ideas. Freud's science is thus just as undialectical and metaphysical as the beliefs of the 'savages' to whom he condescends. Both these discourses are reductive;

they both give priority to one side of the ideal / material binary, and they can therefore both be described as ideological modes of thought.

A CRISIS OF FAITH: STRUCTURALISM AND AFTER

In *Devil on the Cross* (1982), the Kenyan novelist Ngugi Wa Thiong'o parodies capitalist ideology, as it is perceived by the bemused inhabitants of the postcolonial world. This book combines a 'rational' critique of economic imperialism with a 'superstitious' subtext which associates capital with the metaphysical forces of Evil. Ngugi's blend of realism and fantasy also allows him to retain the form and tone of conventional rationalizations of imperialism, while altering their content so as to reveal their real significance. Thus, at a 'Devil's Feast' held by 'Satan, the King of Hell' on behalf of the 'Organization for Modern Theft and Robbery', the Master of Ceremonies rises to announce:

> We who come from the developed world have had many years' experience of modern theft and robbery. I might also remind you that we are the owners of the houses and stores and granaries that contain all the money that has ever been snatched from the peoples of the world. You can see for yourselves that even our suits are made of bank notes. Today money is the ruler of all industry and commerce. Money is *the field marshal* of all the forces of theft and robbery on earth. *Money is supreme. Money rules the world.* . . . We believe in freedom, the freedom that allows one to rob and steal according to one's abilities. That's what we call *personal initiative* and *individual enterprise*. And that's why we have always stated that we belong to the *Free World*, a world where there are absolutely no barriers to stealing from others.
>
> (172–3)

This assumption that the wealth of Western civilization made it intrinsically more advanced than the rest of the world grew to seem increasingly dubious and self-interested over the course of the twentieth century, and this was reflected in a series of attempts to re-evaluate the relation of reason to irrational modes of thought. The notions (which had been axiomatic since the eighteenth century) that human history was characterized by progress from a 'primitive' to a 'civilized' condition, and that Europe was further along that route than other parts of the world, began to be challenged. One convincing theoretical rebuke to Western pretensions was provided by the method of analysis known as 'structuralism'. This discipline was inaugurated by the Swiss linguist, Ferdinand de Saussure, whose lecture notes were collected after his death as the *Course in General Linguistics* [1916] (1972). In outlining his definition of linguistics, Saussure pointedly refuses to make any qualitative distinction between human languages: 'Linguistics takes for its data in the first instance all manifestations of human language. Primitive peoples and civilized nations, early periods, classical periods, and periods of decadence, are all to be included' (6).

Saussure's method does not presuppose that 'civilized' languages are the most sophisticated, or the best suited to the expression of complicated ideas. He insists that synchronic and diachronic linguistics must be kept separate, claiming that the study of a language's 'diachronic' development through time is a quite different area from the analysis of its 'synchronic' structure at any particular time. However, these two methods 'are not of equal importance. It is clear that the synchronic point of view takes precedence over the diachronic, since for the community of language users that is the one and only reality' (89).

The synchronic approach reveals that words acquire meaning, not through any intrinsic correspondence with the objects they represent, but through their place within the linguistic structure. Saussure thus suggests that representation is autonomous and that, in fact, signs produce the objects they designate. He finds that this 'arbitrary nature of the sign' (68) pertains in every society:

> any means of expression accepted in a society rests in principle upon a collective habit, or on convention, which comes to the same thing. Signs of politeness, for instance, although often endowed with a certain natural expressiveness (prostrating oneself nine times on the ground is the way to greet an emperor in China) are none the less fixed by rule. It is this rule which renders them obligatory, not their intrinsic value.
>
> (ibid.)

Saussure's linguistics, then, indicates that meaning is not inherent in the sign, but is arbitrarily produced out of a structured system of signs. This is an idea with extremely radical implications. If the significance which any given society attaches to certain signs is indeed a matter of arbitrary convention, then it becomes difficult for any particular society to claim that its ideas are inherently truer than those of any other, no matter how ostensibly primitive they may seem. What is more, Saussure presents his linguistics as a model for a much wider field of study:

> A language is a system of signs expressing ideas, and hence comparable to writing, the deaf-and-dumb alphabet, symbolic rites, forms of politeness, military signals, and so on. It is simply the most important of such systems. It is therefore possible to conceive of a science which studies the role of signs as part of social life. It would form part of social psychology, and hence of general psychology. We shall call it semiology. . . . It would investigate the nature of signs and the laws governing them.
>
> (15)

Saussure thus claims that all aspects of social life, to the degree that they are significant, are structured like a language. Since he believes that linguistic meaning is arbitrary, it therefore follows that all social behaviour is merely conventional. The inescapable conclusion is that, in the words of the structural anthropologist Claude Lévi-Strauss, 'man has always thought equally well', and that there can be no grounds for dismissing the thought systems of other societies as more 'primitive' than our own. In *The Savage Mind* [1962] (1966), Lévi-Strauss applies Saussure's method of analysis to the kinds of 'magical' systems which Freud studied in *Totem and Taboo*. As we might expect, he is led to very different conclusions. He refuses to call magic a more 'primitive' mode of thought than reason:

> These are certainly not a function of different stages of the development of the human mind but rather of two strategic levels at which nature is accessible to scientific enquiry: one roughly adapted to that of perception and the imagination: the other at a remove from it.
>
> (15)

The definitive characteristic of modern science is that it separates itself from the object studied, thus reflecting and confirming the splits between subject and object and between matter and spirit. In post-Baconian empiricism, the subjective condition of the observer is supposed to have no influence on the objective data being observed. Like Freud, Lévi-Strauss noted that 'primitive' societies do not recognize these dichotomies, but conceive of subjective ideas as inherent in their objects. Unlike Freud, however, Lévi-Strauss does not regard this as a superstitious error; rather, he perceives in it an insight which the Enlightenment does not achieve until Hegel: 'it is in this intransigent refusal on the part of the savage mind to allow anything human (or even living) to remain alien to it, that the real principle of dialectical reason is to be found' (245).

'Primitive' societies, in other words, have not succumbed to the fatal divorce of subject and object which constitutes the central problem for Western philosophy. Of course, for Hegel and Marx this split is itself illusory, and testifies to a mode of fetishism which is no less superstitious than the animistic world-view. While capitalism objectifies the subject, animism subjectifies the object. The result is a strange convergence between ostensibly distinct modes of thought, so that animistic beliefs can be used to make sense of the ideological effects produced by market capitalism. In *The Devil and Commodity Fetishism* (1980), Michael Taussig examines the response of South American peasants to encroaching capitalism, and finds that they can readily interpret the changes in their lives within their pre-existent systems of thought. The places where the newly proletarianized peasants work, and the products of their labour, are invested with the properties associated with the evil spirits, or 'devils', of their 'superstitious' religions. As Taussig demonstrates, this is a perfectly logical transposition:

If we 'thingify' parts of a living system, ignore the context of which they are part, and then observe that the things move . . . as though they were alive . . . reification leads to fetishization. . . . The devil in the Bolivian tin mines offers spellbinding testimony to the fidelity with which people can capture the transformation of fetishization while subjecting it to a paganism that will capture it.

(36, 181)

Structuralist linguistics and anthropology thus opened up the possibility of studying the constitutive role of ideology. All societies represent and give meaning to the lives of their inhabitants by constructing systems of ideas about them. These systems are not optional extras, but constitute the lived reality of the people. It follows that the ideological representations by which we, in advanced capitalist countries, bestow significance on our surroundings, are by no means 'natural' but are instances of the Aristotelian, man-made 'second nature'. It is characteristic of ideology, however, for this second nature to pass itself off as the 'first' nature, so that what has been constructed by human beings is fetishistically regarded as eternal and unchangeable.

The danger for structural analyses of signs is that, by focusing on the formal relations between the various elements of linguistic or semiotic codes, they will exclude or render nugatory the influence exercised on these signifying systems by external reality. Poststructuralist theory often takes the autonomous, constitutive role of representation for granted, or even celebrates it as a ludic liberation from dour referentiality. A salutary warning against this tendency was sounded in one of the earliest responses to Saussure, V.N. Volosinov's *Marxism and the Philosophy of Language* [1929] (1973). Volosinov attacks Saussure's assumption that the structure of language is inherently imprinted on the human mind, and he points out the heritage of this idea in Cartesian rationalism:

> The idea of the conventionality, the arbitrariness, of language is a typical one for rationalism as a whole. . . . What interests the mathematically minded rationalists is not the relationship of the sign to the actual reality it reflects or to the individual who is its originator, but the relationship of sign to sign within a closed system already accepted and authorized. In other words, they are interested only in the inner logic of the system of signs itself, taken, as in algebra, completely independently of the meanings that give signs their content.
>
> (2)

Saussure and his followers, that is to say, take account of neither the individual subjective origin nor the objective referent of signs. Like Descartes, Saussure suggests that the material world is constructed by certain universal properties of the human mind. In Volosinov's view, this ignores the interdependence of ideas, signs and things. His own description of signification locates it at the intersection of subject and object; it consists in a subjective significance being read into a material thing:

> any physical body may be perceived as an image. . . . Any such artistic-symbolic image to which a particular physical object gives rise is already an ideological product. The physical object is converted into a sign. Without ceasing to be a part of material reality, such an object, to some degree, reflects and refracts another reality.
>
> (9)

This 'other reality' Volosinov calls 'the domain of signs', which is 'the ideological sphere' (10). 'Ideology' inhabits the realm of representation; it is an extra, subjective significance, which is added on to the material world by the observer. This act of giving symbolic significance to a material object is analogous to Simmel's description of the formation of financial value: it involves the manifestation of subjective processes in the objective world. Representation is thus neither objective nor subjective; it is the third term in which the two poles of the dichotomy meet. This is what allows Volosinov to equate representation with ideology, which must be embodied in material practices, but which, *contra* Althusser, nevertheless retains a subjective dimension. Thus Volosinov criticizes the polarizing, essentialist tendencies of idealism and materialism alike. In these approaches, he says, 'The individual consciousness . . . becomes either all or nothing':

> For idealism it has become all: its locus is somewhere above existence and it determines the latter. . . . For psychological positivism, on the contrary, consciousness amounts to nothing: it is just a conglomeration of fortuitous, psychophysiological reactions which, by some miracle, results in meaningful and unified ideological creativity. . . . However, the ideological, as such, cannot possibly be explained in terms of either of these superhuman or subhuman, animalian, roots. Its real place in existence is in the special, social material of signs created by man.
>
> (12)

The analysis of this process of constructing ideological meaning, as was foretold by Saussure, has come to be known as semiology. One of the earliest and most successful attempts to apply this rigorous 'science of signs' was undertaken by Roland Barthes, in *Mythologies* [1957] (1994). As the title implies, this book is an anthropology of contemporary French society, which Barthes believes contains a system of modern 'myths' no less extensive, constitutive or superstitious than those held by ancient or 'primitive' peoples. He is interested in the ways in which certain social phenomena are invested with a significance which is at once arbitrary and universally understood, and which, as he says, serves the interests of the 'bourgeois' class. For example:

> I am at the barber's, and a copy of *Paris-Match* is offered to me. On the cover, a young Negro in a French uniform is saluting with his eyes uplifted, probably fixed on a fold of the tricolor. All this is the meaning of the picture. But, whether naively or not, I see very well what it signifies to me: that France is a great Empire, that all her sons, without any color discrimination, faithfully serve under her flag, and that there is no better answer to the detractors of an alleged colonialism than the zeal shown by this Negro in serving his so-called oppressors.
>
> (116)

A fairly complex political and historical point is thus established by the judicious use of bare images. It is the function of such 'mythology', according to Barthes, to make contingent, historical phenomena appear as though they were natural, and thus inevitable. Of course, it would be very difficult to win an argument about the virtues of colonialism by simply pointing to this picture. That is not the point. Such representations are not supposed to be amenable to reasoned proof or rebuttal: this is why Barthes says that they work on the level of myth. In our society, representations of this kind have nevertheless become more effective in moulding people's opinions than rational persuasion, as for example in today's methods of political campaigning. The mythological elements within Enlightenment have finally cast aside the mask of reason, and step proudly into the spotlight.

There is really nothing new in this mode of ideological indoctrination: Marx discusses a similar use of representation in *The Eighteenth Brumaire*, as we saw in Chapter 4. However, it may well be that the development of technology, the extent of mass communications, and the increased research into marketing and advertising techniques, have established this mythical use of representation on a firmer basis today than ever before. Representation becomes indistinguishable from reality to the degree that the commodity form obscures the true nature of things. One way of defining 'the postmodern condition' is as the state of mind which results from the final triumph of the commodity, the ultimate victory of exchange-value, and thus the elevation of representation over reality. In the next chapter, we will need to consider whether it makes any kind of sense to describe such a universal consciousness as 'false'. Or, to put the question another way: have we reached the 'end of ideology'?

6

POSTMODERNISM

living people have become bits of ideology.
(Theodor Adorno, *Negative Dialectics*, 1990, 267–8)

No more ideology, only simulacra.
(Jean Baudrillard, *Symbolic Exchange and Death*, 1993, 2)

NIETZSCHE: THE PRECURSOR

Friedrich Nietzsche is the major nineteenth-century source of the ideas which characterize today's postmodern condition. In particular, the ethical and epistemological relativism of the postmodern world, its scepticism about the possibility of distinguishing truth from falsehood, finds its prototype in Nietzsche's radically nihilistic thought. In *On the Genealogy of Morals* [1887] (1969), Nietzsche sets out to subvert the most deeply held pieties of the 'enlightened' Western world, by speculating about the origins of Judaeo-Christian morality and of rational Greek philosophy. Both these pillars of civilization ultimately rest, according to Nietzsche, on a single foundation:

Greek thinking begins with and for a long time holds to the proposition that mankind is divided into 'good' and 'bad', and these terms are quite

as much social, political, and economic as they are moral. . . . The
dichotomy is absolute and exclusive for a simple reason: it began as the
aristocrats' view of society and reflects their idea of the gulf between
themselves and the 'others'.

(27–8)

With arresting cynicism, Nietzsche traces the entire tradition of Western
philosophy to a self-interested legitimation of hierarchical power-
structures. In Chapter 1 we saw how Aristotle deduced the necessity for
the domination of certain people by others from the hierarchy between
ideas and matter. Here, Nietzsche contends that the original purpose of
the binary opposition between good and bad is to justify and perpetuate
the division of society into a privileged group of Greek, aristocratic men,
and the excluded 'others': women, slaves and barbarians. The dichotomy
rationalizes this situation, making it appear natural and reasonable. And
yet it also forms the very basis of rational thought, which proceeds by
positing such binary opposites and resolving them in syntheses. The
whole of Western philosophy is thus originally an ideology, in so far as it
is a ruse designed to serve the interests of a particular group of people.

As one might expect, those excluded from the exalted circle of rulers
frequently felt aggrieved at their position. As Nietzsche puts it, the
oppressed experienced a sense of '*ressentiment*'. This French word translates into English as 'resentment', but it also carries stronger connotations
of hatred and desire for revenge. This desire was expressed, according to
Nietzsche, in theological Judaism:

It was the Jews who, with awe-inspiring consistency, dared to invert the
aristocratic value-equation (good=noble=powerful=beautiful=happy=
beloved of God) and to hang on to this inversion with their teeth, the
teeth of the most abysmal hatred (the hatred of impotence), saying
'the wretched alone are the good; the poor, impotent, lowly alone are
the good; the suffering, deprived, sick, ugly alone are pious, alone
are blessed by God, blessedness is for them alone – and you, the
powerful and noble, are on the contrary the evil, the cruel, the lustful,
the insatiable, the godless to all eternity; and you shall be in all eternity
the unblessed, accursed, and damned!'

(34)

The message which Nietzsche attributes to 'the Jews' is also delivered by Christ in the Sermon on the Mount, and Christianity is a particular target of Nietzsche's wrath. The greatest confidence – trick in history, he claims, took place when the wretched of the earth were able to turn the tables, and pass off their own empirical qualities – humility, poverty, meekness, suffering – as universally positive values. With the rise to prevalence of this Judaeo-Christian morality, the dichotomy good / bad is transmuted into an opposition between good and evil, with the latter denoting the characteristics of the oppressors: pride, power, aggression and luxury.

Many people would argue that this 'transvaluation of values' constitutes the greatest achievement of human history. But Nietzsche is infuriated by his discovery that Western morality has its origins in primitive impulses to revenge and destruction, and he takes this as evidence of his civilization's unmitigated hypocrisy. Having kicked away the foundation, he glories in the total collapse of the edifice. Among the wreckage are such chimeras as the individual self, or 'subject', which Nietzsche holds to be merely an effect of the grammatical first person singular combined with the hierarchical, binary structure of reason, which presupposes that there must be a subject where there is an object:

> A quantum of force is equal to a quantum of drive, will, effect – more, it is nothing other than precisely this very driving, willing, effecting, and only owing to the seduction of language (and of the fundamental errors of reason that are petrified in it) which conceives and misconceives all effects as conditioned by something that causes effects, by a 'subject', can it appear otherwise . . . there is no 'being' behind doing, effecting, becoming; 'the doer' is merely a fiction added to the deed – the deed is everything.

(45)

The belief in an autonomous self is one of the fundamental characteristics of the Western 'metaphysics' which Nietzsche despises. His extreme scepticism drives him to debunk all such metaphors of depth, which assume that human history and human life have some profound, under-lying significance or final meaning: the suggestion that ideology is the reflection of a material base, for example, or the notion that the material world is a manifestation of ideal forms, would be anathema to Nietzsche.

He envisages the imposition of such hierarchies on the world as an act of aggression, the manifestation of the will to power.

For instance, Nietzsche traces the origin of such subjective qualities as memory and guilt to the demand of creditors that debtors should be accountable for their debts. With a characteristic appeal to German etymology, he claims that 'the major moral concept *Schuld* [guilt] has its origin in the very material concept *Schulden* [debts]' (62–3). All legal theories of guilt and punishment, 'the idea that every injury has its *equivalent* and can actually be paid back, even if only through the *pain* of the culprit' (63), rest upon 'the contractual relationship between *creditor* and *debtor*, which is as old as the idea of "legal subjects" and in turn points back to the fundamental forms of buying, selling, barter, trade, and traffic' (ibid.). Nietzsche differs from Marx in many respects, but they share the belief that an exchange-based economy constructs a false kind of subject, by imposing on it an illusory equivalence with the objective sphere. Nietzsche recalls how, in the ancient world,

> the creditor could inflict every kind of indignity and torture upon the body of the debtor; for example, cut from it as much as seemed commensurate with the size of the debt – and everywhere and from early times one had exact evaluations, *legal* evaluations, of the individual limbs and parts of the body from this point of view, some of them going into horrible and minute detail.
>
> (64)

In Shakespeare's *The Merchant of Venice*, Shylock assumes just such an equivalence between the pound of Antonio's flesh to which he is legally entitled and the debt he is owed. Shakespeare associates Shylock with every kind of objectification. As a Jew, he is linked to the 'fleshly' dispensation of the Old Testament; he puts his faith in justice and the human law rather than in divine redemption; his avarice ties him to the material things of this world; and he is constantly figured in terms of death and the flesh, as when the play's Christians refer to him as 'old carrion'. However, Nietzsche might point out that Shylock is at least honest about the objectifying effects of finance: he does not bother to conceal his reified assumptions behind the hypocritical platitudes of Christianity.

Like Althusser, Nietzsche contends that the individual subject can only maintain its integrity through its faith in an absolute subject. This originary, seminal entity is the *logos*, the ultimate source of all meaning and truth. Thus Nietzsche remarks that we are still deluded by 'the Christian faith, which was also Plato's, that God is truth, that truth is *divine*' (152). This faith, in his view, will not trouble us much longer. What, he eagerly speculates, would happen 'if God himself turns out to be our *longest lie*?' (ibid.). It is the task of Nietzsche's philosophy to answer this question, to criticize the 'will to truth' which he sees as the cause of hierarchy and oppression, and to raise the revolutionary possibility that truth may not, finally, even be a good thing.

Depending on which way you look at it, Nietzsche can be seen either as abolishing the concept of ideology, or as expanding it to include all Western thought. False consciousness can only be identified by comparison with some standard of truth. But according to Nietzsche, the belief in an ultimate truth is in fact the 'longest lie'. All philosophy since Plato has been logocentric; centred on the illusion of an absolute source and guarantor of meaning. Since Nietzsche believes that he has unmasked this illusion as a disguise for base and selfish interests, and thus as facilitating domination and oppression, it would seem that there is no consciousness which is not false, and that the notion of 'ideology' has thus become meaningless and obsolete.

MICHEL FOUCAULT: *DEUS ABSCONDITUS*

The work of Michel Foucault blends Nietzschean history with poststructuralist linguistics, a combination which has come to define philosophical 'postmodernism'. In *The Order of Things* [1966] (1970), Foucault identifies two major eras in the history of the human sciences: the 'classical' phase, running from 1660 to 1800; and the 'modern' epoch, which begins with the nineteenth century and which, according to Foucault's apocalyptic pronouncement, is drawing to a close even as he writes. His contention is that, during each of these periods, such disciplines as biology, linguistics and economics shared a common 'well-defined regularity', and obeyed 'the laws of a certain code of knowledge' (xi). It is with this 'code' that Foucault is concerned, and this fact may lead an innocent reader to assume that he is engaged in an essentially structuralist project. Foucault's neurotically vehement denial of this characterization (xiv) indicates that it contains some truth. But whereas the first generation of structuralists such as Saussure and Lévi-Strauss conceived of 'deep' structures underlying their material manifestations in a metaphysical fashion, Foucault is interested in the specific, concrete results of these abstract 'rules of formation'. He takes Nietzsche's aphorism declaring that there is no subject, no 'doer', that 'the deed is everything', as his methodological basis.

It is immediately clear that there is no room in such an approach for the concept of 'ideology'. Foucault is an ultra-materialist: he refuses to admit the existence of any 'ideal' sphere. It is significant in this regard that Foucault was a pupil of Althusser, whose reductive materialism was discussed earlier. However, Althusser retained the notion of ideology as false consciousness, essentially equating it with idealism. For Foucault, it is no longer possible to use terms such as 'true', 'false' or even 'consciousness' in any absolute sense. There have been 'discourses' which have given rise to 'truth-effects', but the very fact that they have been produced by human beings is enough, for Foucault as for Nietzsche, to deprive them of any objectively veridical character. Similarly, there are institutions and practices – the family, the school, the Church – which function so as to produce the sense that we are individual subjects with independent consciousnesses, but this effect is neither eternal nor inevitable.

What are real are the sets of rules, the patterns of classification, which allow us to make sense of the chaotic wealth of empirical data which daily rushes in on us from all sides. Foucault aims to confront Western culture with 'the stark fact that there exists, below the level of its spontaneous orders, things that are themselves capable of being ordered, that belong to a certain unspoken order; the fact, in short, that order exists' (xx). It is this ultimate 'order', the 'conditions of possibility' (xxii) for knowledge at any given historical moment, which allows us to make sense of the world. This is clearly a Kantian position, and Foucault acknowledges this when he says that he is concerned to discover the 'historical a priori' of the classical and modern human sciences. Unlike Kant, however, Foucault emphasizes the historical aspect. Where Kant wanted to identify the conditions which make possible experience in general, Foucault is interested in what allows the formation of particular, historically specific types of knowledge. He wants, as he puts it, to study the process which 'makes manifest the modes of being of order'. But it is difficult to escape the conclusion that Foucault's 'order' is a transcendent, determining entity, albeit one which is never fully present in the world. It is, in fact, a twentieth-century version of *deus absconditus*, the departed god who governs our actions without being fully manifest to us.

The philosophical implications of Foucault's method in *The Order of Things* are so intriguing that they rather overshadow his contentious readings of actual historical discourses. Foucault seems to acknowledge this by dedicating his next important work, *The Archaeology of Knowledge* [1969] (1972), to an exposition of methodological problems. His declared aim is to escape from the teleological, totalizing, subject-centred approach, which has dominated Western philosophy since Plato; he rebels against the notion that history is a narrative acted out by a coherent subject: 'Making historical analysis the discourse of the continuous and making human consciousness the original subject of all historical development and all action are the two sides of the same system of thought' (12). When we try to shape the flux of events into a coherent narrative, according to Foucault, we simultaneously impose upon it the ostensibly unified, apparently conscious form of our own subjectivity. In fact, however, the subject is neither unified nor fully conscious: it can only come to appear so when it is artificially removed from the objective context which generates it. This is the source of idealism, the philosophy which illegitimately imposes an ideal order on material reality. Like Althusser, Foucault is opposed, above all, to

the notion of 'spirit', which enables us to establish between the simultaneous or successive phenomena of a given period a community of meanings, symbolic links, an interplay of resemblance and reflexion, or which allows the sovereignty of collective consciousness to emerge as the principle of unity and explanation.

(22)

What is being attacked here is the Hegelian concept of the Idea, whose developing relationship with the material dimension guides and moulds the course of history. However, Foucault does not suggest that, in the absence of a coherent narrative of history, events are purely random and indeterminate. On the contrary his notion of 'discourse' is rigidly determinist. In identifying a discourse, he writes, 'we must show why it could not be other than it was, in what respect it is exclusive of any other, how it assumes . . . a place that no other could occupy' (28). His objection is to the notion that a discourse is formed by any 'spiritual' or 'ideal' influences. On the other hand, Foucault is also concerned to distance his work from the naive empiricism which assumes that we can have unmediated access to the material world. As he puts it, he aims 'To substitute for the enigmatic treasure of "things" anterior to discourse, the regular formation of objects that emerge only in discourse' (47).

It thus seems that, like such dialectical thinkers as Hegel and Marx, Foucault is attempting to transcend the polarity between idealism and materialism. But Foucault rejects the Hegelian dialectic, portraying it in Nietzschean terms as a tyrannical imposition of human logic on the recalcitrant blur of reality. As we saw in the case of Althusser, any non-dialectical attempt to abolish the idea / matter opposition risks reducing one pole of the dichotomy to the other – declaring either that matter is, in reality, an idea (as with Berkeley); or that ideas are, in fact, material (as with Hume). Foucault sometimes suggests that his realm of 'discourse' occupies a middle ground between these binary alternatives:

> We shall not return to the state anterior to discourse – in which nothing has yet been said, and in which things are only just beginning to emerge out of the grey light; and we shall not pass beyond discourse in order to discover the forms that it has created and left behind it; we shall remain, or try to remain, at the level of discourse itself.
>
> (48)

As soon as Foucault offers a precise definition of the term 'discourse', however, this balance begins to collapse. Thus he announces that 'We shall call discourse a group of statements in so far as they belong to the same discursive formation' (117). But when we ask what a 'statement' is, we are told that

> it must have a material existence. Could one speak of a statement if a voice had not articulated it, if a surface did not bear its signs, if it had not become embodied in a sense-perceptible element? . . . Could one

speak of a statement as an ideal, silent figure? The statement is always given through some material medium.

(100)

In order to exist 'for us', the 'statement' must take on a material form. A 'discourse' is a regular pattern, or 'formation', of such 'statements'. To all intents and purposes, then, 'discourse' is itself material. And yet Foucault has already positioned discourse as the factor which mediates between the ideal and the material. We can thus see that the attempt to find a third term has failed. Like Althusser, like Freud and, beyond them, like the *philosophes* of the French Enlightenment, Foucault can only move beyond the ideal / material dichotomy by collapsing one of its terms into the other, and he too arrives at the familiar position of materialist determinism.

In his later work, Foucault concerns himself less with 'discourse', and more with 'power'. Like discourse, power is always already material, and in texts such as *Discipline and Punish* [1975] (1977), power is ascribed the role of moulding the subject itself. Not only is the subject ultimately material (and thus, in effect, an object), but it is formed out of a process of subjection to a dominating power. The notion of 'ideology' as false consciousness is therefore necessarily redundant, for two reasons. First, it refers to 'consciousness' which is not material and therefore not real; and second, it assumes the possibility of falsehood, a concept which can have no meaning if the thinking subject is itself merely the objective product of power. There is nothing to be regretted in the dominance of power (it could not be shown to rest on false assumptions), since it is power which creates the very individuals who recognize it as such.

It would thus seem that 'power' is a creative force for Foucault. However, he is careful to avoid a 'logocentric' description of power, which would discover a single, central source from which it flows: God, the King, or the bourgeoisie, for example. In the first volume of *The History of Sexuality* [1976] (1990) Foucault gives the following account of power:

Power's condition of possibility . . . must not be sought in the primary existence of a central point, in a unique source of sovereignty from which secondary and descendent forms would emanate; it is the moving substrate of force relations which, by virtue of their inequality, constantly engender states of power, but the latter are always local and unstable. The omnipresence of power: not because it has the privilege of consolidating everything under its invincible unity, but because it is produced from one moment to the next, at every point, or rather in every relation from one point to another. Power is everywhere; not because it embraces everything, but because it comes from everywhere.

(93)

What, then, is this 'power' which is everywhere and creates all human subjects? Michael Hardt and Antonio Negri suggest a Foucauldian definition of 'power' as a force which is 'distributed throughout the brains and bodies of the citizens. The behaviors of social integration and exclusion proper to rule are thus increasingly interiorized within the subjects themselves' (2002, 23). Certainly, it is clear that Foucault thinks of 'power' as a psychological as well as a material force, and that he believes its psychological operations in some sense facilitate or enable its material manifestations. Power, as Foucault says, constitutes the subject. He evades the profound implications of this insight, however, by insisting, like Althusser, that the subject is material. In *Power / Knowledge* (1980), he declares

I'm not one of those who try to elicit the effects of power at the level of ideology. Indeed I wonder whether, before one poses the question of ideology, it wouldn't be more materialist to study first the question of the body and the effects of power on it.

(58)

Undoubtedly it would be more materialist, though the fact that Foucault takes this as in itself sufficient reason for following this course indicates that his materialism is ultimately dogmatic and metaphysical. As a result, the conflicts and issues which earlier philosophy discussed under the rubric of 'ideology' are simply internalized. The claim that 'The individual is an effect of power' (98) implies that power should be analysed within the individual. Thus Foucault is led into such ostensibly 'idealist' declarations as 'we all have a fascism in our heads' (99). When an interviewer asks Foucault about wider social conflicts – 'who ultimately, in your view, are the subjects who oppose each other?' (208) – his reply is startling:

> This is just a hypothesis, but I would say it's all against all. There aren't immediately given subjects of the struggle, one the proletariat, the other the bourgeoisie. Who fights against whom? We all fight each other. *And there is always within each of us something that fights something else.*
>
> (208, emphasis added)

Are we so far away, here, from the traditional religious conception of the subject as the site of a battle between the cosmic powers of sin and righteousness? We saw earlier how the Frankfurt School applied Lukács's analysis of commodity fetishism so as to understand the 'class struggle' as a fight enacted within each individual consciousness. As Foucault admits, he only became aware of the work of Adorno, Horkheimer and Marcuse 'when I was no longer at the age of making intellectual "discoveries"' (1991, 120). With disarming modesty, Foucault defers to the Frankfurt School, while maintaining that his own work is very similar to theirs:

> Now, obviously, if I had been familiar with the Frankfurt School, if I had been aware of it at the time, I would not have said a number of stupid things that I did say and I would have avoided many of the detours which I made while trying to pursue my own humble path – when, meanwhile, avenues had been opened up by the Frankfurt School. It is a strange case of non-penetration between two very similar types of thinking which is explained, perhaps, by that very similarity.
>
> (1988, 26)

There are certainly some similarities between the Frankfurt and the Foucauldian traditions: the critique of reason as an instrument of oppression and the consequent sense of 'a fascism in our heads' is the most obvious one. But there are also important differences. First, the Frankfurt School remain aggressively dialectical thinkers; it is hard to imagine Adorno reducing the ideal to the material as does Foucault. Second, their thought is based upon Lukács's concept of reification, which in turn is founded upon Marx's anatomy of the commodity in the opening chapter of *Capital*. In *Minima Moralia* (1974), Adorno details the influence of the commodification of labour – that is to say, the commodification of life itself – on individual psychology. People, according to Adorno, 'function in the modern economy as mere agents of the law of value. The inner constitution of the individual, not merely his social role, could be deduced from this' (229). Because he believes that the contradiction between capital and labour is as much ideological as material, Adorno's analysis takes the form of a series of aphoristic reflections on personal, quotidian and commonplace affairs. Surveying his neighbours in Santa Monica, Adorno finds much to fear in the personality-types produced by late capitalism:

> Only when the process that begins with the metamorphosis of labour-power into a commodity has permeated men through and through, and objectified each of their impulses as formally commensurable variations of the exchange relationship, is it possible for life to reproduce itself under the prevailing conditions of production. Its consummate organization demands the co-ordination of people who are dead. . . . The consummation of the division of labour within the individual, his radical objectification, leads to his morbid scission. Hence the 'psychotic character . . .'.
>
> (229–31)

Perhaps the clearest way of illustrating the difference between Adorno and Foucault is to compare their responses to the experience of living in California. The materialist and superficial culture of Los Angeles seems to have induced in Adorno a political pessimism so deep as to verge on the misanthropic. Foucault, on the other hand, found in San Francisco a hedonistic carnality that he evidently regarded as politically, as well as personally, liberating. For Adorno, objectification is psychosis; for Foucault, objectification is freedom. They describe the same cultural phenomena but they reach opposed ethical judgements about them. Temperamental factors aside, the reason for this difference was that Adorno could *explain* objectification; he knew that it was the ideological result of commodification. In contrast, Foucault's work lacks any analysis of commodity fetishism, and he therefore does not perceive that the objectification of the subject is an ideological phenomenon. In fact, he is impelled to the reductive conclusion that human beings are and always were entirely material beings. Taken together, Althusser and Foucault can be said to have completed Spinoza's project of identifying human nature with matter. Their influence remains powerful, and has contributed to the current popularity of theorists who claim to see liberation in the demolition of the subject and the erasure of the distinction between human beings, animals and machines.

DEBORD AND BAUDRILLARD

Foucault's protestations to the contrary notwithstanding (see Foucault, 1988, 26), the Lukácsian analysis of the commodity was current in some French intellectual circles during the 1960s. It offered a way of understanding what Foucault merely records: the fact that the traditional division between the ideal and the material realms is becoming confused and displaced. In *Society of the Spectacle* (1967), Guy Debord announced the 'materialization of ideology', in the form of the 'spectacle', which 'is ideology *par excellence*' (215). We have seen how, in *Capital*, Marx claims that commodity exchange involves the recognition in one object of the image, the representation, of another object, with which it is to be exchanged. When this image is believed to be objectively present within the body of the first object, we have reached the stage of commodity fetishism. This objectified representation is then generalized in the form of money, the universal commodity which secretly represents alienated human activity. In Lukács, this commodity fetishism gives rise to the ideological phenomenon of 'reification', which consists in seeing people as if they were things, while simultaneously attributing a spectral life and ghostly agency to objects. The relationship between the ideal and the material is distorted, and this distortion can be traced to a fundamental belief in the illusory autonomy of representation.

Debord's argument is that, fifty years after Lukács's *History and Class-consciousness*, representation has become autonomous *in fact*. Such was the extent and power of commodity fetishism by 1967 that it no longer made sense to refer to it as an illusion. The result, according to Debord, is the complete dominance of representation – the 'spectacle' – over what had been thought of as 'reality':

This is the principle of *commodity fetishism*, the domination of society by 'intangible as well as tangible things', which reaches its absolute fulfilment in the spectacle, where the tangible world is replaced by a selection of images which exist above it, and which at the same time are recognized as the tangible *par excellence*.

(36)

In the consumer societies of the twenty-first century, exchange-value (a purely symbolic form) has become more real, more objective, than use-value (a material phenomenon). Objects are conceived, designed and produced for the purpose of making money by selling them, rather than for reasons of practical utility. Vast resources are devoted to manipulating the consciousnesses of consumers, and stimulating in them desires which can be met by the acquisition of commodities. As we have seen, to view an object as a commodity is to perceive it very differently from when we see it merely as something to be used. In our society consumers do not buy their clothes, cars or even their food for their use-values alone. Rather, they see in these objects symbolic significances, which determine their patterns of consumption. These patterns in turn dictate the movements of the stock, bond and currency exchanges, and these movements exert a profound influence on the material lives of people all over the world. So the symbolic realm, the realm of representation, literally does determine what goes on in the material world.

Of course, human beings have always attached 'extra', symbolic significance to the objects around them. But the complete dominance of the market, of the exchange of commodities, in today's global economy is unprecedented. Given the Marxian and Lukácsian accounts of the effects of commodification on consciousness, this is a cause for serious concern. Debord notes that to the degree that commodification becomes dominant in a society, an illusory significance, a false appearance, is imposed upon the real world, or the thing-in-itself. The result is a massive distortion of the relationships between ideas, matter and representation. Following Marx, Debord believes that capital represents objectified labour. Furthermore, 'The spectacle is capital to such a degree of accumulation that it becomes an image' (34). The thing-in-itself is obscured by its form of appearance. But the thing-in-itself in this case is *ourselves* – human labour, human activity and, therefore, human life itself, which is hidden and dominated by its simultaneously objectified and symbolic form of appearance: capital.

In a commodity culture, then, we can expect that the human subject will be objectified. What is more, 'When the real world changes into simple images, simple images become real beings and effective motivations of a hypnotic behavior' (18). The commodities themselves, being fetishized, are ascribed an active power. So Debord's 'society of the spectacle' systematically objectifies the subject, and subjectifies the object. Clearly, this is about as false as consciousness can possibly get. But Debord's point is precisely that the triumph of commodification renders the notion of false consciousness obsolete. We are faced, as he says, with 'the materialization of ideology. Society has become what ideology already was' (217). The dreadful truth Debord wants his readers to confront is that a way of thinking which is demonstrably erroneous and harmful is nonetheless an objectively accurate account of a real, material situation.

Debord thus arrives at much the same conclusions as Nietzsche and Foucault. It no longer makes sense to talk of a human 'subject', representation has become autonomous, history has no ultimate end or meaning, there is no way of distinguishing truth from falsehood or appearance from reality, and so on. But Debord has reached this position by a different route. His Marxist assumption that the roots of historical change can be traced to the economy leads him to study the 'postmodern condition' in relation to the predominant form of economic activity in postmodern society: commodity exchange. Since he views such activity as based on systematic error and exploitation, he inevitably sees consumer society as an infernal, fallen condition, in which human beings fetishize the products of their own activity and, in the form of the market, give them absolute power over their lives.

Against this characterization, one might argue that the postmodern world has merely freed us from the repressive effects of Enlightenment reason. Following Nietzsche, one might claim that binary logic, metaphors of depth, the absolute subject and teleological history are in fact instruments of hierarchy and tools of oppression. This, more or less, is the position espoused by Foucault, Derrida, Lyotard and also currently by Jean Baudrillard. Baudrillard's career is especially interesting, for he began as an associate of Debord and the Situationist movement, lamenting the effects of commodification on consciousness. Since the mid-1970s, however, Baudrillard has shifted his attitude, so that he often appears to take a more benign view of postmodern society.

In *For a Critique of the Political Economy of the Sign* [1972] (1981), Baudrillard elaborates on Debord's incisive but brusque analysis of the way commodification influences signification. To do so he modifies the semiotic theory of Saussure, which we discussed in Chapter 5. Saussure claimed that a linguistic sign was made up of two elements: the 'signifier', which was the sign's material form, and the 'signified', which was the concept evoked by the signifier. Baudrillard's argument is that '*the logic of the commodity and of political economy is at the very heart of the sign* in the abstract equation of signifier and signified' (146). Commodification and signification both depend on the recognition of an abstract equivalence, in the first case between the objects to be exchanged, in the second between the internal elements of the sign. In consumer society, this abstract equivalence departs from its previous, humble, enabling role, and steps forth to claim its inheritance. The signified collapses into the signifier; the concept disappears beneath its representation. Following Debord, Baudrillard describes this process as the materialization, the incarnation, of false consciousness: 'Nor is ideology some Imaginary floating in the wake of exchange value: it is the very operation of exchange value itself' (169).

Baudrillard sees his own work as 'decoding the birth of the sign form in the same way that Marx was able to uncover the birth of the commodity form' (112). Marxists, he notes, have not taken account of the autonomy of representation:

> Marxist analysis today finds itself in the same position with respect to the field of ideology as the bourgeois economists before (and since) Marx vis a vis material production: the real source of value and the real process of production are skipped over. It is from neglect of this social labour of sign production that ideology derives its transcendence; signs and culture appear enveloped in a 'fetishism', a mystery equivalent to, and contemporaneous with that of the commodity.
>
> (115)

At this stage, Baudrillard portrays the autonomy of representation as the result of false consciousness. Signs have become divorced from their referents because exchange-value has triumphed over use-value; this phenomenon is definitive of consumer society. Thus 'The definition of an object of consumption is entirely independent of the objects themselves and *exclusively a function of the logic of significations*' (67). If this is the case, then the opposition between ideas and matter no longer holds:

> Marx demonstrated that the objectivity of material production did not reside in its materiality, but in its form. . . . The same analytical reduction must be applied to ideology: its objectivity does not reside in its 'ideality', that is, in a realist metaphysic of thought contents, but in its form.
>
> (144)

'Ideology', for Baudrillard, transcends the artificial, essentialist dichotomy between material and ideal spheres. There is a 'simultaneity of the Ideological operation on the level of psychic structure and social structure' (100), and 'the operation amounts to defining the subject by means of the object and the object in terms of the subject' (71). Thus, 'just as concrete work is abstracted . . . into labour power' (83) in early forms of capitalist economies, so in consumer society, 'desire is abstracted and atomized into needs, in order to make it homogeneous with the means of satisfaction (products, images, sign-objects, etc.) and thus to multiply consummativity' (ibid.). This latter concept of 'consummativity' replaces 'productivity' as the organizing principle of consumer capitalism. Just as labour power abstracts human activity, consummativity abstracts the human spirit. To make a person into a consumer, it is necessary to tamper with his personality, to create and implant new needs and desires within him. And this manipulation of the soul is just as necessary to the functioning of today's economy as the disciplining and regimentation of the body was to the capitalism of the industrial epoch.

To the extent that the needs and aspirations of the postmodern subject are artificially created to serve the interests of the market economy, one can say that the subject has ceased to have any meaningful independent existence. Baudrillard does not hesitate to declare that 'The individual is an ideological structure. . . . The individual is nothing but the subject thought in economic terms' (133). Today's chimerical individual is merely an alibi, necessary to the functioning of consummativity. Baudrillard is able to demonstrate that this is true of the subject in consumer society, but he extends the scope of his argument to suggest that there has never been an authentic human subject. In that case, the question arises of why there is anything actually wrong with the consumer society. If the individual has never existed, then nothing is lost when the subject is objectified. If objects have always genuinely lorded it over subjects, then it makes no sense to argue that commodification bestows upon them an illusory, fetishistic power. If the notion of 'consciousness' is false, how can there be such a thing as 'false consciousness'? Baudrillard's summary of the course of his own investigations is apt: 'we started by meddling with received ideas about fetishism, only to discover that the whole theory of ideology may be in doubt' (90).

In *The Mirror of Production* [1973] (1975), Baudrillard rereads Marx in the light of these postmodern circumstances. He finds that, in his 'critique of political economy', Marx retained many of the fundamental presuppositions of the capitalist system which he criticized. For example, Marx assumes a human essence which is alienated in the labour process, as well as a use-value inherent in the object, which is obscured in the process of exchange. While possibly valid for early capitalism, such essentialist concepts are not applicable to the consumer age, in which representation has become autonomous and non-referential:

> The super-ideology of the sign and the general operationalization of the signifier – everywhere sanctioned today by the new master disciplines of structural linguistics, semiology, information theory and cybernetics – has replaced good old political economy as the theoretical basis of the system. . . . Here there is a revolution of the capitalist system equal in importance to the industrial revolution.
>
> (142)

Baudrillard argues that Saussurian linguistics is ideological, because it retains a concrete referent, located outside the sign, just as Marx retains an essential use-value, distinct from exchange-value. 'In fact', he says, 'the use value of labor power does not exist any more than the use value of products or the autonomy of signified and referent' (30). Exchange-value produces the illusion of use-value to serve its own ends, as the signifier produces the illusion that it necessarily refers to a particular signified. These 'concrete' phenomena are merely the 'ideological ectoplasm' which ground the systems of exchange and signification in a 'hallucinatory reality'.

Baudrillard here defines 'ideology' as referentiality: the belief that signs point to something beyond themselves, that there is a depth beneath the surface. In a suggestive passage from *Simulations* (1983), he recalls the historical struggles over religious images, which we discussed in Chapter 1. Idolatry, as Baudrillard notes, poses the question of the nature of signification in a particularly apposite form:

> what becomes of the divinity when it reveals itself in icons, when it is multiplied in simulacra? Does it remain the supreme authority, simply incarnated in images as a visible theology? Or is it volatilized into simulacra which alone deploy the pomp and power of fascination – the visible machinery of icons being substituted for the pure and intelligible Idea of God? This is precisely what was feared by the Iconoclasts, whose millennial quarrel is still with us today. Their rage to destroy images arose precisely because they sensed this omnipotence of simulacra, this facility they have of effacing God from the consciousness of men, and the overwhelming, destructive truth which they suggest: that ultimately there never has been any God, that only the simulacrum exists, indeed that God himself has only ever been his own simulacrum. Had they been able to believe that Images only masked the Platonic Idea of God, there would have been no reason to destroy them. One can live with the idea of a distorted truth. But their metaphysical despair came from the idea that in fact they were not images . . . but actually perfect simulacra forever radiant with their own fascination.
>
> (8–9)

Baudrillard obviously intends to suggest that the postmodern era presents us with a similar crisis of faith. Not only is there no referent, no absolute or individual subject, but the complete triumph of commodity culture means that the concepts, such as labour power and use-value, which were created as tools to critique the commodity, are also obsolete and 'ideological'. However, this need not necessarily mean that there is no longer any way of distinguishing truth from falsehood. It means, rather, that true consciousness can no longer be distinguished from false by virtue of its closer accordance with some external reality. In *For a Critique of the Political Economy of the Sign*, Baudrillard designated the consumer mentality a 'slave morality' (62). In *The Mirror of Production*, as in Foucault, it becomes clear that the subject is enslaving itself: 'the master–slave couple is interiorized in the same individual without ceasing to function as an alienated structure' (104). Here, perhaps, we can discern a ray of hope. Even though the consumer society reduces its subjects to objects, there remains, apparently, some residual resource within the individual which might enable us to struggle against the all-pervasive power of commodification. In much of his later work, Baudrillard chooses not to follow this course, and instead glories in the disarray of the transcendental subject. The implications of his earlier analyses have, however, been explored by others, most notably by the Slovene philosopher, Slavoj Žižek.

LIVING A LIE: ŽIŽEK AND PRACTICAL FETISHISM

It seems clear that, in the postmodern world, it is no longer useful to divide our experience into the separate 'levels' of ideas, matter and representation. This means that any notion of ideology as residing in a differentiated sphere of ideas must be abandoned. As Ernesto Laclau and Chantal Mouffe note in *Hegemony and Socialist Strategy* (1985), 'the very notion of representation as transparency becomes untenable. What is actually called into question here, is the base–superstructure model itself' (58). Representation no longer mediates between an ideal and a material sphere, it does not refer to any other level of experience than its own. Furthermore, Laclau and Mouffe use Foucault's concept of 'discourse' to denote material practice as well as systems of representation, thereby assuming that there is no significant distinction between these spheres. As with Foucault's 'fascism in the head', this means that the struggle against oppression must take place at all levels, since 'a fragmentation of positions exists *within* the social agents themselves' (84). In the postmodern world the personal is the political, and the individual subject, rather than the broader canvas of world history, is the proper focus of political practice.

The question which postmodern theory often neglects is *why* the material / ideal / representation model has collapsed. There is general agreement among postmodernists that the category of representation is fundamental; there is nothing outside representation. For the early Baudrillard, this triumph of representation is a kind of perversion which is directly traceable to 'the virtual international autonomy of finance capital . . . the uncontrollable play of floating capital' (1975, 129n9). Money is calcified representation, and it is 'the total artificiality of the sign that one "adores" in money' (1981, 93). It is the money-form, the principle of abstract equivalence, which exemplifies, and even embodies, objectified representation. The unprecedented dominance of finance capital thus extends representation into material practice, and also into the minds of human subjects.

This effect of commodity fetishism on the individual psyche is Žižek's primary concern. Due to the fact that he views this effect as malign and distorting, Žižek revives the concept of ideology in order to describe it. He does not, however, return to the notion that ideology consists purely of ideas. Like Debord, he assumes that real life has itself become ideological. Ideology is not false because it does not correspond to material reality; it does this all too well. The problem is with material reality itself, which has taken the grotesque shape of an objectified illusion, and this illusion is duplicated in our consciousness. As Žižek notes in *Tarrying with the Negative* (1993), ideology can only be understood as a phenomenon involving the Hegelian totality:

> For Hegel, the inverted 'topsy-turvy world' does not consist in presupposing, beyond the actual, empirical world, the kingdom of suprasensible ideas, but in a kind of double inversion by means of which these suprasensible ideas themselves assume again sensible form, so that the very sensible world is redoubled . . . he does *not* put forward another, even 'deeper' supra-Ground which would ground the ground itself; he simply grounds the ground in the totality of its relations to the grounded content.
>
> (138–9)

So 'ideology' is not something which affects only our ideas, it is something which happens to the totality of our existence, including material practice. It is not to be conceived as a misapprehension of reality, but as a distortion in the form taken by reality itself. As Žižek puts it in *The Sublime Object of Ideology* (1989):

> ideology is not simply a 'false consciousness', an illusory represen-
> tation of reality, it is rather this reality itself which is already to be
> conceived as 'ideological' – 'ideological' *is a social reality whose very
> existence implies the non-knowledge of its participants as to its essence*. . . .
> *'Ideological' is not the 'false consciousness' of a social being but this being in
> so far as it is supported by 'false consciousness'*.
>
> (21)

We must differentiate here between Žižek's notion of 'false consciousness' and the concept of illusion. There is nothing illusory about ideology,
which accurately corresponds to reality. In that reality, however, we
systematically behave as if an illusion were true. The illusion referred to is
the autonomy of representation, as expressed in the market economy. We
know that money is only a representation of a determinate amount of
human activity, but we nevertheless base our whole economy, and thus
the material activity of our everyday lives, on the assumption that money
is a thing-in-itself: an assumption which we know to be false. In Žižek's
words:

> When individuals use money, they know very well that there is nothing
> magical about it – that money, in its materiality, is simply an expression
> of social relations. The everyday spontaneous ideology reduces money
> to a simple sign giving the individual possessing it a right to a certain
> part of the social product. So, on an everyday level, the individuals know
> very well that there are relations between people behind the relations
> between things. The problem is that in their social activity itself, in what
> they are *doing*, they are *acting* as if money, in its material reality, is the
> embodiment of wealth as such. They are fetishists in practice, not in
> theory.
>
> (1989, 31)

The autonomy of representation is thus empirically true, but ontolog-
ically false, and ethically reprehensible. Žižek has no quarrel with the

postmodern declarations that metaphors of depth are untenable, that we can never 'get beyond' signification, or that the subject is an effect of representation. But he points out that this situation is paralleled in the finance-based economy and he indicates that the effects of this economy on the individual subject are dire indeed. In fact, Žižek goes so far as to say that the commodity economy destroys the subject. This is the point at which Žižek's divergence from the neo-Foucauldians is most pronounced. Foucault, as we have seen, also announces the death of the subject. But he does not connect this event to commodification, and he therefore sees it as an entirely positive development. This position is enthusiastically endorsed by postmodernist theory as a whole. In *Tarrying with the Negative*, Žižek raises his standard against this kind of theory:

> Far from containing any kind of subversive potentials, the dispersed, plural, constructed subject hailed by postmodern theory (the subject prone to particular, inconsistent modes of enjoyment, etc.) simply designates *the form of subjectivity that corresponds to late capitalism*. Perhaps the time has come to resuscitate the Marxist insight that Capital is the ultimate power of 'deterritorialization' which undermines every fixed social identity, and to conceive of 'late capitalism' as the epoch in which the traditional fixity of ideological positions (patriarchal authority, fixed sexual roles, etc.) becomes an obstacle to the unbridled commodification of everyday life.
>
> (216)

Once we admit that such postmodern phenomena as the objectified subject, the autonomy of representation, the impossibility of teleology, and the disappearance of the referent are effects of commodity fetishism, then postmodern ideology begins to look decidedly unappetizing. When we recall that commodity fetishism involves the triumph of dead labour over living labour, the postmodern world begins to seem positively sinister. If we remember the metaphysical horror with which previous eras confronted the fetishism of objects, as well as the moralistic dismay with which they viewed usury and finance, we must conclude that they would have seen the triumph of abstract representation which characterizes postmodernism as the victory of pure evil. Why does it not seem that way to us?

THE LATE ADORNO

Žižek, then, agrees with Foucauldian postmodernism that ideology is material practice. This contention can be traced to Althusser's slide from the legitimate claim that ideas must be *expressed in* material form before they can be known, to the illegitimate and contradictory assertion that ideas *are* material, an assumption which then informs Foucault's influential account of 'discourse'. However, there are two vital differences between Žižek's view of this situation and the way it is portrayed by conventional postmodernism. First, Žižek sees the materialization of ideology as an unmitigated catastrophe. It means, he thinks, that we are literally living a lie. Because we live it, however, the lie becomes real. The postmodern condition is thus one in which reality itself is false; and not merely false but dehumanizing, destructive and evil in the profoundest sense of the word. Second, Žižek arrives at the view that ideology is material through a dialectical analysis of the totality. He does not collapse the ideal into the material in an Althusserian reduction. Instead, he describes a process of fetishism which operates on the material, representational and ideal levels simultaneously, without any one of these levels 'determining' this process. This is necessarily so, because he defines fetishization as a perversion of the relationships between these levels. The material world is organized in a manner which presupposes that the ideal and the representational are themselves material. Logically, of course, the ideal and the representational are not material. But the dreadful prospect which Žižek confronts is that this mode of practical organization turns out to be self-fulfilling: it reduces the ideal and the representational to the material in practice. And this can and does occur despite the fact that the ideal and the representational are demonstrably not material in theory.

If it is to remain true to itself, then, theory must be rigorously and consistently opposed to the real, to the factual. The most promising attempt to elaborate such a theory is undertaken by Theodor Adorno, in his late masterpiece *Negative Dialectics* [1966] (1990). As he puts it in his introduction, 'dialectics is the ontology of the wrong state of things' (11); it is the study of the real as the false. The central image which haunts this book was coined by Max Weber, at the end of *The Protestant Ethic*. Weber remarks that in the seventeenth century, when capitalist forms of economic practice were just beginning, it was assumed that 'the care for external goods should only lie on the shoulders of the "saint like a light cloak, which can be thrown aside at any moment." But fate decreed that the cloak should become an iron cage' (Weber, 1930, 181). As this image implies, commodity fetishism has become all-encompassing. The formal structure of the commodity determines our hopes and dreams, our philosophical systems, our modes of signification, our economic practice. It hardly matters which 'level', if any, determines the others, since the problem is one of form, and it affects all levels simultaneously and to the same degree. As Adorno puts it:

> Where ideology is no longer added to things as a vindication or complement – where it turns into the seeming inevitability and thus legitimacy of whatever is – a critique that operates with the unequivocal causal relation of superstructure and infrastructure is wide of the mark.
> (268)

Negative Dialectics is an attempt, if not to unlock Weber's cage, then at least to make us aware of its existence. In the book's introduction, Adorno makes it clear he does not accept the notion, which was espoused by Baudrillard, that use-value is merely an ideological effect produced by exchange-value. The cage, that is to say, is not empty; there is something real imprisoned within it. In the Marxist conception, exchange-value is the principle of false identity. It renders different use-values identical for the purposes of exchange. Baudrillard would say that these use-values are illusions, produced retrospectively in the act of exchange. Adorno recoils in horror from such an idea, going so far as to declare that 'the ineffable part of the utopia is that which defies subsumption under identity – the "use-value" in Marxist terminology – is necessary anyway if life is to go on at all' (11). Of course, it is by no means necessary that life *should* go on at all. In fact, Adorno is decidedly pessimistic about the long-term prospects for life, and his pessimism is deduced from the undeniable prevalence and power of exchange-value. Because of his belief that use-value is truer than exchange-value, however, Adorno does not see the current dominance of the market as natural or inevitable. In a passage which criticizes the postmodernism of Foucault or Lyotard *avant la lettre*, he points out that

Determinism acts as if dehumanization, the totally unfolded merchandise character of the working capacity, were human nature pure and simple. No thought is given to the fact that there is a limit to the merchandise character: the working capacity that has not just an exchange-value but a use-value. To deny free will outright means to reduce men unreservedly to the normal merchandise form of their labour in full-fledged capitalism.

(264)

However, Adorno would certainly agree that, under capitalism, people really have become objectified. His aim is to register this fact, while simultaneously showing that it is wrong, and that it could have been and might still be otherwise. This is the paradox of ideology: 'Barter as a process has real objectivity and is objectively untrue at the same time. . . . This is why, of necessity, it will create a false consciousness: the idols of the market' (190). Among these Baconian 'idols' is the subject itself:

The universal domination of mankind by the exchange-value – a domination which a priori keeps the subjects from being subjects and degrades subjectivity itself to a mere object – makes an untruth of the general principle that claims to establish the subject's predominance. The surplus of the transcendental subject is the deficit of the utterly reduced empirical subject.

(178)

It is important to do justice to the full complexity of Adorno's thought here. He claims that human beings are originally both subject and object. Under capitalism, however, they are made into mere objects. Their subjectivity is, as it were, squeezed out of them, and it reconstitutes itself in the fantasy form of a transcendental subject. In our society, this transcendental subject is 'man': a supposedly eternal and irreducible apotheosis of human nature. As though to compensate for their loss of real subjectivity, each of the individual 'subjects' (who are in fact no longer subjects but objects) then acquires an illusory, ideological 'appearance' of subjectivity, which is based on an identification with the fantastic transcendental subject. On an individual level, we end up with fully objectified subjects who take their very objectivity as a form of subjectivity.

For example, a postmodern individual may well construct his or her 'personality' out of an amalgam of consumer goods, fashion statements, 'lifestyle' choices, identification with real or fictional celebrities – in other words, out of objective phenomena which are administered to them by the 'culture industry'. And yet this utter loss of subjectivity is combined, in our society, with a resounding emphasis on the 'individual', on the uniqueness of each and every 'person'. As Adorno shrewdly sees, this is a shabby ideological ruse: 'to a great extent the subject came to be an ideology, a screen for society's objective functional context and a palliative for the subject's suffering under society' (66–7).

There are thus two subjects: a 'real' subject, which is repressed by exchange-value, and an 'objective' subject, which is not real, and which is the product of exchange-value. This might not even matter, except for the fact that the relationship between these two subjects is antagonistic: we are faced with 'the subject as the subject's foe' (10). The 'objective' subject is like a zombie in a horror movie, preying upon and destroying the 'real' subject. We can find an early parable of this development in Mary Shelley's *Frankenstein* [1818] (1823). When Dr Frankenstein is confronted by the monster he has created, the creature reminds him that 'thou hast made me more powerful then thyself' (206), and suggests that the only way the doctor can be rid of him is literally to close his eyes to the monster's presence. The doctor cries:

> 'Begone! relieve me from the sight of your detested form.' 'Thus I relieve thee, my creator,' he said and placed his hated hands before my eyes, which I flung from me with violence; 'thus I take from thee a sight which you abhor.'
>
> (210)

Ridley Scott's movie *Blade Runner* suggests an intensification of this process, in which the sinister Tyrrel Corporation has succeeded in creating 'replicants' of human beings who are unaware of their own artificial status. The ubiquitous theme of death-in-life, of the living dead, in recent popular culture is highly revealing, and highly disturbing. In *Nineteen Eighty-Four* (1949), George Orwell connects the motif of the unsuspecting zombie to totalitarian politics. The book's hero, Winston Smith, cannot understand his lover's optimism:

> 'We are the dead,' he said. 'We're not dead yet,' said Julia prosaically.
> 'Not physically. . . . But it makes very little difference. So long as human
> beings stay human, death and life are the same thing.'
>
> (137)

In *Negative Dialectics*, Adorno takes Marx's description of capitalism
as the domination of dead labour over living labour to its terrible
conclusion. The consequences of this position are so frightening that it is
easy to understand why many thinkers, including Althusser and Foucault,
recoil from them, and take refuge in the notion that the subject was
actually an object all along. Adorno considers this option, and pointedly
rejects it:

> But it is not the purpose of critical thought to place the object on the
> orphaned royal throne once occupied by the subject. On that throne
> the object would be nothing but an idol. The purpose of critical thought
> is to abolish the hierarchy.
>
> (181)

We must remember, however, that postmodern capitalism has already
abolished the hierarchy of subject and object. It has done so, according to
Adorno, in a radically false way: by collapsing the opposition into one of
its poles, and reducing the subject to an object. It is this illegitimate
reduction which constitutes the form presently taken by 'ideology':

> With society, ideology has so advanced that it no longer evolves into a
> socially required semblance and thus to an independent form, however
> brittle. All that it turns into is a kind of glue: the false identity of subject
> and object.
>
> (348)

It follows that a theory which is critical of ideology must resist the
temptation to endorse such an identity:

> The task of criticizing ideology is to judge the subjective and objective
> shares and their dynamics. It is to deny the false objectivity of concept
> fetishism by reducing it to the social subject, and to deny false

subjectivity, the sometimes unrecognizably veiled claim that all being lies in the mind, by showing it up as a fraud, a parasitical nonentity, as well as demonstrating its immanent hostility to the mind.

(197–8)

Once again, we find 'the subject as the subject's foe'. Adorno obviously perceives the postmodern subject as animated by some mysterious drive to self-destruction. In a highly significant recourse to metaphysical terminology, he refers to this tendency as a 'spell', under which 'Men become that which negates them' (344).

What is this force which 'negates' human beings? Adorno tells us that the 'spell' is 'radical evil' (346); that 'In human experience the spell is the equivalent of the fetish character of merchandise' (ibid.); and that 'In the spell, the reified consciousness has become total' (ibid.). This 'spell', then, clearly involves objectification – it is objectification as applied to human beings. The name which we usually give to this thing is 'death'. Death is the ultimate false (but real) objectification. The fetishism of the commodity, no less than the idolatry of the heathen, brings death in its wake:

As subjects live less, death grows more precipitous, more terrifying. The fact that it literally turns them into things makes them aware of reification, their permanent death and the form of their relations that is partly their fault. The integration of death in civilization, a process without power over death and a ridiculous cosmetic procedure in the face of death, is the shaping of a reaction to this social phenomenon, a clumsy attempt of the barter society to stop up the last holes left open by the world of merchandise.

(370)

To fetishize a commodity or to worship an idol is to treat dead labour, dead life, as though it were alive. It is to misconstrue the relationship between death and life. If this were merely an ideological error, it might not be very important. But, before Adorno's stricken gaze, this ideology reveals its practical results. First of all, the instrumental reason to which the commodity form gives birth shows every sign of culminating in nuclear annihilation or rendering the earth ecologically uninhabitable.

This is what happens when we fetishize our own reason, making of it a 'second nature' (67). At least these catastrophes have not yet actually happened. However, Adorno believes that we have already witnessed the consequences of objectifying human activity, in the Nazi Holocaust:

> The earthquake of Lisbon sufficed to cure Voltaire of the theodicy of Leibniz, and the visible disaster of the first nature was insignificant in comparison with the second, social one, which defies human imagination as it distils a real hell from human evil . . . since, in a world whose law is universal individual profit, the individual has nothing but this self that has become indifferent, the performance of the old, familiar tendency is at the same time the most dreadful of things. There is no getting out of this, no more than out of the electrified barbed wire around the camps. Perennial suffering has as much right to expression as a tortured man has to scream; hence it may have been wrong to say that after Auschwitz you could no longer write poems. But it is not wrong to raise the cultural question whether after Auschwitz you can go on living – especially whether one who escaped by accident, one who by rights should have been killed, may go on living. His mere survival calls for the coldness, the basic principle of bourgeois subjectivity, without which there could have been no Auschwitz; this is the drastic guilt of him who was spared. By way of atonement he will be plagued by dreams such as that he is no longer living at all, that he was sent to the ovens in 1944 and his whole existence since has been imaginary, an emanation of the insane wish of a man killed twenty years earlier.
>
> (361–3)

The one who 'was spared' referred to in this passage is, of course, Adorno himself. He speculates that the words he is writing may be nothing more than the dreams of a dead man. And there is a sense in which his philosophy bears this out. The ultimate message of *Negative Dialectics* is that 'we are the dead': our economic system presupposes it, our consciousness reflects it, and our material activity puts it into practice. Like the Philistines summoning Samson to the temple, we have called forth our own destroyer.

7

IDEOLOGY AFTER 11 SEPTEMBER

The total obliteration of the war by information, propaganda, com-
mentaries, with camera-men in the first tanks and war reporters
dying heroic deaths, the mish-mash of enlightened manipulation
of public opinion and oblivious activity: all this is another expression for the withering of experience, the vacuum between men and
their fate, in which their real fate lies. It is as if the reified, hardened, plaster-cast of events takes the place of events themselves.
Men are reduced to walk-on parts in a monster documentary
film which has no spectators, since the least of them has his bit
to do on the screen. It is just this aspect that underlies the much-
maligned designation 'phoney war'. . . . The war is really phoney,
but with a phoneyness more horrifying than all the horrors, and
those who mock at it are principal contributors to disaster.

(Theodor Adorno, *Minima Moralia*, 1974, 55)

CAPITAL AND EMPIRE

Adorno wrote the above passage more than fifty years before Jean
Baudrillard outraged the literal minded with his essay *The Gulf War Did*

Not Take Place (1995). The title was frequently and glibly parodied, but Baudrillard's point is perfectly sound. He meant that the Gulf War had been so effectively transformed into an image that people outside the combat zone had difficulty in conceiving it as fully real. In many people's minds, the war occupied the same ontological category as a video game. We witnessed a similar effect following the terrorist attack of 11 September. When shell-shocked New Yorkers returned home after watching the twin towers burn, they switched on their televisions to find that the event had already been packaged, branded and presented after the manner of a feature film. As Mike Davis puts it in *Dead Cities* (2002):

> The hijacked planes were aimed to impact precisely at the vulnerable border between fantasy and reality. . . . Thousands of people who turned on their televisions on 9–11 were convinced that the cataclysm was just a broadcast, a hoax. They thought they were watching rushes from the latest Bruce Willis film. . . . The 'Attack on America', and its sequels, 'America Fights Back' and 'America Freaks Out', has continued to unspool as a succession of celluloid hallucinations, each of which can be rented from the corner video shop.
>
> (5)

In fact, Adorno and Baudrillard are saying exactly the same thing, but there is an important difference between their attitudes. Adorno sees hyper-reality as the conquest of the world by what, *mutatis mutandis*, we can without exaggeration call 'Satan'. Baudrillard's ethical position on hyper-reality is certainly debatable, but he has left ample interpretative room for his followers to revel in its libidinal liberation from *logos* and *telos*.

The weakness of the postmodernist case does not lie in a false description of the empirical situation but in the way this situation is evaluated. There is no doubt that, in the twenty-first century, images really do determine reality, the human subject really is objectified, and the global market really is likely to remain the only significant world power for the foreseeable future. But the market's success does not have to be applauded. Many people who celebrate the market and its ideology do so because they believe that its triumph is inevitable, that, as Margaret Thatcher used to say, 'there is no alternative'. But that is no reason to suppose that the victory of the market is a benign development. There is no plot narrative dictating that human history must have a happy ending.

The most comprehensive analysis of the global market's ideology to be published in recent years is Michael Hardt and Antonio Negri's *Empire* (2000). The authors point to the importance of ideology, as opposed to overt repression, in sustaining the postmodern form of imperialism. 'Empire is formed', they write, 'not on the basis of force itself but on the basis of the capacity to present force as being in the service of right and peace' (15). The power they call 'Empire' will certainly exert material force where necessary, but the real battles take place in the realm of perception. Governments devote unprecedented attention to constructing ideological narratives that 'spin' their adventures in appropriate fashion. Following the violent ejection of the Taliban from power, for instance, the Western media incongruously hailed 'the first peaceful transfer of power in Afghanistan for decades' (*Guardian*, 14 December 2001).

In domestic affairs, Western governments rule by opinion poll and focus group, which are devices for the alienation of thought, turning rational cognition into statistics by subjecting it to the empirical methods of the natural sciences. These techniques originate in commercial marketing and, with their migration into politics, the citizen becomes a customer. It is this method, rather than an appeal to any absolute principle or value, that provides the ideological justification for power in our relativistic era. The formal characteristics of political campaigns are more significant than any substantive issues they may raise: all parties agree that people are to be regarded as consumers, whose choices are determined by non-rational factors such as images and soundbites. Consumer choice, which is driven by desire and not by reason, is the truly sovereign power in the age of 'Empire'. As Hardt and Negri comment, Empire is 'legitimated not by right but by consensus' (18).

Thus brings us to the most pressing question raised by Hardt and Negri's book: what exactly *is* 'Empire'? The authors make it clear that it is, above all, a new phenomenon, and that its newness consists in the extent of its power: 'Our basic thesis is that sovereignty has taken a new form, composed of a series of national and supranational organisms united under a single logic of rule. This new global form of sovereignty is what we call Empire' (xii). This globalization of Empire is more than the supersession of national by global sovereignty, however. It also involves the annexation of sovereignty itself by capital: '*imperial sovereignty marks a paradigm shift*. . . . We believe that this shift makes clear and possible today the capitalist project to bring together economic power and political power, to realize, in other words, a properly capitalist order' (8–9).

Nor are capital's ambitions limited to the seizure of political power. Hardt and Negri suggest that capital is bent on colonizing every aspect of social life and subjective experience. Like Gramsci's 'hegemony' or Foucault's 'power', the concept of 'Empire' designates a force which is at once ideological, economic and political; simultaneously subjective and objective. To convey the pervasive nature of empire, Hardt and Negri resurrect the ancient concept of the microcosm, whereby society constitutes a 'body politic' that is analogous to an individual person: 'Society, subsumed within a power that reaches down to the ganglia of the social structure and its processes of development, reacts like a single body' (24). Their argument recalls Foucault's interest in 'micropolitics' and the effects of power on the body. But unlike Foucault, whose description of 'power' is so vast and vague that it can be made to mean almost anything, Hardt and Negri clearly understand that this unification of experience results from capital's colonization of areas of life that were once thought of as lying outside the economic sphere: 'in the postmodernization of the economy, the creation of wealth tends evermore toward what we will call biopolitical production, the production of social life itself, in which the economic, the political, and the cultural increasingly overlap and invest one another' (xiii).

As we have seen, capital's insatiable lust for conquest was diagnosed by Marx. But Marx saw that capital faced a powerful adversary in labour, which in his time was incarnated in the proletariat. Since capital *was* labour in objectified form – since it was the illusion of which labour was the reality – Marx thought that its defeat was inevitable. Hardt and Negri also believe that 'Empire' is confronted by a strong foe, but rather than the proletariat they identify the nemesis of 'Empire' as the 'multitude'. This term is another allusion to the pre-Enlightenment world-view. In the sixteenth and seventeenth centuries, the 'multitude' was often held up as an example of dangerous irrationalism. In Thomas Browne's *Religio Medici* [1643] (1972), the usually mild-mannered author declares:

> If there be any among those common objects of hatred I do condemn
> and laugh at, it is that great enemy of Reason, Virtue and Religion, the
> Multitude: that numerous piece of monstrosity, which, taken asunder,
> seem men, and the reasonable creatures of GOD; but, confused
> together, make but one great beast, and a monstrosity more prodigious
> than Hydra.
>
> (64)

It is just this sense of monstrous multiplicity, deplored by Browne, that
makes the concept of the 'multitude' appealing to Hardt and Negri.
Whereas the 'proletariat' was often imagined as a unitary, monolithic
subject, the 'multitude' allows for the inclusion of various social groups
and perspectives. Nevertheless, it still seems that the 'multitude' stands in
relation to 'Empire' as, in traditional Marxism, labour does to capital:

> The multitude is the real productive force of our social world, whereas
> Empire is a mere apparatus of capture that lives only off the vitality of
> the multitude – as Marx would say, a vampire regime of accumulated
> dead labor that survives only by sucking off the blood of the living.
>
> (2000, 62)

In the nineteenth and twentieth centuries, the proletariat was mainly
identified with the industrial working class of the Western nations, but
we can now see that this was a temporary historical phase. The logical,
dialectical contradiction is between capital and labour, not between
bourgeoisie and proletariat. In the age of Empire, Hardt and Negri
declare, 'we understand *proletariat* as a broad category that includes all
those whose labor is directly or indirectly exploited by and subjected to
capitalist norms of production and reproduction' (52). The postmodern
proletariat, in fact, is labour in general: 'In effect, the object of exploitation and domination tend not to be specific productive activities but the
universal capacity to produce, that is, abstract social activity and its
comprehensive power' (209). Hardt and Negri's analysis is thus closely
attuned to the nuances of Marx's labour theory of value. As we have seen,
Marx's advance on Adam Smith lay in his recognition that, in order to
function as financial value, labour must first be conceived of in general, as
an abstract category for human activity as a whole.

In Marx, the proletariat is at once capital's opposite, its true nature and its gravedigger. In the late nineteenth and early twentieth centuries, the proletariat could be identified with a social class, which channelled its anti-capitalist energies into socialist political parties and labour unions. At the beginning of the twenty-first century, this social class has arguably been assimilated into capitalism to the degree that it no longer constitutes an oppositional force. Almost everyone today sells his or her labour power, and thus almost everyone meets the definition of a proletarian. One way to look at this would be to say that the proletariat has disappeared; another would be to say that it has become universal. Hardt and Negri note this paradox: 'Just as the proletariat seems to be disappearing from the world stage, the proletariat is becoming the universal figure of labor' (256). However, this capacious definition of the proletariat necessitates a similar expansion in what has traditionally been understood by the term 'labour': 'As the proletariat is becoming the universal figure of labor, the object of proletarian labor is becoming equally universal. Social labor produces life itself' (258).

It seems, then, that the opposition between 'Empire' and 'Multitude' is the same as the contradiction between dead labour and living labour, or between 'capital' and 'people'. It is true that capital is owned and administered by people, since there certainly remain 'capitalists', but even these people frequently sell their labour for wages, and in any case their economic actions are determined according to the logic and interests of capital. The fact that human beings take these decisions is effectively irrelevant; it is capital itself that decides how the economy is to be run. The fact that capital is dead labour, that it is objectified human activity, thus begins to take on ethical and spiritual implications. If capital is death and labour is life, we will need to move beyond the materialist terms of most current debate in order to understand the nature of the conflict between them. This, unfortunately, is a step that Hardt and Negri are unwilling to take. They shrink from the implications of their position, and they seem not to appreciate the inferences to be drawn from the fact that, today, 'Capital and labor are opposed in a directly antagonistic form', shorn of their mediation through social classes. The resulting confusion in their thinking is encapsulated in the following *non sequitur*. In the postmodern 'Empire', they contend: 'Having achieved the global level, capitalist development is faced directly with the multitude, without mediation. Hence the dialectic, or really the science of the limit and its organization, evaporates' (237).

But dialectic is not 'the science of the limit', it is the science of contradiction. In the nineteenth and twentieth centuries, many ideological contradictions operated simultaneously: there were, for example, contradictions of class, race, gender and nationality. The notion of 'ideology' grew increasingly complicated towards the end of this period, as it became evident that the proletariat was not the only ideologically oppressed section of society. As Hardt and Negri put it, 'We can now see that imperial sovereignty . . . is organized not around one central conflict but rather through a flexible network of microconflicts. The contradictions of imperial society are elusive, proliferating, and nonlocalizable: the contradictions are everywhere' (201). However, with the globalization of the economy (which is simultaneously an internalization of economics, a transformation of economics into ideology) Hardt and Negri observe that this multiplicity of contradictions is congealing into the single, essential contradiction between capital and labour, or in their terms, between Empire and Multitude. It does not follow from this, however, that the dialectic 'evaporates' as a useful mode of analysis. To the contrary, a dialectical approach is more necessary than ever if we are to grasp the interpenetration and mutual definition of the capital / labour opposition.

Why, then, are Hardt and Negri reluctant to employ a dialectical analysis? The answer lies in their materialist view of the subject. They understand that dialectics presupposes a distinction between subject and object. From a dialectical point of view, it is reductive to claim that the subject is merely the product of objective forces. This is, however, precisely the claim made by such influential thinkers as Althusser and Foucault, and the deleterious effect of such arguments lingers in the work of Hardt and Negri. They assert that 'the modern critical response of opening the dialectic between inside and outside is no longer possible' (210). In fact, Hardt and Negri seem almost enthusiastic about the 'posthuman' subject, calling for a

> recognition that human nature is in no way separate from nature as a whole, that there are not fixed and necessary boundaries between the human and the animal, the human and the machine . . . when the dialectic between inside and outside comes to an end, and when the

separate place of use value disappears from the imperial terrain, the new forms of labor power are charged with the task of producing anew the human (or really the posthuman).

(215, 217)

But these 'new forms of labor power' involve its generalization, from the specific paid work of the industrial proletariat to the abstract form of life activity as a whole. Furthermore, by *Empire*'s own account, the 'posthuman' already exists – it is *capital*. Capital is alienated, objectified life activity, and the ideological manifestation of capital is the alienation and objectification of the subject. Hardt and Negri acknowledge this at several points in their book, noting for instance that in postmodern American society 'productive subjectivities are forged as one-dimensional functions of economic development'. But they seem unable to accept that this subjugation of the human personality to the objective force of capital is the cause of the 'posthuman' condition that they elsewhere applaud. They retain, in other words, the pseudo-scientific, reified assumption that, as Hegel mockingly put it, 'the Spirit is a bone'. The objectification of the subject, which is the primary ideological effect of market capitalism, is not a problem for them because they believe that the subject was an object all along. They are therefore prevented from using the dialectic to place the opposition between 'Empire' and 'Multitude' in its ideological context. They ignore the fact that capital is reproduced within our minds as the psychological tendency to objectification.

Despite this, *Empire* is an important book. Its success both within and beyond the academy has rekindled an intellectual anti-capitalism that will surely grow more coherent and more prominent as popular awareness of the totalitarian aspirations of the global market becomes more pronounced. Hardt and Negri offer few proposals for political practice, but their scattered speculations about the current possibilities for resistance are suggestive, not least because many of them stand in bold contrast to their materialist approach to subjectivity:

Allow us, in conclusion, one final analogy that refers to the birth of Christianity in Europe and its expansion during the decline of the Roman Empire. In the process an enormous potential of subjectivity was constructed and consolidated in terms of the prophecy of a world to come, a chiliastic project. This new subjectivity offered an absolute alternative to the spirit of imperial right – a new ontological basis. From this perspective, Empire was accepted as the 'maturity of the times' and the unity of the entire known civilization, but it was challenged in its totality by a completely different ethical and ontological axis. In the same way today, given that the limits and irresolvable problems of the new imperial right are fixed, theory and practice can go beyond them, finding once again an ontological basis of antagonism – within Empire, but also against and beyond Empire, at the same level of totality.

(21)

What conclusions can we draw from Hardt and Negri's 'analogy'? Christianity did not attack the Empire physically, but ideologically. Over three centuries, Christianity gradually but inexorably undermined the psychological foundations of the greatest and apparently most impregnable power the world had ever seen, achieving what Nietzsche calls a 'transvaluation' that ensured the Empire's political collapse. But this victory was won through a profound and uncompromising anti-materialism: a repudiation of the things of this world, a rejection of the pleasures of the flesh, a renunciation of the pagan obsession with glory on earth, and a repugnance for gods who could be physically represented. At this point, the 'analogy' with Hardt and Negri's politics fails. Like other 'post-Marxist' thinkers such as Laclau and Mouffe, Hardt and Negri espouse a materialist view of the subject, and they consequently miss the real ethical and psychological implications of the all-encompassing contradiction between life and money.

DIALECTIC AND DIFFERENCE

No one would dispute that, in the twenty-first century, money rules the world. But few people understand what money is. Money is an objectified representation, not of human labour, but of human life. To say that money rules the world is to say, with Adorno in *Minima Moralia*, that 'life has become appearance' (15), that we are witnessing 'the dissolution of the subject' (16) and the replacement of true personality by 'the idol of personality' (79). Although some theorists gamely attempt to enjoy the cult of celebrity and the other accoutrements of mass culture, they can neither escape nor disguise the fatal *ennui* that has enveloped them. Adorno shows how commodification infects even the most immediate of our sense impressions, rendering impotent the *jouissance* that postmodernists celebrate as a ludic alternative to referentiality:

> The quality of things ceases to be their essence and becomes the accidental appearance of their value. The 'equivalent form' mars all perceptions. . . . Our organs grasp nothing sensuous in isolation, but notice whether a colour, a sound, a movement is there for its own sake or for something else; wearied by a false variety, they steep all in grey. . . . Disenchantment with the contemplated world is the sensorium's reaction to its objective role as a 'commodity world'.
>
> (1978, 227)

Adorno concludes that, since the market has rendered reality radically false, authentic art must renounce, or 'negate', reality. He cites as examples the plays of Samuel Beckett and the atonal music of Schoenberg, of which he remarks that 'This music is no longer an ideology' (10). The ideological implications of Adorno's musical theory have been explored in such diverse texts as Thomas Mann's *Doctor Faustus*, in which the emergence of atonal music is ascribed to the influence of Satan, and Griel Marcus's *Lipstick Traces*, which draws a bold comparison between Adorno's *Philosophy of Modern Music* and the Sex Pistols.

In the Introduction, I argued that the purpose of ideology in the postmodern epoch is to erase the fundamental contradiction between capital and labour. Today, these forces are not only embodied in distinct social classes or different regions of the globe. The contradiction between capital and labour has also become internalized within the minds of individuals. It has become, in other words, an ideological phenomenon. In the course of this book I have tried to show that capital is objectified labour, and that labour is subjective human activity considered as a whole. The contradiction between capital and labour has thus become a psychological opposition between the forces of life and the forces of death. The history of human thought is replete with lengthy and profound meditations on this struggle, but they are often dismissed today because they depart from the materialist presuppositions that dominate the thought of our age. These assumptions are themselves the most glaring results of psychological objectification, however, and it is always rash to consign the thought of earlier eras to obsolesence. Consider the following two passages:

> Good and evil we know in the field of this world grow up together almost inseparably; and the knowledge of good is so involved and interwoven with the knowledge of evil, and in so many cunning resemblances hardly to be discerned, that those confused seeds which were imposed on Psyche as an incessant labor to cull out and sort asunder, were not more intermixed. It was from out the rind of one apple tasted, that the knowledge of good and evil, as two twins cleaving together, leaped forth into the world. And perhaps this is that doom which Adam fell into of knowing good and evil, that is to say, of knowing good by evil.
>
> (Milton, *Areopagitica* [1644], 1962)

> Terrorism is immoral. The occurrence at the World Trade Center, this symbolic act of defiance, is immoral, but it was in response to globalization, which is itself immoral. We are therefore immoral ourselves, so if we hope to understand anything we will need to get beyond Good and Evil. The crucial point lies in precisely the opposite direction from the Enlightenment philosophy of Good and Evil. We naively believe in the progress of Good, that its ascendance in all domains (science, technology, democracy, human rights) corresponds to the defeat of Evil. No one seems to have understood that Good and Evil increase in power at the same time and in the same way.
>
> (Baudrillard, 2002)

These two statements occupy positions at opposite ends of the modern era. Their apparent similarities conceal a vital difference. Both authors recognize the logical truth that good and evil constitute a mutually definitive binary opposition, in which it is impossible to conceive of one pole without also bringing the other into conceptual existence. But Milton insists on the imperative to seek the good, even though that necessitates the experience of evil, while, following Nietzsche, Baudrillard suggests that the inseparability of good and evil is grounds for abandoning these categories altogether. Milton, in other words, holds a dialectical view of knowledge: he believes that knowledge must move through the conflict and resolution of logical oppositions. For Baudrillard, however, the tendency to think in binary oppositions is a problem to be over-come, and in this he is typical of postmodernist philosophy. This is why postmodernists are unwilling to speak of 'ideology', since this category implies a binary opposition between true and false modes of thought. The neo-pragmatist philosopher Richard Rorty denies the possibility of ever identifying a systematically distorted consciousness, since '"distortion" presupposes a medium of representation which, intruding between us and the object under investigation, produces an appearance that does not correspond to the reality of the object' (1993, 17).

There can be no distortion if there is no referent beyond or outside representation, for in that case there is nothing to be distorted. But Rorty's argument implies, like Kant's, that our inability to perceive the thing-in-itself is an eternal and inevitable condition, so that the pretence that we can perceive it becomes the very definition of superstition. This argument takes no account of the particular historical conditions under which materialist relativism and belief in the determining power of representation have arisen and come to seem plausible. In partic-ular, it ignores the influence on consciousness of *money*. Money is a system of representation that achieves determining power in *practice*. In a world dominated by money, then, we should expect that repre-sentation might also be accorded determining power in the realm of theory. If it is true that the autonomy of representation in philosophy is part of the same process as the seizure of global power by money, then the fact that money is an alienated and objectified form of human life implies an ethical condemnation of Rorty's faith in signification's constitutive role.

The dialectical nature of reason, the fact that it works through the interpenetration of opposites, has been a commonplace since Socrates. In his *Essay on Man*, Alexander Pope argues that this process of dialectical reason is the definitive characteristic of humanity:

> Extremes in Nature equal ends produce,
> In Man they join to some mysterious use;
> Tho' each by turns the other's bounds invade,
> As in some well-wrought picture light and shade;

> And oft so mix, the diff'rence is too nice
> Where ends the Virtue or begins the Vice.
>
> (ll. 205–10)

This is, in essence, the position arrived at by Baudrillard and Rorty. Since ideas such as good and evil, or vice and virtue, only have significance because of the mutual relation of the poles of the oppositions, it is held to be impossible to draw any essential or absolute distinctions between them. In the lines that follow, Pope strongly protests against such relativism:

> Fools! Who from hence into the notion fall
> That Vice or Virtue there is none at all.
> If white and black blend, soften, and unite
> A thousand ways, is there no black nor white?
>
> (ll. 211–14)

Baudrillard differs from Pope, and from most thinkers before the twentieth century, in that where they believe that the mutually dependent relation of good to evil enhances the imperative to distinguish between them, he claims that binary thinking itself is the root of the problem. Unlike some of his followers, however, Baudrillard is not reckless enough to imagine that the abolition of binary thinking is a practical possibility. The polarity between good and evil may be reprehensible and destructive, but he insists that such habits of thought are becoming more and more deeply ingrained in our psyches. He does not, for example, see the destruction of the World Trade Center as an act of revenge by those excluded from the benefits of the new world order. Rather, he claims, the desire to destroy that order 'resides in the hearts even of those who have shared in the spoils' (2002, 13). The fall of the towers was an ideological inevitability, the external manifestation of a secret 'profound complicity' (13) lurking within us all: 'it was they who did it but we who wished it' (13). The same issue of *Harper's* that carries Baudrillard's article prints a passage from the diary of Eric Harris, one of the perpetrators of the 1999 Columbine High School massacre ('Duke' and 'Doom' are video games):

it will be like the LA riots, the oklahoma bombing, WWII, vietnam, duke, and doom all mixed together. maybe we will even start a little rebelion or revolution to fuck things up as much as we can. . . . if by some weird as shit luck me and V survive and escape we will move to some island somewhere or maybe mexico, new zealand, or some exotic place where americans can't get us. if there isn't such a place, then we will hijack a hell of a lot of bombs and crash a plane into NYC with us inside firing away as we go down. just something to cause more devistation.

(14)

Movies such as *Fight Club* speak to the same involuntary, visceral revulsion from Empire within the minds of its most privileged citizens. Here, 'real' historical events are experienced as Debordian 'spectacles'. For Eric Harris, clearly, the Gulf War did not take place, neither did the Second World War, the LA riots, nor indeed the Columbine High School massacre. This inability to distinguish between reality and representation, the condition which Baudrillard calls 'hyper-reality', has catastrophic moral consequences. We might profitably wonder what, in Harris's pseudo-world, is denoted by the term 'americans'. As with the real bombers of the World Trade Center, one gets the impression that, for Harris, 'americans' is a floating signifier, a trope or figure for something less tangible. Most of the victims of those who acted out Harris's fantasy assault were Americans, but they were not 'americans' in his sense of the term. I think that Harris's 'americans' designates the same thing as Hardt and Negri's 'Empire': the system of global exchange, of world trade, whose external centre may have been destroyed, but whose real, ideological life flourishes within each of us. As Baudrillard puts it:

> Terrorism is the act that restores an irreducible singularity to the heart of a generalized system of exchange. All those singularities (species, individuals, cultures) that have been sacrificed to the interests of a global system of commerce avenge themselves by turning the tables with terror. Terror against terror – this is no longer an ideological notion. We have gone well beyond ideology and politics. The energy that nourishes terror, no ideology, no cause, not even an Islamic one, can explain. The terrorists are not aiming simply to transform the world. Like the heretics of previous times, they aim to radicalize the

world through sacrifice, whereas the system aims to convert it into money by force.

(14)

In the days immediately following 11 September, Western politicians and media commentators went to some lengths to deny such connections. In fact, any attempt to give the event a meaning, a significance – to read it as a sign of something – was condemned as disloyal and immoral. It seemed important to insist that the event had no depth, no referent, that it was an empty, surface phenomenon, that it was emphatically *not* a sign. We were told that the only terms in which it was permissible to understand the event was as an attack on Good by Evil. And it is true that 9 / 11 cannot be understood as a clash between competing ideologies. Like Eric Harris, the terrorists made no demands, registered no protests, proposed no programme. Perhaps 'Good versus Evil' is indeed the only way of comprehending this conflict. But in that case we must take full account of a fact we all know but can easily forget: Good and Evil reside together within each of us.

Is Baudrillard right to claim that 11 September represents the end of 'ideology'? As he says, the attacks were not carried out in the name of any ideology. We might, however, deduce from this an intensification rather than an amelioration of ideological tension. We might conclude, as Baudrillard's reference to 'heretics of past times' suggests, that as was recognized in past ages, the real site of political struggle is the human mind. Perhaps what was in the nineteenth and twentieth centuries a visible contradiction manifested in the external struggle between social classes has, in our time, reverted to an ideological conflict manifested internally. If that is the case, close attention to the history of ideology is more relevant than ever to our predicament.

GLOSSARY

Rather than attempt to list every meaning that has ever been given to these terms, I have defined them here as they are used in this book, and located them in philosophical history by giving the name of the thinker with reference to whom they are discussed.

A posteriori (Kant): knowledge derived from sensory experience, judgement based upon empirical observation.

A priori (Kant): knowledge prior to sensory experience, judgement based upon abstract reason.

Absolute Spirit (Hegel): the unitary Idea or Mind that both transcends and makes possible our experience, and which is manifested to us in the history of our individual and collective thought; the philosophical descendant of the Judaeo-Christian God.

Alienation (Hegel, Feuerbach, Marx): in Hegel, the objectification of the Absolute Spirit in the material world; in Feuerbach, the projection of the human race's species-being into the figure of God; in Marx the representation of labour power in the form of money.

Base (Engels, Gramsci, Althusser): the material actions of human beings, the economy.

Bourgeoisie (Marx): people who live off income from capital investments.

Capitalism (Marx): an economic system in which all things, including labour, are exchangeable for money, and in which money is held to be able to reproduce itself in the form of interest.

Commodity (Marx, Lukács): a thing for sale; a thing whose exchange-value obscures or displaces its use-value.

Concept (Plato, Hegel): the imposition of a general term on a particular thing; the subsumption of a particular thing under a general term.

Cool (Frank, Klein): a marketing tool whereby rebellion is commodified.

Custom (Aristotle, Machiavelli): habitual behaviour ossified to the degree that it appears natural; a second nature.

Deconstruction (Derrida): a mode of textual analysis that views logic as a rhetorical effect.

Determinism (Althusser, Foucault): the idea that a particular course of events is preordained by some factor external to those events.

Dialectic (Plato, Hegel, Marx): in Plato, the progress of reason towards truth through logic; in Hegel, the progress of Spirit towards self-consciousness through history; in Marx, the progress of humanity towards Communism through class struggle.

Discourse (Foucault): a set of statements obeying specific conventions and addressed to a determinate field of enquiry.

Dualism (Plato, Descartes, Hegel): in Descartes, the belief that the universe is divided into the two distinct entities of matter and spirit; in Plato and Hegel, the illusion that the universe is so divided.

Economy (Goux, Shell): once the system of material production and trade, but today used in a more general form to refer to any system of exchange.

Empire (Hardt and Negri): capitalism as it has expanded to include not only politics but psychology.

Empiricism (Hobbes, Locke): the belief that all knowledge is caused by experience.

Enlightenment (Voltaire, Adorno): in Voltaire, the liberation of humanity from religious superstition; in Adorno, the enslavement of humanity to fetishized reason.

Epistemology (Kant, Hegel): the study of what and how it is possible to know.

Essence (Aristotle): properties of a thing which define it as such, without which it would not be what it is.

Ethics (Milton, Adorno, Baudrillard): the evaluation of human behaviour according to the criteria of morality; judgement between good and evil.

Exchange-value (Aristotle, Marx): the value of one object perceived in the body of another.

Expressionism (Lukács, Adorno): early twentieth-century artistic movement that aspired to express subjective experiences rather than to depict the objective world.

Fetishism (Freud, Lévi-Strauss, Marx): the attribution of supernatural power to a natural thing.

Globalization (Hardt and Negri, Klein, Baudrillard): the extension of market capitalism to every corner of the world.

Hegemony (Gramsci): the institutions and techniques whereby a dominant social group exercises and retains power over others.

Idealism (Plato): the belief that the material world is an illusion created by ideal forms.

Ideological State Apparatuses (Althusser): the institutions, such as schools and churches, that administer ideology.

Ideology: a systematically false consciousness.

Idolatry (Luther, Milton): worship of the products of human labour.

Indulgence (Luther): a certificate sold by the papacy denoting a determinate amount of penitential human labour, and fetishized as having the power to reduce the time a soul would spend in purgatory.

Labour (Marx, Lukács): human activity exchanged for money.

Market (Hardt and Negri, Baudrillard): organized exchange of commodities.

Materialism (Thales, Democritus, Condillac, Lenin, Althusser): the belief that ideas are merely reflections caused by material phenomena.

Money (Aristotle, Marx): the objectified representation of labour.

Monism (Plato, Hegel, Althusser, Foucault): the belief that only one kind of thing exists. In Plato the belief that ideas constitute reality; in Althusser and Foucault, the belief that only matter is real; in Hegel, the belief that the division of the world into matter and spirit is an illusion disguising the universality of Spirit.

Multitude (Hobbes, Hardt and Negri): in Hobbes, the irrational and selfish mass of individuals requiring control by an external power; in Hardt and Negri, the crowd of irreducible subjectivities resisting the impersonal tyranny of Empire.

Myth (Lévi-Strauss, Barthes): the conveyance of an ideological message through the rhetorical manipulation of signs.

Nihilism (Nietzsche, Dostoevsky): the belief in nothing, an aggressive and extreme form of relativism.

Object (Kant, Hegel, Marx, Adorno): that which is experienced.

Ontology (Democritus, Plato): the study of how existence is possible.

Overdetermination (Althusser, Macherey): the belief that effects have more than one cause.

Phenomenology (Hegel): the study of things as they appear or are revealed to us, the study of our experience of things.

Postmodernism (Rorty, Baudrillard): the current historical period, whose origin has been variously located (1945, 1968 and 1989 being plausible suggestions); our age's characteristic philosophy, politics, aesthetics and economics.

Pragmatism (Rorty): the belief that truth is what works in practice, usually associated with capitalism, which is often legitimized on the grounds that it 'works'.

Proletariat (Marx, Lukács, Gramsci): people who live by selling their labour for money.

Rationalism (Descartes): the belief that knowledge of the world is made possible through the operation of reason.

Reductionism (Plato, Condillac, Althusser): the tendency to interpret one pole of the matter/spirit opposition as a mere reflection of the other.

Reification (Lukács): the mistaking of subjective phenomena for objective things; commodification as it affects psychological or intellectual life.

Relativism (Rorty): the belief that the veridical status of ideas is determined by the context in which they occur.

Ressentiment (Nietzsche): sublimated feelings of hostility felt by the weak towards the powerful, which are expressed in the form of Judaeo-Christian religion.

Rhetoric (Plato): the art of persuasion by non-rational means.

Romanticism (Rousseau): the belief that passion is more authentic than reason.

Satan (Luther, Milton, Adorno): the enemy of human life, the source of fetishism, the cause of death.

Scepticism (Hobbes, Descartes, Hume): the belief that it is impossible for human beings to attain objectively true or accurate knowledge.

Semiotics (Saussure, Barthes): the science of signs.

Simulacrum (Baudrillard): a sign without a referent, an autonomous sign.

Species-being (Feuerbach): the concept of the human race as a whole.

Spectacle (Debord): the visible manifestation of the commodity form.

Structuralism (Saussure, Lévi-Strauss, Barthes): in Saussure, the belief that linguistic meaning is produced by the location of words within the structure of language; in Lévi-Strauss and Barthes, the belief that cultural meanings are produced in an analogous fashion by the meta-language of mythology.

Subject (Kant, Hegel, Marx, Adorno): that which experiences.

Sublime (Kant): aesthetic beauty that transcends sensory experience.

Superstructure (Engels, Gramsci, Althusser): the sphere of ideas; in Engels and Althusser it is supported by the material 'base'.

Teleology (Aristotle): the study of *telos*.

Telos (Aristotle): the end, purpose or final cause of any thing.

Thing-for-us (Kant): an object as we experience it, the phenomenon.

Thing-in-itself (Kant): an object as it exists independently of our experience, the noumenon.

Use-value (Aristotle, Marx, Laclau and Mouffe): the inherent capacities of any object, what an object can be used for.

Usury (Aristotle): the making of money with money, allowing money to reproduce, lending money at interest, capitalism.

FURTHER READING

The following is a selection of other secondary and introductory volumes which consider many of the same issues as this book.

Barth, Hans (1976) *Truth and Ideology*, trans. Frederic Lilge; University of California Press; Berkeley. [An original and opinionated overview, relating Marxist thought to the nihilistic tradition of Nietzsche.]

Eagleton, Terry (1990) *The Ideology of the Aesthetic*; Basil Blackwell Ltd; Oxford. [Deals with the relations between ideology, pleasure and idealist philosophy.]

—— (1991) *Ideology: an Introduction*; Verso; London. [The definitive introduction to the subject. Takes a Marxist, historical approach, and simultaneously puts forward the author's own thesis.]

—— (1994) *Ideology*; Longman Group UK; Harlow, Essex. [A selection of readings by authors ranging from Marx to Clifford Geertz. Offers a wide variety of definitions.]

Goodheart, Eugene (1997) *The Reign of Ideology*; Columbia University Press; New York. [Far-ranging survey of the possibilities for ideology critique in postmodernity.]

Ingersoll, David E. and Matthews, Richard K. (1986) *The Philosophic Roots of Modern Ideology: Liberalism, Communism, Fascism*; Prentice Hall Inc.; Englewood Cliffs, NJ. [Traces the evolution of various forms of ideology, as well as considering the phenomenon as a whole.]

Larrain, Jorge (1979) *The Concept of Ideology*; Hutchinson & Co.; London. [Penetrating and undogmatic historical account of ideology's various permutations.]

Mannheim, Karl (1936) *Ideology and Utopia*, trans. Louis Wirth and Edward Shils; Harcourt, Brace & Co.; New York. [Brilliant early attempt to theorize ideology across various periods. Defines it against the rival force of 'utopia'.]

McLellan, David (1986) *Ideology*; University of Minnesota Press; Minneapolis. [Brief, schematic but extremely lucid outline of the topic, which addresses the issue of its continuing relevance.]

Rosen, Michael (1996) *On Voluntary Servitude: False Consciousness and the Theory of Ideology*; Harvard University Press; Cambridge, Mass. [Detailed historical argument denying that ideology can be identified with false consciousness.]

Thompson, John B. (1990) *Ideology and Modern Culture: Critical Social Theory in the Age of Mass Communication*; Stanford University Press; Stanford, Calif. [Masterly analysis of the role of the mass media in the definition and transmission of ideology.]

Van Dijk, T.A. (1998) *Ideology: a Multidisciplinary Study*; Sage Press; London. [Argues that existing boundaries between academic fields must be broken down in order to grasp the role of ideology in forming social cognition.]

BIBLIOGRAPHY

Adorno, Theodor (1974) *Minima Moralia: Reflections from Damaged Life*, trans. E.F.N. Jephcott; New Left Books; London.
—— (1990) *Negative Dialectics*, trans. E.B. Ashton; Routledge; London.
Adorno, Theodor and Horkheimer, Max (1972) *Dialectic of Enlightenment*, trans. John Cumming; Herder & Herder; New York.
Althusser, Louis (1969) *For Marx*, trans. Ben Brewster; Pantheon Books; New York.
—— (1971) *Lenin and Philosophy and Other Essays*, trans. Ben Brewster; Monthly Review Press; New York.
Amis, Martin (1984) *Money*; Penguin Books; London.
Appleby, Joyce Oldham (1978) *Economic Thought and Ideology in Seventeenth-century England*; Princeton University Press; Princeton, NJ.
Arac, Jonathan (ed.) (1986) *Postmodernism and Politics*; University of Minnesota Press; Minnesota.
Arato, Andrew and Gebhardt, Eike (eds) (1978) *The Essential Frankfurt School Reader*; Urizen Books; New York.
Aristotle (1984) *Complete Works*, ed. Jonathan Barnes; Princeton University Press; Princeton, NJ.
—— (1984) *Politics*, trans. Carnes Lord; University of Chicago Press; Chicago.
Bacon, Francis (1959) *Novum Organon*, trans. R. Ellis and James Spedding; George Routledge & Sons Ltd; London.
Baron, Hans (1966) *The Crisis of the Early Italian Renaissance*; Princeton University Press; Princeton, NJ.
Barth, Hans (1976) *Truth and Ideology*, trans. Frederic Lilge; University of California Press; Berkeley.
Barthes, Roland (1994) *Mythologies*, trans. Annette Lavers; Hill & Wang; New York.
Baudrillard, Jean (1975) *The Mirror of Production*, trans. Mark Poster; Telos Press; St Louis, Mo.
—— (1981) *For a Critique of the Political Economy of the Sign*, trans. Charles Levin; Telos Press; St Louis, Mo.
—— (1983) *Simulations*, trans. Paul Foss, Paul Patton and Philip Beitchman; Semiotext(e); New York.
—— (1993) *Symbolic Exchange and Death*, trans. Iain Hamilton Grant; Sage Publications; London.
—— (1995) *The Gulf War Did Not Take Place*, trans. Paul Patton; Indiana University Press; Bloomington, Ind.
—— (2002) 'L'Esprit du Terrorisme', trans. Donovan Hohn, *Harper's Magazine* (Feb. 2002), 13–18.
Beck, Lewis White (ed.) (1966) *Eighteenth-century Philosophy*; Free Press; New York.
Bernstein, J.M. (2001) *Adorno: Disenchantment and Ethics*; Cambridge University Press; Cambridge.

Bloom, Alan (1987) *The Closing of the American Mind*; Simon and Schuster; New York.

Bonefeld, Werner and Holloway, John (eds) (1995) *Global Capital, National State and the Politics of Money*; St Martin's Press; New York.

Breckman, Warren (1999) *Marx, the Young Hegelians and the Origins of Radical Social Theory: Dethroning the Self*; Cambridge University Press; Cambridge.

Brown, Stephen (1995) *Postmodern Marketing*; Routledge; London.

Browne, Thomas (1972) *Religio Medici*, ed. R. H. Robbins; Clarendon Press; Oxford.

Bunyan, John (1984) *The Pilgrim's Progress*; Oxford University Press; Oxford.

Burke, Edmund (1965) *Reflections on the Revolution in France*, ed. William B. Todd; Holt, Rinehart & Winston; New York.

Burnham, Peter (2000) 'Globalization, Depoliticization and "Modern" Economic Management', in *The Politics of Change: Ideology and Critique*, eds Werner Bonefeld and Kosmas Psychopedis; Palgrave; New York.

Callinicos, Alex (1989) *Against Postmodernism: a Marxist Critique*; Polity Press; New York.

Carlyle, Thomas (1956) *Sartor Resartus: on Heros and Hero-worship*; Dutton; New York.

Coleridge, S.T. (1912) *Complete Poetical Works*, ed. Ernest Hartley Coleridge; Clarendon Press; Oxford.

—— (1969) *Biographia Literaria*, ed. J. Shawcross; Oxford University Press; Oxford.

de Condillac, Etienne Bonnot (1966) 'Essay on the Origin of Knowledge', in *Eighteenth-century Philosophy*, ed. Lewis White Beck; The Free Press; New York.

—— (2001) *Treatise on the Sensations*; Clinamen Press; Concord, Mass.

Coupland, Douglas (1991) *Generation X*; St Martin's Press; New York.

Darwin, Charles (1999) *The Origin of Species*; Bantam Books; New York.

Davis, Mike (2002) *Dead Cities*; The New Press; New York.

Debord, Guy (1967) *Society of the Spectacle*; Black & Red; Detroit, Mich.

Descartes, René (1911) *Philosophical Works*, trans. Elizabeth S. Haldane and G.R.T. Ross; Cambridge University Press; Cambridge.

Destutt de Tracy (1986–7) *Elémens d'Idéologie*; A. Wahlen; Brussels.

Docherty, Thomas (ed.) (1993) *Postmodernism: a Reader*; Columbia University Press; New York.

Dostoevsky, Fyodor (2000) *Devils*, trans. Michael Katz; Oxford University Press; Oxford.

Dupre, John (2001) *Human Nature and the Limits of Science*; Clarendon Press; Oxford.

Eagleton, Terry (1981) *Walter Benjamin, or, Towards a Revolutionary Criticism*; Verso; London.

Eliot, T.S. (1970) *Collected Poems*; Harcourt, Brace & World; New York.

Ellis, Brett Easton (1985) *Less Than Zero*; Viking Press; New York.

Engels, Friedrich (1942) *The Correspondence of Karl Marx and Friedrich Engels*; International Publishers; New York.

Feuerbach, Ludwig (1957) *The Essence of Christianity*, trans. George Eliot; Harper & Brothers Publishers; New York.

Fitzgerald, F. Scott (1991) *The Great Gatsby*; Cambridge University Press; New York.

Foucault, Michel (1970) *The Order of Things: an Archaeology of the Human Sciences*, trans. Alan Sheridan-Smith; Pantheon Books; New York.

—— (1972) *The Archaeology of Knowledge*, trans. A.M. Sheridan Smith; Pantheon Books; New York.

—— (1977) *Discipline and Punish: the Birth of the Prison*, trans. Alan Sheridan; Pantheon Books; New York.

—— (1980) *Power/Knowledge: Selected Interviews and Other Writings 1972–7*, ed. Colin Gordon, trans. Colin Gordon, Leo Marshall, John Mepham and Kate Soper; Pantheon Books; New York.

—— (1988) *Politics, Philosophy, Culture: Interviews and Other Writings, 1974–84*, ed. Lawrence D. Kritzman, trans. Alan Sheridan *et al.*; Routledge; New York.

—— (1990) *The History of Sexuality*, vol. I, trans. Robert Hurley; Vintage Books; New York.

—— (1991) *Remarks on Marx: Conversations with Duccio Trombadori*, trans. R. Jame Goldstein and James Cascaito; Semiotext(e); New York.

Frank, Thomas (1997) *The Conquest of Cool*; University of Chicago Press; Chicago.

—— (2000) *One Market Under God*; Doubleday; New York.

Freud, Sigmund (1950) *Totem and Taboo: Some Points of Agreement between the Mental Lives of Savages and Neurotics*, trans. James Strachey; W.W. Norton; London.

—— (1962) *Three Essays on the Theory of Sexuality*, trans. James Strachey; Basic Books Inc.; New York.

Fukuyama, Francis (1992) *The End of History and the Last Man*; The Free Press; New York.

Gagnier, Regina (2000) *The Insatiability of Human Wants: Economics and Aesthetics in Market Society*; University of Chicago Press; Chicago.

Gibson, Nigel and Rubin, Andrew (eds) (2002) *Adorno: a Critical Reader*; Blackwell Publishers; Malden, Mass.

Goethe, Johann Wolfgang von (1957) *The Sufferings of Young Werther*, trans. Bayard Quincy Morgan; Frederick Ungar Publishing Co.; New York.

—— (1962) *Faust*, trans. Peter Salm; Bantam Books; New York.

Goux, Jean-Joseph (1990) *Symbolic Economies*, trans. Jennifer Curtiss Gage; Cornell University Press; Ithaca, NY.

—— (1994) *The Coiners of Language*, trans. Jennifer Curtiss Gage; University of Oklahoma Press; London.

Gramsci, Antonio (1971) *Selections from the Prison Notebooks*, ed. and trans. Quintin Hoare and Geoffrey Nowell-Smith; International Publishers; New York.

Grant, James (1992) *Money of the Mind*; Farrar Strauss Giroux; New York.

Greenblatt, Stephen (1983) *Renaissance Self-fashioning from More to Shakespeare*; University of Chicago Press; Chicago.

Hardt, Michael and Negri, Antonio (2000) *Empire*; Harvard University Press; Cambridge, Mass.

Haug, Wolfgang Fritz (1986) *Critique of Commodity Aesthetics: Appearance, Sexuality and Advertising in Capitalist Society*; University of Minnesota Press; Minneapolis.

Hawkes, David (2001) *Idols of the Marketplace: Idolatry and Commodity Fetishism in English Literature, 1580–1680*; Palgrave; New York.

Hegel, G.W.F. (1977) *Phenomenology of Spirit*, trans. A.V. Miller; Clarendon Press; Oxford.

Helvetius, Claude (1970) *Essays on the Mind*; Burt Franklin; New York.

Henwood, Doug (1997) *Wall Street*; Verso; New York.

Hobbes, Thomas (1985) *Leviathan*, ed. C.B. MacPherson; Penguin Books; London.

Holbach, Baron d' (1970) *The System of Nature*, trans. H.D. Robinson; Burt Franklin; New York.

Hook, Sidney (1962) *From Hegel to Marx*; University of Michigan Press; Ann Arbor.

Hoxby, Blair (1998) 'The Trade of Truth Advanced: *Areopagitica*, Economic Discourse, and Libertarian Reform', *Milton Studies* 36, ed. Albert C. Labriola; Pittsburgh, Pa.

Jameson, Frederic (1991) *Postmodernism, or, the Cultural Logic of Late Capitalism*; Duke University Press; Durham, SC.

Kant, Immanuel (1934) *Critique of Pure Reason*, trans. J.M.D. Meikelejohn; J.M. Dent & Sons; London.

—— (1987) *Critique of Judgment*, trans. Werner S. Pluhar; Hackett Publishing Co.; Indianapolis.

Keats, John (1958) *The Letters*, ed. Hyder Edward Rollins; Harvard University Press; Cambridge, Mass.

Kennedy, Emmet (1978) *Destutt de Tracy and the Origins of 'Ideology'*; American Philosophical Society; Philadelphia.

Kim, Joohan (2000) 'From Commodity Production to Sign Production', *Semiotica* 132:1, 75–100.

Klein, Naomi (2000) *No Logo: Taking Aim at the Brand Bullies*; Picador; New York.

Laclau, Ernesto and Mouffe, Chantal (1985) *Hegemony and Socialist Strategy: Towards a Radical Democratic Politics*; Verso; London.

Leach, William (1993) *Land of Desire: Merchants, Power and the Rise of a New American Culture*; Pantheon Books; New York.

Leavis, F.R. (1930) *Mass Civilization and Minority Culture*; The Minority Press; Cambridge.

Lenin, V.I. (1927) *Materialism and Empirio-Criticism*; International Publishers; New York.

Lévi-Strauss, Claude (1966) *The Savage Mind*; University of Chicago Press; Chicago.

Locke, John (1867) *An Essay Concerning Human Understanding*; William Tegg; London.

Lukács, Georg (1971) *History and Class-consciousness*, trans. Rodney Livingstone; MIT Press; Cambridge, Mass.

Luther, Martin (1959) *Works*, ed. Jaroslav Pelikan and Helmut T. Lehmann; Fortress Press; Philadelphia.

Lyotard, Jean-François (1984) *The Postmodern Condition: a Report on Knowledge*, trans. Geoff Bennington and Brian Massumi; University of Minnesota Press; Minneapolis.

—— (1993) *Libidinal Economy*, trans. Iain Hamilton Grant; Indiana University Press; Bloomington.

—— (1993) *The Postmodern Explained: Correspondence 1982–1985*, ed. Julian Pefanis and Morgan Thomas, trans. Don Barry, Bernadette Maher, Julian Pefanis, Virginia Spate and Morgan Thomas; University of Minnesota Press; Minneapolis.

McCloskey, Dierdre N. (1994) *Knowledge and Persuasion in Economics*; Cambridge University Press; Cambridge.

Macherey, Pierre (1978) *A Theory of Literary Production*, trans. Geoffrey Wall; Routledge; London.

Macherey, Pierre and Balibar, Etienne (1981) 'On Literature as an Ideological Form', in Robert Young (ed.) *Untying the Text*; Routledge; London.

Machiavelli, Niccolò (1969) *Works*, trans. Anthony J. Pancini; Greenvale Press; Greenvale, NY.

McNally, David (1993) *Against the Market: Political Economy, Market Socialism and the Marxist Critique*; Verso; New York.

MacPherson, C.B. (1969) *The Political Theory of Possessive Individualism, Hobbes to Locke*; Oxford University Press; Oxford.

Mann, Thomas (1992) *Doctor Faustus*, trans. H.T. Lowe-Porter; Alfred A. Knopf; New York.

Marcus, Griel (1990) *Lipstick Traces: a Secret History of the Twentieth Century*; Harvard University Press; Cambridge, Mass.

Marcuse, Herbert (1964) *One-dimensional Man: Studies in the Ideology of Advanced Industrial Society*; Beacon Press; Boston, Mass.

Marx, Karl (1973) *Grundrisse*, trans. Martin Nicolaus; Penguin; Baltimore, Md.

—— (1976) *Capital*, vol. I, trans. Ben Fowkes; Penguin Books; London.

Marx, Karl and Engels, Friedrich (1975) *Collected Works*; International Publishers; New York.

Mehlman, Jeffrey (1979) *Revolution and Repetition*; University of California Press; Berkeley.

Milton, John (1962) *Complete Prose Works*; Yale University Press; New Haven, Conn.

—— (1990) *Complete English Poems*, ed. Gordon Campbell; Everyman; Lymington, Hants.

Ngugi Wa Thiong'o (1982) *Devil on the Cross*; Heinemann International; Oxford.

Nietzsche, Friedrich (1911) *Complete Works*, trans. Paul V. Cohn; T.N. Fouls; London.

—— (1954) 'On Truth and Lie in an Extra-moral Sense', *The Viking Portable Nietzsche*, trans. Walter Kaufmann; Viking; New York.

—— (1969) *On the Genealogy of Morals*, trans. Walter Kaufman and R.J. Hollingdale; Vintage Books; New York.

Norris, Christopher (1990) *What's Wrong with Postmodernism*; Johns Hopkins University Press; Baltimore, Md.

—— (1993) *The Truth About Postmodernism*; Blackwell; Oxford.

Orwell, George (1949) *Nineteen Eighty-Four*; Harcourt, Brace & Co.; New York.

Paley, William (1986) *Natural Theology*; Lincoln-Rembrandt Publishing; Charlottesville, Va.

Plato (1974) *The Republic*, trans. G.M.A. Grube; Hackett Publishing Co.; Indianapolis.

Plekhanov, George (1940) *The Materialist Conception of History*; International Publishers; New York.

Pocock, J.G.A. (1975) *The Machiavellian Moment: Florentine Political Thought and the Atlantic Republican Tradition*; Princeton University Press; Princeton, NJ.

Pope, Alexander (1999) *Complete Poems*; Viking Penguin; New York.

Rorty, Richard (1993) 'Feminism, Ideology and Deconstruction: a Pragmatist View', *Hypatia* 8:2 (Spring 1993).

Ross, Andrew (ed.) (1988) *Universal Abandon? The Politics of Postmodernism*; University of Minnesota Press; Minneapolis.

Rousseau, Jean-Jacques (1992) *Discourse on the Origin of Inequality*, trans. Donald R. Cress; Hackett Publishing Co.; Indianapolis.

Sartre, Jean-Paul (1957) *Nausea*, trans. Lloyd Alexander; New Directions Publishing Co.; New York.

Saussure, Ferdinand de (1972) *Course in General Linguistics*, trans. Roy Harris; Open Court; La Salle.

Savonarola, Girolamo (1978) 'Treatise on the Constitution and Government of the City of Florence', in *Humanism and Liberty: Writings on Freedom from Fifteenth-century Florence*, trans. Renee Nea Watkins; University of South Carolina Press; Columbia, SC.

Schama, Simon (1989) *Citizens*; Alfred E. Knopf; New York.

Self, Will (1995) *My Idea of Fun*; Vintage Books; New York.

Shakespeare, William (1974) *The Riverside Shakespeare*, ed. G. Blakemore Evans; Houghton Mifflin Co.; Boston, Mass.

Shell, Marc (1978) *The Economy of Literature*; Johns Hopkins University Press; Baltimore, Md.

—— (1982) *Money, Language and Thought*; Johns Hopkins University Press; Baltimore, Md.

Shelley, Mary (1823) *Frankenstein, or the Modern Prometheus*; G. & W.B. Whittaker; London.

Simmel, George (1978) *The Philosophy of Money*, trans. Tom Bottomore, David Frisby and Kaethe Mengelberg; Routledge; London.

Slater, Don and Tonkiss, Fran (2001) *Market Society: Markets and Modern Social Theory*; Blackwell; Malden, Mass.

Smith, Adam (1994) *An Enquiry into the Nature and Causes of the Wealth of Nations*; Random House; New York.

Stepelevich, Lawrence S. (ed.) (1983) *The Young Hegelians*; Cambridge University Press; Cambridge.

Taussig, Michael (1980) *The Devil and Commodity Fetishism in South America*; University of North Carolina Press; Chapel Hill.

Taylor, Charles (1975) *Hegel*; Cambridge University Press; Cambridge.

Taylor, Ronald (ed.) (1977) *Aesthetics and Politics*; New Left Books; London.

Tennyson, Alfred, Baron (1969) *The Poems*, ed. Christopher Ricks; Longmans; Harlow, Essex.

Traherne, Thomas (1985) *Centuries of Meditation*; Morehouse Publishing; Wilton, Conn.

Volosinov, V.N. (1973) *Marxism and the Philosophy of Language*, trans. Ladislav Matejka and I.R. Titunik; Harvard University Press; Cambridge, Mass.

Weber, Max (1930) *The Protestant Ethic and the Spirit of Capitalism*, trans. Talcott Parsons; Unwin Hyman; London.

Weisskopf, Walter A. (1971) *Alienation and Economics*; E.P. Dutton; New York.

Welsh, Irvine (1998) *Filth*; W.W. Norton; London.

Woodmansee, Martha and Osteen, Mark (eds) (1999) *The New Economic Criticism*; Routledge; London.

Wordsworth, William (1984) *Poems*, ed. Stephen Gill; Oxford University Press; Oxford.

—— (1988) *Selected Prose*, ed. John O. Hayden; Penguin Books; London.

Wu, Chin-tao (2001) *Privatising Culture*; Verso; New York.

Yeats, W.B. (1989) *The Poems*, ed. Richard J. Finneran; Macmillan; New York.

Žižek, Slavoj (1989) *The Sublime Object of Ideology*; Verso; New York.

—— (1993) *Tarrying with the Negative: Kant, Hegel and the Critique of Ideology*; Duke University Press; Durham, SC.

INDEX

For reasons of space, page ranges are used for scattered references as well as for continuous discussion.